SEP 1 2 2005

This
Terrible Business
Has Been Good
to Me

This Terrible Business Has Been Good to Me

AN AUTOBIOGRAPHY

Norman Jewison

THOMAS DUNNE BOOKS
ST. MARTIN'S PRESS ✠ NEW YORK

THOMAS DUNNE BOOKS.
An imprint of St. Martin's Press.

Text design: Peter Maher
Electronic formatting: Jean Lightfoot Peters

www.stmartins.com

ISBN 0-312-32868-0
EAN 978-0-312-32868-9

First published in Canada by Key Porter Books Limited

First Edition: September 2005

10 9 8 7 6 5 4 3 2 1

Contents

Foreword by

John Patrick Shanley

Napoleon Bonaparte was a tremendous reader of books. In his time, which was also the age of Voltaire, it was still possible for a man or woman to read every book that had ever been written in the West. The publication of a new volume was a Continental event. Napoleon, who was always traveling, had his coach outfitted as a kind of rolling office library. Every new book that came out of Europe was in that coach. Napoleon would pick up each volume in turn, read it through, and then throw it out the window. You could always find the emperor by following the books.

If you want to find Norman Jewison, follow the movies. They are not his life. But they are the massive and various evidence that a man of substance and dumbfounding productivity has passed by here. So many genres: social realism, political satire, romance, musicals, issues of race. And so many faces: Steve McQueen, Doris Day, Al Pacino, Sidney Poitier, Sir Michael Caine, Cher, Denzel Washington, Anne

Bancroft, Rod Steiger. All these stories and faces and issues and eras of our lives. They've been flying out the windows of Norman's coach mile after mile, decade after decade. And the coach is still rolling.

I've known Norman since 1986, when I agreed to work with him on a screenplay based on a play I'd written. I flew to Toronto and met him at his office. He was sitting at his desk. Behind him was an imposing bust of a Roman general. I thought, He's inviting me to think of him in this way: As a general. So what am I? A Greek slave? Gee. I was a starving writer living in a tenement in Washington Heights. He looked at me. He said, "You call this *The Bride and the Wolf.* Now why, if you've written a love story, have you given it the title of a horror picture?!" So we changed the title to *Moonstruck.*

He thumbed through the script and looked up at me. "A son who doesn't love his mother? Is that okay?" I said I thought it was okay. He looked morose. "Three reels around a kitchen table and the movie's over. Jesus Christ, is that okay?!" I said I thought it was okay. "All right," he said, "let's read it." And we read the whole script, acting out all the parts. Made some changes. But he wouldn't change anything unless I agreed. He went to Cher. Would she do it? She warned him: "I can be difficult to work with." Norman said, "I've worked with some difficult people. Are you more difficult than Judy Garland?" Cher signed on.

I still work with Norman. He's still very skeptical and treats me like I'm a bizarre person. And he still won't change anything unless I agree. I love the guy and I respect the guy. To put that in perspective, I've loved and respected three men in my life: my father, Joe Papp, and Norman Jewison.

When Madame de Staël, that great estimator of people, met Napoleon, she said, "He is more and less than a man." That's one of the differences between Norman and Napoleon. I have never seen Norman Jewison be less than a man. He keeps his word even when it's not convenient. And he's much, much taller than Napoleon.

Preface

This book is all Jay Scott's fault. He started it, then died on me. Now, eleven years later, I am trying to fulfill a promise to Jay. It's not a straight memoir. It jumps around in time and place the way our minds often do—one memory triggering a reminiscence or anecdote from another moment in one's life. Sometimes there's a strong visual image, vibrant with detail, and other times it's out of focus and hard to clarify. This is not a personal autobiography; it's mostly about my work, my experiences as a filmmaker. I don't think my life, outside of my work as a film director, has been interesting enough to warrant some sort of sober, scholarly treatment. Anyway, I wouldn't want to read it. And my life certainly hasn't been "shocking" enough for an exposé.

I've tried to be truthful and entertaining, to write something that's sometimes serious and sometimes funny, sometimes sad and sometimes joyful, something with passion and anger, laughter and tears, and even the occasional insight…something that's like one of my better movies, in other words.

I would like to express my deepest thanks to Anna Porter for her constant push, advice, and commitment. My thanks as well to Jack Batten, both for his research and for his confidence and encouragement. My talented editor, Meg Taylor, guided me every step of the way. Barbara Sears saved me from factual errors. Liz Broden and Kim Briggs, my personal assistants, deserve special thanks, for without their prodigious efforts this manuscript would never have been completed.

My thanks to all those I have loved and who have loved me. And to all those people out there in the dark.

Norman Jewison
Putney Heath Farm
August 2004

I

Growing Up Jewish

What would you say if I told you
I'm a goy?

—*Norman Jewison, 1969*

For as long as I can remember I've always wanted to be a Jew. For many years I believed, hopefully, that I was Jewish, that my parents were lying when they denied it. When I was six, I started going to the Kenilworth synagogue, in the Beach area of Toronto, with my friend Stanley Zann. I wore my yarmulke proudly and carried on being Jewish until Stanley's mother found me out.

"Stanley, what kind of a Jew is your friend?" she asked during their Friday night dinner a couple of years into my Jewish childhood. "His parents never bring him to shul."

"They do, too," Stanley responded brightly. "They go to Bellefair United Church every Sunday." Since then, betrayal has played an important part in my life and my films.

Until that fateful evening at the Zanns', I had felt betrayed only by my name. How can my ancestors have been called "Jew's son" if they were not at least a little bit Jewish? My classmates at Kew Beach School

11

called me "Jew boy" and "Jewy" and beat me up with all the other Jewish kids when they could catch us. In my case that wasn't very often. I was already a fast runner.

"Why aren't we Jewish?" I demanded of my mother.

"We just aren't, dear," she told me. "And let's not start that again."

"But our name says Jew," I insisted.

"Some people are and some people aren't. We are not. I was born an Anglican, and the Jewisons have always been Methodist." My mother tried to be patient, but she was annoyed with my persistence.

"But I want to be Jewish!" I cried.

Those were the words that sprang to mind in 1969 when I stood in Arthur Krim's New York office. It was on the twentieth floor of the United Artists building, a rather seedy building at Forty-ninth and Seventh Avenue, across the street from two porno theaters. I had been invited, or commanded, to be there by Arthur Krim himself. He said it was a confidential meeting, so confidential I shouldn't tell my agent, my lawyer, or my wife. Arthur Krim was head of United Artists and an icon in the film business. The most powerful film executive in the East, the biggest film distributor in the world, he was also head of the National Democratic Fundraising Committee and an adviser to Kennedy and Johnson. When Arthur Krim called, you jumped.

In 1969 I had already made three successful films for UA, *The Russians Are Coming, In the Heat of the Night,* and *The Thomas Crown Affair.* Still, I was not used to getting calls directly from the top of the pyramid.

I had caught a late-night flight to New York and arrived wearing my rumpled corduroy trousers, a sports jacket, and no tie. In contrast, the assembled United Artists executives were all neatly attired in dark suits. They sat at one end of the large office: Arthur Krim, his partner Bob Benjamin, Arnold Picker and his nephew David Picker, and Bill Bernstein, head of business and legal.

They seated me in front of the massive old-fashioned desk displaying framed photos of Arthur with JFK, Golda Meir, and Dag Hammarskjöld of the United Nations. Arthur opened the meeting with the usual pleasantries: Did I have a good trip? How were the kids? How was my wife, Dixie? Then he got down to business. "Norman," he said, "we called you here to ask if you would be interested in directing a very important picture for our company."

I smiled and nodded. They all nodded together.

"We don't have all the rights yet, but we expect to get them and wanted to know where you stood," Arthur continued. He paused dramatically and leaned forward. "What would you say if we asked you to direct *Fiddler on the Roof*?"

I could hardly breathe. *Fiddler* was a smash hit on Broadway. It was big. I had seen it the first week it opened. Hal Prince found a cushion for me to sit on in the aisle because no one could get a seat. Zero Mostel was extraordinary. The director was a genius. I wept through most of the second act. The first questions that sprang to my mind were Why me? Why not Jerry Robbins? Hal Prince? Blake Edwards? My heart started to pound. Oh my god, they think I'm Jewish!

The room was quiet except for the hum of traffic and distant sirens. I got up from my chair and walked to the window. People were scurrying along Seventh Avenue in a New York kind of rush, the porno theater lights were flashing red and orange. I stood there for so long that someone started to cough impatiently.

In the end I decided to tell them the truth. "What would you say if I told you I'm a goy?"

I had turned and was looking right in their eyes, at the shock on their faces. Bob Benjamin's jaw dropped, Bill Bernstein looked like he was going to faint. Arnold Picker shot a look of concern at David Picker. Arthur Krim recovered first and, to his credit, he folded his hands and said with a smile, "We don't want a Seventh Avenue [Yiddish] production. We want the film to play everywhere in the world, regardless of religion." He was good.

That's how a Methodist/Anglican was entrusted with bringing Sholom Aleichem's classic stories to the screen.

My father's family were Calvinists, non-smoking, no-dancing, no-swearing, hard-working teetotalers. They were members of the

Orange Lodge, a rather joyless lot from a farming area in Yorkshire, England. Since it seems all the Jewisons came from there, it's been easy to trace the family back to 1216. I also found out that the city of York was the last stronghold of the Jews in England before they were expelled from the country in 1290. So who knows? There may be support for my childhood desire to be Jewish after all.

The first Jewison set foot in the New World in the early 1800s. The story goes that my great-grandfather Joseph Jefferie Jewison bought a team of horses and a cow, and moved with his young wife from Port Hope, Ontario, to Bewdley, Ontario, by the shores of Rice Lake, where he worked a hundred-acre farm.

His son, my grandfather Joseph Jewison, had five children. All had interesting names. The eldest was Wilbert Chancellor, then Clara Trafina, then Lila Trafosa, then Bertha Louise, and finally Percival Innis, my father. At least, that was what he was christened in the Methodist Church in Millbrook, Ontario, in 1890. He changed his middle name to Joseph some thirty-five years later. I think he rather liked the sound of PJ; he always signed his name with the middle initial.

My mother's family, the Weavers, immigrated from Bath, England, to Toronto around 1905, when my mother, Dorothy Irene, was just a child. Being Anglicans, they were a great deal livelier than my father's family. The Weavers drank a little, told stories, didn't frown on the sins of the world the way the Jewisons did. Grandpa Weaver had even managed a pub called The Mermaid's Inn in Bath before coming to Canada. My favorite uncle was Uncle Charlie, a sergeant major in the 48th Highlanders, over six feet tall and ramrod straight, with a ready laugh. My handsome Uncle Fred, the youngest sibling, was my mother's favorite brother. She even named me after him—my middle name is Frederick. He was the top surveyor for Ontario and served with the RCMP intelligence during World War II, a secret that was kept from everyone in the family.

My father was a Mason, and my mother was active in the Order of the Eastern Star. They met while tobogganing in Riverdale Park. My father was short, slim, dark-haired, and dark-eyed; my mother was a tall, blue-eyed blonde (her hair turned gray before she was forty, which she of course blamed on me). They opened and ran a dry goods store at the corner of Kippendavie and Queen Street East.

My father liked to call himself the "Beach's corsetier"—he and my mother fitted all the ladies of Toronto's east end with corsets and girdles. He was a great salesman and, despite his strict Methodist upbringing, had a touch of a carnival barker in him.

I was born in my grandmother's house on Lee Avenue, right across the street from Kew Gardens, on the hottest day of the year, everyone said. July 21, 1927. Mrs. Ellis, a Cockney midwife who always had a cigarette dangling from her lips and who later babysat me when my parents were out at lodge meetings, assisted old Doc Edmunds. Everyone in the Beach went to Doc Edmunds. During the Depression, he went from home to home offering bargain tonsillectomies. Only $25.95, including an adenoid removal if you chose. He performed my operation when I was seven on the dining room table, using a big wad of cotton soaked in chloroform to knock me out. The ginger ale and ice cream I got to eat for the next two days almost made up for the evil smell and the sore throat.

Our neighborhood, like most of Toronto during the Depression years, suffered from a poisonous anti-Semitism. The Balmy Beach Canoe Club actually posted Gentiles Only signs on the beach. But the Beach was a working-class area, friendly and quiet but tough, politically left. I remember communist meetings by the boardwalk, near the lake, on hot summer evenings with the moths swarming around the streetlights and young men making passionate speeches about the threat of fascism and the Spanish Civil War.

I have very fond memories of growing up in the Beach. The district stretched from Coxwell Avenue in the west to Neville Park Boulevard in the east, north to Kingston Road and all the way south to Lake Ontario. We kids regarded the lake as our own. All summer we canoed, swam, played ball on the beach, and fished.

We lived in a tiny apartment above my parents' store. My older sister, Betty, and I were expected to help out, which is when I first recognized my knack for selling. I sold everything from wool and thread to women's stockings and men's undershirts. During my teens,

I sold Christmas trees on the sidewalk in front of the store. The store also served as the local post office. I was sworn in when I was sixteen and, like my sister, often served as postmaster—writing out money orders, handling registered mail, selling stamps, weighing parcels, and even doing the books.

Our store was rarely busy during the Depression. Almost every family was on relief. That's what they called it: if your old man was out of work, you were "on relief." Though there was no shame in that in the Beach, it meant you didn't have much of anything to shop with.

I was constantly trying to wheedle ten cents from my parents or pennies from anybody else who happened by so I could go to the Beach Theatre on Saturday afternoons. For a dime, you got the full treatment: a serial, a cartoon, the news, and two features—a big movie and a "B" movie. The show started at 1 p.m. and you were disgorged at 5:30, the pupils of your eyes dilated from sitting so long in the dark, but intensely happy and full of great stories to tell.

At dusk, I would gather our Kew Beach School gang on Kippendavie and tell them the movies. I played all the parts, made all the sound effects, played horrific scenes of violent death—gunned down by the law, taking an Indian arrow in my back, whirling as the shots hit, and falling, hand clutched to my heart. Dying, they said, was the highlight of my repertoire. I remember sitting at dinner with my parents, my mother serving soup, and I would suddenly clutch my chest, eyes bulging, and topple off the chair onto the floor. I'd writhe there for a while, arms over my chest, making horrible sounds while my parents continued to talk, spoon the soup, step over me to take their plates to the kitchen.

We used to invent new ways of dying, the kind where people get shot, do four back flips, go through a series of elaborate gyrations, and land spectacularly on their backs. It was pretty much as the dumbed-down Hollywood movies of today do the scene: guy does cartwheels after the first shot, goes through a plate glass window, falls four stories, and is then impaled on a fence. They're movies made to appeal to eight- to twelve-year-old males and their adult equivalents: guys who have chosen not to grow up.

I believe that those years in the Kippendavie store and my adolescent love of performance prepared me for my future career. Many years later, I found myself in New York with a group of agency and network types, all listening to me pitching a story, sometimes changing it as I went, watching their faces for reaction, pushing a scene or cutting it short (timing is everything), playing all the parts, pacing, prancing, declaiming, whispering to make them lean in closer, menacing, shouting to see them back away, hoping all the time they would like the pitch enough to give me the green light to produce a particular TV special. "Doing my dance," my agent Larry Auerbach called it. It's not much different from the performances I put on in the Beach, only the stakes are higher. And as the decades have rolled by, my dance has become smoother and perhaps more elegant.

Coppola was a terrific dancer, so was Fellini. It's the art of selling, of convincing people to give you millions of dollars to make your dream. Hitchcock may have been the best. He invented a persona for himself, one so credible even he could believe in it and he used it to sell. He manipulated everybody who could make a difference to his projects. That's what studio people call them: "projects." As in "We've got this project Coppola wants to make…says he's got Dustin…" And so the dance begins. In his nineties, Billy Wilder was still slow-dancing, as was John Huston, in his late seventies, when he made his last film, *The Dead*.

As I recall, no one in my family sat down and relaxed much. The store was open from nine in the morning till eight at night, six days a week, even during the Depression. Sales were down so much in those years that my dad began painting and renovating houses while my mom ran the store. And when she wasn't in the store, she was cooking and baking in the apartment. When she actually did sit down in the evening, her hands were always busy knitting or crocheting. Of course, we had the biggest stock of yarn in the area. In those days nobody bought scarves or sweaters or socks. They were made by hand.

Since my parents were always busy at the store, I was left alone a lot. I invented stories to entertain myself, sang, and directed my own dramas, which included a special imaginary friend. He retired after I

became busy with growing up, though I brought him out of retire-
ment once with *Bogus*, a movie starring the effervescent Gérard
Depardieu as the imaginary friend. *Bogus* starred Haley Joel Osment,
only seven years old. He would become one of Hollywood's most celebrated and sought-after child actors, but when we made *Bogus*, he had
almost no experience. Still, I thought he was perfect for the part. He
was about the same age I was when I began to talk to my imaginary
friends. For the sake of simplicity we restricted him to one friend,
Bogus the clown, so perfectly played by Gérard Depardieu I still get
choked up when I think of his last goodbye to the little boy. For me,
that whole movie was an emotional roller-coaster ride.

It started with an idea, a treatment I had optioned about a little
boy whose father dies. I called Alvin Sargent who was in New York
from L.A. Alvin was a friend and Academy Award–winning writer
with scripts as diverse as *Ordinary People* and *Paper Moon* to his
credit. He thought it would be a great idea if I picked him up in
Buffalo and we drove to Los Angeles together. We could work on the
story as we drove.

Like Thelma and Louise, we had a great time. Since we were in no
particular hurry, we started each day with a leisurely breakfast, then
took turns driving while reading each other the *New York Times*. We
talked about the news, argued about the reviews, vented at political
opponents, aired grievances—we had a terrific time driving through
the Midwest, endless miles of flat highway. We'd eat lunch somewhere,
then work on the story through the afternoon.

We stopped at the National Cowboy Museum in Oklahoma City,
in Santa Fe, and in Las Vegas, where the Mirage Hotel rolled out the
red carpet. "Mr. Jewison, are you *really* going to make a movie about
Vegas? And will the Mirage be the real set? Will you need any shots of
our casino?" We were building our story bit by bit, bringing in the
magician, the Cirque de Soleil, the trapeze artists. And of course the
magician would have to be French because he sounded so perfect in
French on the stage at the Desert Inn, and I had been wanting to make
a movie with Gérard Depardieu since I first saw him in *Cyrano de
Bergerac*. Here was my chance to work with him at last.

Arnon Milchan of Regency Pictures was less enthusiastic than Alvin and I when we hit Los Angeles ten days after we had left Buffalo, but he agreed to finance our movie if we could change the leading role from a male to a female and cast Whoopi Goldberg. Apparently, another project had collapsed and he had a "pay or play" deal with Whoopi. It wasn't easy. For one thing, the kid was white and Whoopi was proudly black, so she could hardly be the mother. But we were by then so committed to *Bogus*, we began to change the script and adapt it for her.

Whoopi was filming in deepest Arizona at the time. Alvin and I flew to Phoenix, rented a car, and drove for what seemed like hours through the desert to arrive at an adobe house she'd rented in one of the remotest areas of the state, near Sedona.

It was a hundred degrees in the shade, relentlessly clear-skied, parched, the air vibrating with the heat. I was wearing my Canadian tweed jacket and heavy pants, perfect for Caledon, Ontario, but stiflingly uncomfortable in the Arizona sunshine. Alvin wore his California chinos and looked more comfortable. I said we'd do the dance together.

"No problem, Norm."

There was an open-air bamboo-topped patio over the pool of Whoopi's rented house and that's where we were led to when we arrived. I was sweating so much I considered jumping into the pool as I was. Alvin asked for a cool drink and relaxed, ready for the long wait we both knew was part of the star system.

We had barely settled into our bamboo seats when Whoopi loped in, wearing a caftan, already grinning from the doorway, her hand outstretched. "*Heat of the Night, Soldier's Story*, Norman, so good to see you! And Alvin, *Ordinary People*...I love your movies!"

Whoopi was a joy to work with except for her astonishing desire to start early in the morning. Of course, I didn't discover this till we had started filming. "Gee, Whoopi," I told her, "I'm not too good in the morning. I start cooking around four in the afternoon."

"What are you talking about?" she said. "I'm out of gas by 3:30."

So we started shooting early, and the first day she brought me a bottle of Moët et Chandon. "Here, maybe this will improve your disposition."

I tried. But it didn't. I still don't think that the film we shot between 8:30 and 10:00 is very good.

I spent a lot of time with my spinster aunts, Bertha and Lila Jewison. Bea was a schoolteacher, and Lila was a nurse. They lived in an old red-brick house north of the Danforth on Hurndale Avenue. It had dark, creaky wooden stairs and smelled musty with a faint odor of medicine. Grandma Jewison lay in a bed off the little sunroom on the second floor. She suffered from angina, and Aunty Bea warned us too much noise could upset her, so Betty and I tended to whisper in their house.

The aunts also owned a cottage at Big Cedar Point on Lake Simcoe. In my first ten years, I spent my summers there. Every Saturday night my mother and father would make the four-hour drive up Yonge Street—Highway 11—to visit and then go home on Sunday evening. It was their only vacation spot, and those twenty-four hours, their only vacation time.

Aunty Bea was a tiny, wiry woman with a determination that still amazes me. While I was yearning to play hockey with my friends at Kew Beach Park, she insisted I practice piano and read Dickens and Sir Walter Scott. She was as unswerving in her belief in my ability to succeed as she was in her Methodist faith. (She also pushed my sister in these endeavors, but I was seen as more important, being the youngest and a boy. And I carried the Jewison name.) Bea loved English literature and the New Testament in equal measure. At age ninety-two she could still recite Gray's *Elegy Written in a Country Church-yard* without a pause or hesitation. And I, some seven decades after her insistence that I memorize long passages from the New Testament, can still recite most of her favorite psalms.

It was Aunt Bea's idea to send me to the Royal Conservatory of Music to learn to play piano and study music theory. She was a school-teacher, after all. She wanted me to acquire some of what she thought of as "accomplishments." She taught me to read early and insisted I learn poetry by heart. Tucked in my old iron bed in the cottage attic, I was introduced to Robert Louis Stevenson, *Ivanhoe*, and *The Count of Monte Cristo*. She got me hooked on Macaulay's *History of England*. I would stay up late reading, long after the rest of the family went to sleep. I still love lying in the dark, reading poetry by the light of coal oil lamps, ducking my head at the dry swoosh of bat wings.

Bea was thrilled when I developed a passion for Robert Service. During the Depression, declaiming poems was thought to be a fitting occupation for most children, and I excelled at the long Service poems with their galloping rhythms and addictive rhymes.

By the time I was seven, I was used to rousing applause for my renditions of "The Shooting of Dan McGrew," "The Cremation of Sam McGee," and my encore, "Willie Gets the Neck," to beaming audiences of Masons and the ladies of the Eastern Star. I loved performing. I remember standing on the stage, wearing my black lace-up boots and hand-knit sweater shouting and whispering the strange tale of Sam McGee in the Yukon. I could swear that all the grown-ups held their breath as I stuffed Sam's frozen body into the boiler of the derelict boat on the shore of Lake Lebarge.

Thirty-four years later I discovered in actor Warren Oates another Robert Service fan. On a hot summer evening somewhere in southern Illinois, we sat in a car waiting for a camera set-up for *In the Heat of the Night* and recited together, relishing each word, each rhyme, all the cadences of Sam McGee: "There are strange things done in the Midnight sun/By the men who moil for gold…"

Since my sister Betty was six years older than me, by the time I was in my teens, we didn't spend much of our free time together. She was working and dating while I was off at the movies or playing with my friends. But she often protected me when I got into trouble. My father was strict, and we were always careful not to get him angry, as he would use the belt if pushed too far.

In the Beach every boy's dream was to own his own canoe. I got mine through the death of a friend, a fellow Boy Scout. I was fourteen and a great paddler. My friend Bobby Blair was a little older and lived on Kippendavie, not far from our store. He got caught in a summer storm off the water treatment plant in Scarborough, paddling his canoe back from an overnight trip to Highland Creek. His parents decided on a Boy Scout funeral. A scout at the head of the coffin and one at the foot. It was a sweltering July day, and we were in full uniform, sweat running down our faces, the smell of the lilies mixed with the smell of embalming fluid, as we stood at attention, determined not to keel over.

Bobby was still and waxy. I watched a fly land on his lip, crawl up his nose, come out again, and crawl across his forehead. It was hard to believe that he was not just pretending, that he would not sit up, whack the fly, and laugh at us all in our uniforms. For the first time in my life, I was faced with the death of a close friend.

I waited ten days after the funeral—I just couldn't wait any longer. I went to Bobby's house and tapped on the screen door. When Bobby's mother opened the door, I said, "Hi, Mrs. Blair. I was just wondering... what you're going to do with Bobby's canoe."

There was silence, then she started to cry. I said I was sorry.

I paid $35 for the canoe, earned by delivering groceries for Mr. Marchment's store on Queen Street and working weekends for the Greek butcher at Devon Meats. The canoe was cedar strip. Beautiful. Hand-built by the Indians on Rice Lake. I still have it. It's one of my most prized possessions. My children had it stripped and restored about twenty-five years ago as a surprise for me.

I think of Bobby every time I go for a paddle at sunset.

2

Another Kind of Justice

You tryin' to be smart, sailor?

—*Tennessee bus driver, 1946*

I blame living in the Beach right next to Lake Ontario and my love of Bobby Blair's canoe for my decision to join the Canadian Navy.

I was a skinny kid full of teenage angst. I wanted to be taller, bigger, more athletic. I wasn't. I was thin and wiry with tiny brown ferret eyes and a small pointed face with big ears. I was rarely chosen for pickup games of football or hockey, and the girls did their best to ignore me. Joining the Sea Cadets was one way to get attention.

The other was through my Saturday matinee performance skills. I had already discovered I could make people laugh. Being the class clown made me almost as popular as the star football player. Egged on by success, I started writing and directing comedy sketches for the annual Christmas events at my high school. I learned to sing and dance. I particularly excelled at the Balmy Dip, a move that involved thrusting your pelvis tight against your partner's as you dipped her back to the swinging beat of Glenn Miller's "String of Pearls." I may not have been as attractive as some of the other guys at Malvern Collegiate, but I was just as hormone-driven, and faster than most when it came time to pick your partner for the Tea Dance.

There were so many nights when I was left alone in the apartment over the store that I had a lot of time to listen to the radio. My favorites were comedy shows—*Fibber McGee and Molly*, Jack Benny and Fred Allen, *Amos 'n' Andy*, and W.C. Fields. And dramatic shows ran a close second: *Lux Radio Theater* with host Cecil B. De Mille. Orson Welles's The Shadow, asking his enthralled listeners "Who knows what evil lurks in the hearts of men?" When he broke into his trademark maniacal laugh, I would shudder with terror. Little Orphan Annie, the Asp, Sandy, and Daddy Warbucks delighted me, too. I used to sing the theme song along with the show every night. I can still sing it.

At Malvern in the early forties, we used to gather in the auditorium once a week to hear announcements and news from the staff. Once I managed to talk four husky guys into carrying me on stage. I was dressed, somewhat inelegantly, in a white sheet and green leaves around my head as I reclined on the stretcher—a rather skinny Nero. While the teachers and faculty sat frozen in shock, I grabbed the microphone and announced the next Tea Dance would be a toga party. What saved me from instant expulsion, I think, was that I did it all in fractured Latin, a feat that made even the sternest of our teachers howl with laughter.

I loved to perform, loved the applause and the attention, never tired of it from my first days on stage when I was only six, to last year in New York when I accepted the Billy Wilder Award from the National Board of Review. My dad loved show business almost as much as I did, and especially vaudeville. On the rare occasions that he managed to get away from the store, we would go to Shea's downtown, one of the last movie houses in Toronto that still had live shows.

One show in particular made a big impression on me, and it may have been when I was only eight or nine. It was at the Loew's Hippodrome. From the second the lights went down and the giant Wurlitzer rose from the orchestra pit, I was spellbound. While Quentin McLean at the organ played "Deep Purple," the curtains flickered with purple lights. It was magical. You could almost hear the audience sigh with delight. Then the curtains parted and the dog act came on. There was always the one dog who wouldn't do what he was told, and he was the one who stole my heart. Then a booming voice announced the headliner: "Ladies and Gentlemen, Mr. Red Skelton!" One of the highlights of Red's act was his impersonation of a woman struggling out of her girdle. It was done behind a lit screen, and when he was through, everyone was convulsed with laughter. Willy Wes and McGinty rounded out the bill that day. As my father and I left the theater, I knew I wanted to be in show business when I grew up, and I imagined my father going to see me on stage.

As a teenager, when I wasn't attending school, seeing movies, or listening to the radio, I worked, and not just in my parents' store. One summer I lifted egg crates at Loblaw's warehouse down on Front Street. The summers of 1942 and 1943, I worked on a vegetable farm on the Holland Marsh, north of the city. So many men had been called up for service that the farmers were in desperate need of help to get the produce to market. The Ontario government had organized student farm labor. With my boyhood friends Harry Thornton and Reid Scott, I lived in a bunk-filled dormitory in the middle of the Marsh, on the Verkaik brothers' farm, and from dawn till dusk we weeded, fertilized, and picked or dug lettuce, onions, carrots, and potatoes.

I had my commercial driver's license by then and was allowed to drive the tractor, and later the farm's ten-ton truck, which was used to deliver crates of vegetables to markets all across southern Ontario. It was a tough job, since the crates were heavy and piled high. I started at midnight and began my deliveries at dawn. But I relished doing a man's work and found the hours on the road peaceful.

From the time I was thirteen, however, Canada was a country at war. My dad, at forty-nine, was in the reserve regiment of the 48th Highlanders. He had been with the Queen's Own Rifles when he was in his twenties. He was a crack shot with the 303 Lee-Enfield rifle and always brought home the Christmas turkey from the sniper competition.

I was already a keen member of the Sea Cadets, the training ground for high school boys destined for active service in the Navy.

The older boys in the neighborhood were marching off in their smart uniforms, and we listened to Hitler shrieking on the radio and Churchill commanding the Empire to join Britain in defense of liberty. The Union Jack still flew above the school, and we stood to attention every morning to sing "God Save the King." All my friends were chomping at the bit to join up.

At seventeen, I decided to join the Navy before I was called up; my Sea Cadet experience would give me priority. My parents didn't object, and I was excited and anxious to prove myself. I was accepted for the Navy at a flat-roofed, low-lying building on the Toronto waterfront.

We were shipped out to HMCS *Montcalm* in Quebec City for our six weeks of basic training. Many French Canadians were against the war and had voted against conscription. So we were not that popular in the pubs. But our chief petty officer was French Canadian, and he was one tough cookie. I tried a few bits of shtick on Petty Officer Cloutier as we marched around the Plains of Abraham on the heights of Quebec City.

"You fucking pimply-faced little shit!" he screamed into my face, our noses almost touching. "You mock me?"

"No, sir!" I lied.

Then he started yelling in earnest: "Your mother is a whore, your sister is a whore..." He tried to make me hit him. When that failed, he tried to get me crying, if not in grief, then in frustration that I couldn't hit him. Finally, he ordered me to raise my Lee-Enfield rifle at arm's length above my head and start running double-time down the Plains of Abraham. He ran me up and down for what felt like an hour, shouting, "Get that fucking rifle up!" every time my arms started to sag. What I learned from that nasty experience was that I had enormous endurance—a wonderful asset for a director—and that there are times when you should keep your mouth shut—a great asset in the military.

Everyone in the Navy yells at you and you are not allowed to talk back. Everything is double time. The discipline inherited from the British Royal Navy and laid out in the "King's Regulations and Admiralty Instructions" had us marching, tying knots, running like idiots, eating, sleeping, even pissing when ordered, and moving in lockstep with others in our company. After six weeks of basic training, I barely missed my individual human rights.

For all the effort, my sole glimpse of the enemy was after Germany had surrendered in 1945 and we escorted a bunch of sorry-looking German prisoners from a submarine that had sailed into a Canadian port to give themselves up. They were tired, their fearsome white turtleneck sweaters filthy with oil and sweat. They stank. When we herded them into a train bound for an internment camp somewhere up north, I gave one of them a pack of cigarettes.

With the war over in Europe, I was ordered to take my sixty days' leave, then demobilize. Rumor was that younger recruits would take the place of older men in the Pacific fleet, but it seemed I was not considered essential to the war effort. I was eighteen years old, ambitious to learn and raise my horizons. I thought perhaps I would go to university, become a journalist, maybe one day a war correspondent. I didn't think about the stage or the movies anymore. Acting, while exciting and fun, didn't seem like a legitimate profession.

I decided to ponder my future while taking my long leave hitchhiking around America. I packed my sea bag and put on my best uniform. My light blue collar was scrubbed and washed, my jumper was skin-tight, my black silk (worn in honor of the death of Lord Nelson) neatly tied in front with regulation tapes. I sported gold Canada badges and kept my cap shining white with shoe polish. My bell-bottom pants were so wide they flapped as I strode out of our barracks. The Navy would have said I was "tiddley," the naval expression for being in best dress uniform.

I hit the road. In uniform, I had no trouble getting rides. My first stop was Chicago, where my Aunt Jo and Uncle George lived. Aunt Jo was my mother's younger sister. She was pretty and funny and loaded with energy. In my view, she and my uncle were terribly hip compared to the Canadian faction of the family. Why were Americans always so much livelier and fun to be around? I wondered. In America they seemed to embrace success and accomplishment. In Canada we seemed to be suspicious of anything too successful.

I recall being amazed at the amount of alcohol we consumed that weekend. I was introduced to all the neighbors and friends. Everyone thought my uniform was so cute and different. I sang all the raunchy navy songs and was an instant hit. The raunchier, the better. The whole weekend was such an *adult* experience for me—everyone older than me but treating me as an equal.

Aunt Jo eventually ended up a helpless alcoholic. She broke my mother's heart and alienated my father. Ultimately Jo and George lost everything, including their lives. They died in 1973 in Florida, only three blocks from my retired parents' little house in St. Petersburg.

After Chicago, I hitchhiked to St. Louis, where I found free lodgings through the USO. Unfortunately I was assigned to share a tent with an overweight, six-foot-five marine sergeant, a Southerner and an aggressive drunk, who also happened to be homosexual. It seems he decided I would be the perfect partner for the night and assumed I'd be willing. Or even if I wasn't, he'd see to it that with enough booze in me, I'd be compliant. I still remember making a run for it as he was ordering more booze at a bar happy to serve naval men free drinks, racing at full speed, my black boots pounding the pavement, the enormous sergeant in full pursuit. I was so terrified of being caught I seemed to take wing and landed on a city bus just as the doors closed. The sergeant chased the bus for several blocks, screaming, but the driver, thank God, never heard him.

My life changed on a hot, hazy day on the outskirts of Memphis, Tennessee. I was waiting for the out-of-town bus. An old black man sitting outside the small grocery store nearby gave me a piece of sugar cane, which he whittled and peeled for me. Another man brought me a slice of watermelon. Everywhere I went people gave me free food and drinks. People were so gracious and polite. I loved the South—the magnolias, the plantation houses with their white columns and wide shade trees. In most towns mine was the only foreign uniform anyone had seen outside of the movies. While no one seemed to know exactly where Canada was, they all knew we were in the war together and that we were still British and lived somewhere up north where it was cold.

I stood there waiting for the bus, watermelon juice still dripping down my chin, the white shoe polish on my cap starting to melt and run down my forehead, my uniform sticking to me, the dark material holding in the heat. When the bus finally came, I was so relieved to be in the shade, I offered to pay. The driver, all smiles, told me my money was no good. I walked to the back, threw my sea bag over a seat, and slouched down by an open window.

After a few minutes the bus came to a jarring stop. When I looked up I saw the driver looking at me in his mirror. He had a wide ruddy face, sweat running down from under his cap. There were two women in the front seats, and they, too, turned and looked at me. "You tryin' to be smart, sailor?" the driver shouted.

I was caught off guard. I didn't know what to say.

"You tryin' to be funny, sailor?" he shouted again with his Tennessee twang.

I looked around, puzzled. A couple of people sat just in front of me. They were black. When they turned, they gave a quick glance only, no emotion showing. The two women and a man close to the front were staring at me, grim-faced, disapproving. The women held their handkerchiefs to their noses as if I were something thoroughly unpleasant.

"This bus ain't moving until you do," the driver shouted next. "Can't you read?"

One of the black passengers pointed at a sign hanging from two twisted wires near the center of the bus. It read: "Colored persons to the rear." That's when it dawned on me. Sure, I had read about the Civil War and heard about segregation, but I had seen black men in uniform. In Detroit. In Chicago. I had seen newsreels showing black soldiers and white being shipped off to war. It had never occurred to me that they would still have to sit in the back of a bus in Tennessee.

The bus waited in silence as I grabbed my bag and got off at the back door. I stepped out onto the side of the road and watched the bus pull away, leaving me in a cloud of dust.

I think it was then, along the highways of Tennessee, Alabama, Mississippi, and Louisiana, that the desire to make films such as *In the Heat of the Night* and *A Soldier's Story* took root. It was still with me when I made *The Hurricane* about Hurricane Carter, a black man wrongly convicted of murder. I have always wanted to tell stories that grab an audience, stories that hold your attention. But what really fascinates me are the ideas behind the stories. Racism and injustice are two themes I have come back to, again and again, in my films.

Traveling in the South, I understood the meaning of being victimized even more than I had as a boy. In a small town near the Louisiana border, a raw-faced farmer gave me a lift in his pickup truck. "See that truck over there?" he asked, pointing at a beat-up blue truck parked in front of the general store. "That's the one that dragged the niggah through town at the end of a rope," he said proudly. "An' that's after they hanged him."

3

Directing Puppets

Kid, nobody's looking at *you* in this movie!

—*Edwin Marin, director, on location in Banff*

In 1981 the University of Western Ontario presented me with an honorary doctorate. I have never taken honorary degrees very seriously, though I have been grateful for every one of them on behalf of my very strange profession, but this one was special.

In 1946, after my discharge from the Navy and my trip around the southern United States, I applied to Western for admission to its school of journalism, the only one in the country at that time. With some other veterans, I had taken some extra high school credits at a special school in Kitchener. I went to classes during the day and worked nights at the B.F. Goodrich plant, where I spliced rubber moldings for refrigerators. It was a dirty, smelly job, but I needed the cash. In August I bought a fine wool suit, shirt, and tie for my interview with the dean, and hitchhiked the 100 miles from Toronto to London to meet him.

The dean's office where I sat, waiting for my interview, was hot, humid, and unfriendly. I had arrived early. The dean had set 11:30 for my moment, but I was there at 10:30. Around 12:30 the dean appeared. He hurried past me and disappeared down a long corridor. I continued to wait for a while, then asked the secretary if the dean would see me shortly.

"Afraid not," she said, barely looking up from her papers.

I showed her the letter confirming my 11:30 appointment. She shook her head firmly and informed me he had gone to lunch and would not be back for a couple of hours. "You'll have to come back later," she suggested in frosty tones.

I didn't. I wrote a letter to the dean telling him I didn't want to go to his lousy university after all. And he wrote back telling me he was glad. While accepting his university's honorary degree some thirty-five years later, I realized I owed him a debt.

I ended up at the University of Toronto, at Victoria College, because that's where all the United Church and Methodist students went. The Catholics went to St. Mike's, the Anglicans to Trinity, the Presbyterians to Knox, and the Jews to University College. The U of T campus was an exciting place in the 1940s. I made friends with Don Harron and future senator Keith Davey. Johnny Wayne and Frank Shuster graduated the year I got there. I had the privilege of being taught by Northrop Frye and Marshall McLuhan. Yet despite such worthy lecturers and my desire to be a journalist, I found myself increasingly drawn to campus musical productions. I wrote, directed, and performed in the Vic Bob, the annual satirical revue at Victoria College. I followed this up with the All-Varsity Revue at University College, where I sang, danced, did the lighting, the staging, wrote the songs and comedy sketches. I spent more time in the theater than in lecture halls. I was never involved, however, in straight drama productions, preferring to be my own producer, director, and writer. I am still not sure how I managed to graduate, but I did. In 1949—veterans could graduate in three years instead of the usual four—I walked away with a Bachelor of Arts degree and an honorary award. I was the first person in my family to get a university degree.

As I told the University of Western Ontario's graduating class in

1981, had the dean kept his appointment with me, I might have become a not-very-effective journalist. Or one of those foreign correspondents leaning up against a grim hotel bar in some strange country, hoping to pick up enough news over drinks to file another column.

During the summers I worked as a waiter, under the tutelage of the autocratic Italian maître d' George Allora from the Royal York Hotel in downtown Toronto. He taught me to always carry a clove of garlic in my pocket to add to the salad dressing at the last moment. "It is," he said, "worth that extra $5 tip you may not be getting." He was in charge at another Canadian Pacific institution, the Banff Springs Hotel in the Rocky Mountains. A Hollywood western called *Canadian Pacific* was being shot in Banff the summer of 1948 and all the movie people stayed at the hotel, easy prey for an attentive waiter's services. I poured extra glasses of water, snapped forward to light cigars, ran to bring ice, changed ashtrays, emptied glasses, and begged to be allowed on the set as an extra.

A casting director finally noticed and hired me for a crowd scene. It's the 1880s. A bunch of fiendishly phony Indians were attacking railroad workers who were laying track. I played a railroad worker. Right up my alley, I thought, especially if the script said anything about an arrow in the back.

Randolph Scott, a somewhat famous western star, was playing a surveyor against the magnificent backdrop of the real Rockies. Most movies didn't bother with the real thing if a painted backdrop would do. They still don't. Now they use blue screen and computer imaging. Anyway, the surveyor romanced Jane Wyatt and Nancy Olson in his spare time, but mostly, he fought off war-painted Indians and protected the railroad guys, which was where I came in, me and the hundred other extras.

The location of the crowd scene was a big, sloped field outside Banff. I felt like I was at the center of the movie universe. Huge arc lights dominated the area. Four or five men struggled with a massive old Mitchell movie camera on wheels that dug into the soft earth. At the top of this solid, cumbersome structure a guy on a seat was looking through a lens, talking to a couple of dozen technicians. And on the field's most prominent rise was the director, master of all he surveyed. His name was Edwin Marin, a veteran from the days of silent pictures, a B-movie guy—second features, thrillers, minor comedies, westerns—but as far as I was concerned, on that day of my introduction to movie-making, Edwin Marin shone with the luster of a John Ford or Howard Hawks.

The crowd of extras had been given period costumes. Dark, frayed, crumpled suits, boots, and old hats for the railway workers, feathered headgear for the Indians. Many of them were native people from the local reserve, now dressed and painted in Hollywood's version of wild Indians.

Randolph Scott, handsome, suntanned, big-shouldered, sat ruggedly on his steed.

An assistant director shouted instructions and signaled the extras to take our places at one end of the field. This presented a problem for me. The clothes I'd been issued for the scene were way too large. I had told the costumer who gave me the gear that the boots didn't fit, but he'd just looked at me: "Don't worry about it, kid. You're an extra." He said I could hold the pants together with some rope. Didn't matter if I looked a bit like Charlie Chaplin.

I was so excited about being in a movie, I let it go. Now, I figured, it was too late to do anything about it. I clumped to my spot and waited for the moment when I could start my performance.

Another assistant director turned to me: "Carry this dynamite charge. Just run across here and take it over there by the shed."

Oh God, I thought, I have a real acting piece! Then the director said, "This is where there is an attack on the train and I want you all to run across here and..." I heard someone shout, "Roll camera!" Heard the clacker board smack shut. Heard "Action!" Shots were ringing out everywhere. The Indians were all howling. And, as instructed, I started running with the other extras across the open space toward a railroad shed.

Around me, there were cries from the attacking Indians, the thud of horses' hooves, the wham of dynamite blowing up the railroad tracks. It was rackety and chaotic and thrilling. Just one trouble: the damned extra-large boots got tangled with my extra-long pants and sent me sprawling.

Jesus, I thought, I've ruined the scene.

Twenty-five extras pounded past me. I struggled to my feet, grabbed my fallen hat with one hand, hoisted my pants up with the other and joined the stampede to the shed.

"Cut! Cut!" Edwin Marin shouted over the din.

Uh-oh, I thought, here's where I catch hell.

"Great scene!" Marin shouted. "Print it!"

I pushed my way over to him. "But Mr. Marin," I said, "you can't print it. I fell in the middle of the scene and dropped the dynamite!"

"You fell?" Marin said. "Kid, nobody's looking at *you* in this movie!"

I felt completely deflated. And that wasn't the end of my disappointment. When *Canadian Pacific* came out, I sat through two screenings in a theater at home in Toronto, and I couldn't find myself. I wasn't there. I must have been left on the cutting room floor. There was no "me" in the movie.

Oddly enough, though, none of that squelched my ambitions.

Eighteen months later, after I graduated from university, I hitchhiked across the continent to California. With me was a list of the people who worked on *Canadian Pacific*. They would be my first Hollywood contacts—Nat Holt, Randolph Scott, Edwin Marin, and others. After all, Nat Holt, the producer, had told me, "Look me up, kid, if you ever get to Hollywood."

They'd get me my break into movies, I fantasized.

Hollywood looked like just another city. Nothing magical about it. I stayed at a cheap motel on Pico Boulevard somewhere in Santa Monica. The studios were far enough away to make traveling to them difficult and time-consuming. I phoned around town, but couldn't get past the receptionists and secretaries and assistants. I left my name. Nobody returned the calls. I stuck it out in L.A. for as long as my budget let me, seven or eight days. No job offers came in, no call backs, nothing. When I ran out of money for my room, I slept on the beach near the Santa Monica Pier. By two in the morning it got so cold, I slipped into an apartment lobby and curled up under the stairs with my Gladstone bag as a pillow and a Mexican shawl I'd bought as a souvenir for my mother as a blanket.

I could imagine what the people back in Hollywood thought when they looked at the messages I'd left.

"Who the hell's Norman Jewison?"

After hitchhiking all the way back to Toronto I was broke and frustrated. My dad was pushing me to apply for a government job in External Affairs. Every month our sub–post office would get these employment notices.

"You could travel to other countries and see the world," my dad said. "Look at what it says." He placed a notice in front of me.

"Junior Foreign Affairs Officer," I read. "University degree required. Also a second language. Starting salary $3,500 annually."

"Gee, Dad, I don't know," I muttered. "My French isn't that good."

"Just apply and write the exam. You have a university degree. Don't waste your time."

I knew my father was worried that I would never make a living in show business. To please him I filled out the application and sent it off to Ottawa. And then, since I had a commercial driver's license from my days delivering vegetables, I applied to Diamond Taxi and started driving a cab on the night shift. From five o'clock every night till seven the next morning I cruised the darkened streets of downtown Toronto.

If you ever wish to study human behavior up close, drive a cab. It puts you in personal contact with all kinds of different people, especially at night. When people sit in a darkened cab, the driver is often seen as a confidant and trusted friend. They don't have to look at you and know you'll have to listen. Like a bartender, a driver's a captive audience. Furthermore, a *paid* captive audience. One moment it would be a wealthy middle-aged couple heading for a mansion in Rosedale. The next passenger would be a smelly drunk trying to find his way home. Millionaires, musicians, hookers, and deadbeats. After six months I had met them all, heard their stories. Some I had actually taken home and helped to the sofa. It was a fascinating period and I would use these observations of human behavior time and time again over the course of my career as an actor, writer, and director. I still have my driver's medallion from 1950, number 14222. I have it framed and in my study, just in case I have to go back to driving cab one day.

It was during this time that I met Stuart Griffiths, a man who was to become a mentor to me. He was the new programming head of CBC television—except there were no studios and no transmitter yet. I had applied for an interview and met with Stuart at his office in downtown Toronto, at 354 Jarvis Street, an old white mansion known affectionately as the Kremlin. I told him of my interest in this new medium of communication. How I had watched television in the Silver Rail Tavern on Yonge Street, a terrible black and white signal from Buffalo, and realized it was some sort of miracle. That this was the greatest medium of communication ever devised by man and would completely change our lives.

Griffiths liked my enthusiasm. He suggested I go to England where the BBC had been on the air with live TV since the end of the war. "That's where you'll be able to learn something," he counseled.

It was good advice and I took it. Especially since the government interviewer at External Affairs in Ottawa, where I'd gone for my oral exam, told me, "Why don't you do what you really want to do with your life? If you really are serious about acting and writing, go for it!"

Sometimes you get the right advice at the right time for the wrong reasons. I think he probably felt I didn't have the stuff to make a good civil servant. So with the money I had saved driving cab I bought a ticket for $140 on a Greek immigrant ship sailing out of Quebec City bound for Southampton, England.

This meant leaving not only my family and friends, but my first true love. Inge Hansen was a Danish girl I had met at university, a trim little brunette with a gamine look. I thought my exile would make her heart grow fonder, and I imagined I would return as a better prospect—certainly in the eyes of her parents, who saw me as just an unemployed actor.

Thinking back on the journey now, I must have been crazy to imagine I'd be luckier there than I'd been in Hollywood, but I was determined to give this terrible business the best shot I could. Mere reality wasn't going to put me off. I pinned my hopes on a guy called Bernie Braden. He had a late-night show on BBC Television—a sophisticated half-hour of light comedy, filmed live with three cameras. It starred Bernie and his wife, Barbara Kelly, an attractive blond actress with smart comedic timing. She was also Canadian. Both of them wrote the show and Bernie did all the staging.

BBC Television in the early fifties was not only years ahead of Canadian television, it was leaps and bounds ahead of America. The huge botanical gardens at Alexandra Palace in London had been converted into studios. Since the corporation was non-commercial and funded by a direct-tax license on radios and television sets, it maintained a true independence from sponsors or ratings systems, and was a real haven for creative types.

In addition to *The Goon Show*, a wild radio comedy featuring the brilliant artists Peter Sellers, Harry Secombe, Spike Milligan, and Michael Bentine, there were great live theatrical dramas and musical variety shows. New program ideas were being explored as more and more people bought TV sets and the number of broadcasting hours increased daily.

Somehow I talked Bernie Braden into hiring me as one of the writers for his show. I was also his stand-in for rehearsals. Handsome and witty, sort of Jack Paar with a little bit of Steve Allen thrown in, Bernie both acted in and directed the show, moving from one role to the other effortlessly. He was an extraordinary man and a great teacher. I learned from him just by hanging around the control booth, listening to him planning camera angles and directing the other actors. I picked up a lot of technical stuff about how a TV show got on the air. The pay was a pittance, but the thirteen weeks I spent there provided me with invaluable experience in live television.

To make ends meet I also wrote comedy sketches for a BBC Radio show called *Starlight Hour*, starring Alfie Marks and Beryl Reid. I scanned the newspapers every day for topical ideas to use in comedy sketches. One piece I wrote involved "swan upping." That's the ritual where young swans are grabbed on the Thames so that their beaks can be notched. Which means they now belong to the Queen. Great stuff for a comedy piece.

I also babysat for Don Harron, who had moved to London by then and embarked on a successful career as an actor. A gifted writer, he encouraged me and often helped me with some of my comedy writing. We would later work together on stage in the Canadian comedy revue *Spring Thaw*, for Dora Mavor Moore.

I wrote a children's show for BBC Radio that was well received and for which I was paid a guinea a minute. I auditioned for every American part I could find. My English and Irish accents didn't fool anybody in England, but my New York and Southern U.S. accents were passable. I did get a call back from Josh Logan on *South Pacific*, but lost out to a tall Irish tenor. I ended up that year as the ass end of a cow in a third-rate British panto production of *Aladdin* at the Woolwich Armoury Theatre.

Christmas 1951 was a tough, cold one for me in my attic room in Mrs. Harris's boardinghouse on Inverness Terrace in Notting Hill Gate. Dinner was rabbit stew and onions, and I didn't have a shilling for the gas fire. Shivering in the dark, I tried to imagine Christmas at home. Everybody around the table with Dad carving the turkey and Mom all red in the face rushing in with the gravy and pudding. For the first time in my life, I was hungry, poor, and scared. What's worse for someone in show business, I was losing my confidence. The day I picked up a tiny withered turnip off the floor at the greengrocer's and put it in my pocket, I knew I was in trouble.

A couple of days later I received a letter from Stuart Griffiths in Toronto. He said CBC-TV was hiring the best young Canadian talent from radio, theater, dance, and music. A training program was about to start. Did I want to be a trainee? I was twenty-four, out of work, and penniless. It was time to go home.

My parents never said much about my struggle to get into show business. In the Beach, people acted in high school or service club shows, but they didn't act for a living. This was outside my parents' experience and they were never completely comfortable with my involvement in any form of show business. Nevertheless, they sent me

$500—an enormous sum of money in those days—for my steerage ticket home on the *Empress of Canada*. My old couch in the alcove off the living room was made up for me when I arrived. I settled in, ready to start a job and take up where I had left off with Inge.

But Inge had other plans. She had met a sportswriter for a Toronto newspaper. An upstanding guy who didn't put his ambition before their relationship. She was committed to him. Luckily I landed a part in a play produced by Dora Mavor Moore and her New Play Society. It kept my mind off Inge and made me some money (about $60 a week) while I waited for the new CBC-TV studios on Jarvis to be finished and the training session to begin. On stage I played the young romantic lead in *The Biggest Thief in Town*. Off stage I played the jilted lover and struggling bohemian artist.

When Tom Dryden, an old college chum, heard I was back in town, he invited me to a party. At the end of the evening, in what can only be called a set-up, it was suggested that Margaret Ann Dixon could give me a ride home since we both lived in the Beach. "Dixie," a petite brunette with large dark eyes, adorned billboards all over town as the "Black Cat" cigarette girl. I couldn't believe my luck. But the more I tried to impress her on the drive across town, the more she resisted. Dixie parked her father's yellow convertible in the driveway of her lovely home in the poshest part of the Beach and politely said goodnight. I hiked ten blocks home to my tiny alcove over the store. A stockbroker's daughter and a shopkeeper's son. It didn't look promising.

I called her the next day and suggested we go to a movie. She just laughed and said she was busy. I called again and kept calling until eventually she agreed to a date. This time I relaxed and dropped the sophisticated world traveler bit. I talked about my dreams of show business and since her father, Jim, was also a dreamer, we were into familiar territory.

Over the next few months we fell in love.

When the CBC's training program finally began, they were still pouring concrete for Studio A, so we learned how to put on a live TV show in a Quonset hut up the street. Radio people like Ross McLean,

Drew Crossan, and Arthur Hiller were thrown together with theater people like Silvio Narizzano, Hank Kaplan, Don Hudson, and myself. NBC's Pat Weaver, Sigourney's dad, sent up some advisers. We had dummy cameras for a while because the real equipment hadn't arrived yet. Then just three months later, on September 8, 1952, we stumbled onto the airwaves—and I do mean stumbled.

The first image that appeared on Canadian TV was an upside-down CBC logo. Fortunately I wasn't responsible. I was in too much of a panic even to notice. The powers-that-be had made me a floor director, which meant I worked on the floor with the actors and cameras, taking direction through earphones from the director in the booth perched one floor up. All I remember was running around in total chaos.

Live TV is an amazing adrenaline rush. I started working on an hour-long weekly variety show called *The Big Revue*. It starred performers like Wally Koster, George Murray, and Phyllis Marshall, and employed dozens of singers and dancers. Lorraine Thomson, future broadcast journalist and wife of CBC newsman Knowlton Nash, was a dancer, and Ted Kotcheff, the noted Hollywood film director, was a stagehand. We were all under the tutelage of a screaming, intense producer-director, Don Hudson. Sets collapsed. Cameramen fainted. Actors threw up. But when it worked, the high was incredible.

Once I had the hang of my new job, I thought it was time to impress Dixie's parents. I invited Dixie to bring Jim and Thelma to watch a live broadcast of *The Big Revue*. They joined about two hundred people in the bleachers set up at one end of Studio A. Dixie was nervous because her parents would have preferred she not get involved with someone who wore sandals and sold Christmas trees on Queen Street to supplement his meager show business income.

Just before the show began, I strode out onto the floor to give everyone a three-minute warning. Howard Cable's orchestra finished tuning up and the singers began to assemble. I grabbed a broom and began to sweep the floor because I was always afraid a nail or a stray pencil would trip up a dancer or camera. I looked up to see Thelma nudging Jim. Dixie looked embarrassed as her mother's voice carried down to the studio floor: "So *that's* what he does at the CBC—he sweeps the floor!"

That summer I took Dixie on a canoe trip to Algonquin Park, a wilderness area four hours north of Toronto. She turned out to be a good paddler. All those fancy girls' camps, I thought. When we arrived at the first portage, Dixie calmly put her pack's tumpline on her forehead and got under the bow to help carry the canoe a half mile to the next lake. We set up camp on an island, all alone on the lake. It was a true Canadian romantic evening. Dinner cooked over an open fire, the sound of water lapping on rocks, a sky full of stars and two people snuggled down in a double sleeping bag.

The next morning, the sun streaming into the tent woke me up. Dixie wasn't there. I sat up and looked through the mosquito netting. She was picking blueberries in the nude. As she bobbed up and down picking berries for our breakfast, I knew this was the woman I would marry.

After three months as a floor director on *The Big Revue*, I was asked to direct and stage all the comedy sketches on the show because Don was too busy with the musical numbers. I never really missed performing in front of the camera. I had discovered that the power that comes with controlling things from behind the camera is just as exciting. In the spring of 1953, I became the producer-director of my own show. A fifteen-minute puppet show: *Uncle Chichimus*, starring a balding, middle-aged puppet.

A bizarre mix of satirical comment, weather forecast, and domestic comedy—similar to *Kukla, Fran, and Ollie* from the U.S., *Uncle Chichimus* appeared before the evening news. Frank Fice and I wrote a new show every day with assistance from the talented character actor Larry Mann, who was Uncle Chich's human foil. As the weeks went by, the show got loopier and more controversial. The little puppet became a kind of political commentator when we discovered you could get away with almost anything as long as it came out of a puppet's mouth. He even had his own network, the Chichimus Broadcasting Corporation, a satire of our own employers.

After *Uncle Chichimus* I moved on to produce and direct a musical program called *Jazz with Jackson*. It was the first big band jazz program on live television and starred Cal Jackson, a black conductor-arranger from Los Angeles. The show attracted a lot of attention in the music world of New York, Chicago, and L.A. Soon word got around, and our signal was picked up in Buffalo. When important musical artists like Oscar Peterson and the Modern Jazz Quartet, Mel Torme, Kenny Hodges, and George Shearing began making the trip north, I said a silent thank you to Aunt Bertha every night. Because I could read a musical score, I could make my camera cuts at the perfect musical moment. This ability to "watch" music became my métier and kept me in demand as a variety musical and comedy director.

After twenty-six weeks working on *Jazz with Jackson*, I moved on to produce and direct General Electric's *Showtime*. This was the big Sunday-night weekly variety hour. Frank Peppiatt, John Aylesworth, and Sol Ilson served as the writing team. Robert Goulet and Shirley Harmer were the singing stars. This was followed by my favorite show, *The Barris Beat*, a late-night show with great jazz and some highly original and unpredictable comedy. Phil Nimmons and his nine-piece orchestra backed up Gloria Lambert and various guest singers. Alex Barris was a columnist for the *Toronto Telegram* and became a rather charming and articulate host.

Montreal-born Reuben Shipp was a Hollywood writer for a popular American sitcom, *The Life of Riley*, starring William Bendix. Shipp was deported from the States during the McCarthy hearings. Rumor was he was a leftist and had been forced out of his network job and blacklisted. I hired him immediately because he was an extremely talented comedy writer. But some months later the long hand of the FBI or Senator McCarthy somehow reached up to Ottawa. We were informed that poor Reuben Shipp would be fired due to political pressure.

I made a difficult decision. I told Reuben that he could keep writing, but his name would be changed on the credits. I felt angry and ashamed that the blacklist also existed in Canada.

So Reuben secretly kept working and was supported by the creative community. The following year he wrote a fantastic satirical political drama about McCarthyism, *Point of Order*. It was broadcast on CBC Radio and copies of the program were smuggled to New York. It created quite a furor, and I admired Reuben for standing up for his rights.

Someone once told me they had counted how many shows I had directed during those early days at the CBC. It came to three hundred. That could be right. At one point it seemed as though I was working with half the acts that appeared every Sunday night on *The Ed Sullivan Show*. Wayne and Shuster, Robert Goulet, Shirley Harmer, Steve Lawrence and Eydie Gorme, not to mention dozens of great comedy acts from New York—everybody from Jerry Lester to Morey Amsterdam and Shelley Berman. I was enjoying myself so much I lost count of the hours and the shows.

The American networks began to seduce Canadian talent with offers to join their networks, and with audiences ten times the size and salaries double or triple those paid by the CBC, they were hard to resist. But artists also left Canada because the Canadian public and press were so negative at that time. Artists need to feel that their work is appreciated. They need approval. When the encouragement to produce their best work doesn't exist in their own country, they go somewhere else, in this case the United States. In 1957 I was one of the ones who headed south.

4

Do You Want It Good or Do You Want It Wednesday?

Oh, and Frank, bring Dean, will ya?

—*Norman Jewison*

In 1957 an agent named Larry Auerbach at the William Morris Agency in New York called and asked if he could represent me. He had seen some kinescopes of my work with the American singer Gloria Lambert on *The Barris Beat* and he said he liked what I was doing. It was exciting and disturbing to get that call. Was I really as good as Larry said I was? I had never had an agent. Back then, nobody in Toronto had an agent. And nobody bothered to tell you how good they thought you were. Maybe that was why people like Robert Goulet and Shirley Harmer had left. So had the drama director Arthur Hiller. He was now directing live drama in New York. They left Canada, never to return. I drove the eleven hours to New York and took a cab to the William Morris Agency at Fifth-sixth and Sixth Avenue.

Larry Auerbach didn't keep me waiting. As soon as I was announced, he came out of his office to shake my hand. We exchanged a little small talk. He said he had started with the agency in the mailroom and had worked his way up. Now he was trying to sign up some new young talent.

"What we're going to do, Norman," he said, "is to send your clips over to CBS and if they respond, we'll go and take a meeting." Larry was a tall, good-looking guy about my age but brimming with such confidence he seemed older.

I shuffled nervously and gazed out at the Manhattan skyline, both excited and fearful of the possibilities. I had a secure job at CBC-TV, made $12,000 a year, one of the highest-paid directors. I had two young kids—Kevin was four and Michael only a month old—and an old house in the east end of Toronto with an upstairs tenant whose rent helped pay the mortgage. A familiar and established environment. It was all a long way from taking my chances in New York. "I don't think I can hang around, Larry," I said. "I've gotta get back to Toronto."

"Let's just see if they have any interest," he said and put his hand on my shoulder as if to reassure me that perhaps they wouldn't and I could head back home without having to make any hard decisions. "Come, I'll take you to lunch."

Larry drank two martinis before he'd even examined the menu. He seemed to know everyone in the restaurant and greeted them all by name, introducing me to the comedian Fat Jack Leonard as a hot new television director. I was amazed at how smooth he was.

After a long lunch we headed back to his office. Another agent rushed in, very excited, and shouted, "Come on, let's get your client over to CBS quick. Mike Dann has seen the clips and likes them. He wants to make a deal."

Larry jumped up and grabbed me. "See? Wha'd I tell ya?"

An hour later I was on the thirty-fifth floor of the black CBS tower, flanked by my two new agents in their tailored suits. I was rumpled from my long drive, dizzy from lunch and the sheer speed of it all. We marched into Mike Dann's office. The East Coast program director of CBS television, Dann was in shirtsleeves, his tie undone. He had sandy hair and reminded me of Bugs Bunny. He spoke very fast when he offered me a job.

It took more than four months for our green cards to come through. Endless trips to the U.S. consulate in Toronto, special clearance from Scotland Yard (because I had lived in England), medical examinations, and even a passport for Michael, who was only eight weeks old when he had his passport photo taken. We had to prop him up for his picture.

Although I had visited New York many times to see Broadway shows, I was uneasy about moving my family to Manhattan. It's no place for kids or dogs. Larry Auerbach and I finally found a small two-bedroom apartment across from Van Cortlandt Park in the North Bronx, at 252nd Street. It meant an hour's commute to the end of the subway line and then a bus. The CBS rehearsal studios and the *Hit Parade* office were in an old building at Seventy-fifth and Tenth. Live television with a new show every week required long hours and late dinners every night, with only one day of rest and play with the kids. Almost every night, I'd fall asleep on the subway train and had to be awakened at the end of the line.

It was a difficult transition for Dixie. Two small children, rented furniture, a tiny kitchen, and the never-ending battle with the New York City cockroaches. But we did have the park across Broadway, and we were only committed to a one-year lease. We missed our house on Bingham Avenue in Toronto with the big backyard.

CBS in the fifties was all variety shows—*The Garry Moore Show* and *The Ed Sullivan Show* on Sunday nights. I was going to be directing *Your Hit Parade.* It was a long-running show featuring each week's top ten songs across America. There were two talented soloists, Dorothy Collins and Johnny Desmond, with a cast of thirty backup singers and dancers. My job was to "freshen up" the show. Give it a new look. At first the task seemed impossible. The songs were lousy, stuff like "Rockin' Robin," repetitious, uninteresting. I think we did more than twenty different versions of that one.

Then I spotted an opportunity. It was a love ballad with a catchy melody called "It's All in the Game." It hovered around number 15 in the charts. I suggested to the producer, Perry Lafferty, that if we booked the song and its singer, Tommy Edwards, as a guest a month ahead and if the song moved up the charts, we'd look brilliant. He agreed. We made the booking and, sure enough, the song shot to number 1 and stayed there for six weeks. But there was a catch. The man who sang on the record, the man we had booked for the show, Tommy Edwards, was black.

Kenny Greengrass, the show's contact with our sponsor, Lucky Strike Cigarettes, called me down to the Madison Avenue offices of Young and Rubicam, the ad agency with the lucrative Lucky Strike account. When I got there, he introduced me to an executive from South Carolina. He had a beefy handshake and a ready smile, but the minute he started talking I was taken back to that dusty road in Tennessee where the bus had separate seats for blacks and whites. He had the same sound in his voice as the bus driver and the man in the pickup truck.

"We been doin' *Your Hit Parade* on the radio and on television for many a year," he said to me. "We had Sinatra, rock 'n' roll, and soft stuff, but we never had a black and, young fella, we ain't about to start now."

Back at CBS I raged and shouted, heard a whole lot of placating words, but none that meant they would ignore Lucky Strike's demands. Then Kenny Greengrass came to the studio during a rehearsal and asked what I was going to do.

"Suppose Lucky Strike bans Tommy Edwards," I said to him, "and suppose the story gets out? What if it turned up on the front page of the papers? Or *Time* magazine, for example?" I knew someone at *Time*, but hadn't thought of the particular strategy until Greengrass arrived.

"You'd let the papers know?" he asked, incredulous. "Is that what you're telling me?"

I shook my head and shrugged. "It won't matter, Ken. It's bound to leak out to the press. I'm just worried about the reputation of the American Tobacco Company." I turned and went back to rehearsals.

On the night of the show, Tommy Edwards appeared as scheduled, live on camera, singing "It's All in the Game," and everyone in the studio went crazy. It was a wonderful song. And I learned that Lucky

Strike wanted a newspaper story about their attitude to blacks even less than they wanted a black singer on *Your Hit Parade*.

The lesson, though I didn't quite see it then, was to push back, to not let injustice persist, to understand that bigots often don't like the light to shine in their dark corners.

This lesson would be useful again when I started doing specials for CBS. I produced and directed specials for Danny Kaye, Jimmy Durante, and Jackie Gleason. Then *The Broadway of Lerner and Loewe*, when I had the opportunity to work with Richard Burton, Stanley Holloway, Julie Andrews, and Maurice Chevalier. And then came *Tonight with Belafonte*, the first special on American television starring a black performer. It was followed by *Belafonte N.Y.* As Harry saw it, the point of the shows was to give Americans back a part of their culture they were not able to see anywhere else on television. When the camera scanned the faces of the actors, they were both black and white. And they shared the same chemistry, the same joy in the music. No racial tension, no mutual distrust. The star was Belafonte. Many of the backup singers and the dancers were white. In one part, Harry sang to a bunch of little kids, black and white, and he was great—having fun, laughing with them, making them feel the songs, sing along with him. The audience loved Harry's singing, his humanity, his ability to make everyone feel comfortable.

Years later Harry told me he thought we showed life as it should be in America. We offered hope. Harry knew how revolutionary that was.

More than twenty of CBS's Southern affiliates went off the air during our first Belafonte special. When the show went off the air, I was proud of that, and when Harry got his first Emmy for *Tonight with Belafonte*, I was proud of that, too.

When I had finished the second Belafonte special, I had a call from Freddie Fields and David Begelman. Their personal management company represented a number of actors, including Paul Newman, Henry Fonda, Joanne Woodward, and Judy Garland. They wanted to talk to me about Judy.

"Have you heard her Carnegie Hall LP?" Freddie asked when we met.

"Everybody's talking Judy's back," added David. "It's time for Judy to do a television special."

I didn't say anything.

"Judy's due for a comeback," Freddie said, in case I had missed his message the first time.

Judy Garland had endured more comebacks than anyone else in show business. She had begun as a child actor. She became an international movie star at MGM, along with Mickey Rooney.

"You *have* heard Judy sing?"

Of course I had. The last time I saw her was at the Palladium Theatre in London eight or nine years before. The Palladium was packed. I was poor and sitting in the third balcony, enthralled by this tiny legend filling the enormous stage. She was, even then, almost middle-aged, a little overweight in the hips, a little awkward on her long thin legs, but she still generated more magic, more energy, and more honest emotion than any other musical performer I had ever seen with the exception of Edith Piaf. Like Piaf, she could grab your heart. Way up there on the third balcony with the not-so-great acoustics, I could feel the hair on the back of my neck stand up.

And what a performance she gave! After six curtain calls, she came back out, sat down on the edge of the stage and, as the audience fell silent, she sang "Over the Rainbow" with only the piano accompanying her. *Judy at Carnegie Hall* would go on to win five Grammys and stayed in *Billboard*'s Top 40 for a year.

Still, it would be a gamble. Hollywood studios had given up on Judy years ago. She had ricocheted from stardom to failed marriages, to drug addiction, back to stardom, to alcohol, to some of those concerts like the one I had seen in London. I was afraid. I had avoided her Carnegie Hall performance for fear I would be disappointed after what I had seen at the Palladium. I wanted her to remain a legend.

"Something elegant, something classy," Freddie was saying. He moved around the room quickly and he talked very fast. He was a terrific agent and a great dancer.

David was taller, dark, very good-looking. He was soft-spoken and carried himself like a young Cary Grant. Black suit, gray tie, white button-down shirt. He always wore the same thing. Like a costume. They both insisted this was Judy's moment. The Carnegie Hall recording provided the opportunity. An important television special would revitalize her career.

At the end of the meeting I reluctantly agreed to attend Judy's next concert in Haddonfield, New Jersey, on the following Saturday night. It was May 1961. Freddie and David sent a limo for Dixie and me. A torrential rain was falling, and the driver had a lot of trouble finding the sports arena they had booked for the evening.

"Why is she performing in a sports arena?" Dixie asked, getting, as she so often does, to the heart of the matter.

"It's a gig," I answered. I knew what she meant. It's a long way from Carnegie Hall to the Haddonfield, New Jersey, ice rink.

The place was packed. Over three thousand people were jammed into the barnlike hall. The ice rink had been covered with chairs. Upstairs around the back it was standing room only. There was no curtain, just a black velour backdrop, an orchestra, and a microphone in a spot center stage.

The orchestra, under the direction of Mort Lindsey, began with his superbly arranged Carnegie Hall overture that opens her recording of that concert. The audience—many of them were still dripping from the downpour—hushed with anticipation.

When Judy entered in her black tights and short, sequined jacket they went wild. And she sang her heart out. She pranced and danced around that stage with such energy and exuberance that when she had finished I was on my feet, clapping and shouting for encores along with everyone else. Hordes of young men ran to the stage with bouquets of flowers and Judy leaned down to touch their hands.

When she came to "Birds fly over the rainbow, why, then, oh why can't I?" the place began to feel like a religious revival meeting, and I found myself crying along with the rest of the audience.

After the show I was ushered backstage into her dressing room. Close to forty, she still had that gamine look. Her eyes were enormous in a small face, child's eyes, full of trust and innocence despite all she had endured in the past couple of decades. I was already thinking of how to arrange the lighting for our show to capture Judy's best features, to reduce the bit of extra weight, to focus on that extraordinary face, the huge, black-fringed eyes. We began to talk.

She was open, curious, earthy, and very funny. She had a bawdy laugh that she used to punctuate many of her sentences, often at her own expense.

About five minutes into our talk, she looked at her watch and said, "Excuse me, Norman, but I have to make a call." She picked up the phone on the table between us. Dialed. A few seconds went by, then she said into the receiver: "This is Judy Garland. May I speak to the president, please."

The president? What president? I was looking at Dixie. Of CBS perhaps?

"Good evening, Mr. President," Judy said after the briefest pause. "How are you tonight?"

She chatted easily, cheerfully. A few moments later it dawned on me that it was the real president she was talking with: the President of the United States. She'd been put straight through to John F. Kennedy, and he had, obviously, accepted her call.

As we stared in awe, she cleared her throat and began to sing into the receiver. "Somewhere over the rainbow, way up high..." She sang the first sixteen bars in a soft voice, then she said, "Good night, Mr. President, and happy birthday." And she hung up.

She turned to me without a word of explanation and asked as if nothing unusual had happened, "Now, where were we, Norman?"

I knew I was hooked.

The team we put together for the show had some of my people and some of Judy's. Gary Smith was the production designer on all my shows; his work was minimalist and sophisticated. I also hired two trusted writer friends from Toronto, Frank Peppiatt and John Aylesworth. Her people included Mort Lindsey, her musical director of many years, and Kay Thompson, a woman of many talents, elegant, opinionated, and totally eccentric.

Kay flew into New York from her apartment in Rome for our first planning meeting.

"This has been great," I said at the end of the meeting. "Let's get together again tomorrow."

"I can't," Kay said.

"Why not?"

"I have to fly back to Rome," Kay said. "I think I left my front door unlocked."

She flew home. The front door *was* unlocked. She locked it and came back to New York.

Kay was a great vocal coach. She had worked as a club act with the Williams Brothers and had become Andy Williams's mentor. She had a real talent for lyrics and special material. She was the one who taught Judy to take some edge off her power, to sneak in a subtle phrase or two. Kay knew how to relax Judy. All Kay had to do was go into her little girl's voice and tell funny stories about Eloise, the kid who grew up in the Plaza Hotel, and everyone would break up. Those were the stories Kay published in her children's books.

Judy was so fond of Kay that she made Kay godmother to her daughter Liza Minnelli. As far as I was concerned, Kay had only one flaw. It was her dog. It went everywhere Kay went. I swear that dog, a pug named Fenice, farted every thirty seconds.

I'd heard the stories about Judy's insecurity, Judy's need for hand-holding from her director. That wasn't the Judy I dealt with. My Judy was in good emotional shape. She told bawdy stories. She had a wicked laugh. She arranged treats for her friends.

One afternoon I drove up to her place for a rehearsal. Dixie and the kids and I had moved to an old Tudor-style house that I had rented in Larchmont, north of New York City. Judy was twenty minutes farther north in Scarsdale. I arrived, and Judy told me to sit in the living room.

"Now don't move, Norman," she said.

Mort Lindsey was at the grand piano, just the two of us in the room. Judy disappeared upstairs. A couple of minutes went by, five, ten...what the hell was happening? Mort just shrugged and smiled. Suddenly Judy's voice rang out: "Hit it, Mort."

Mort began a jazzy introduction on the piano and around the corner from the hall came Judy and Liza, the two of them belting it out, Liza fifteen years old, the voice almost the size of her mother's. The song sizzled. It was "Two Ladies in de Shade of de Banana Tree." It was Harold Arlen, and a song I had been urging Judy to do. Judy loved Harold Arlen. Judy and Liza danced, they sang, all for an audience of one.

Seventeen years later, I saw the same scene in a movie, in Bob Fosse's *All That Jazz*, a woman and a teenage girl singing and dancing in a living room for a director. It was great in the movie, but it was even better in real life in Scarsdale. It was Judy's treat. I guess that meant she had begun to think of me as a friend.

Gary Smith and I planned a very spare show. No elaborate sets, no big ensemble numbers. Almost stark. Theatrical with lots of footlights, a thrust stage built out into the audience. Shades of the old Palladium. Music would carry the hour. That was the way I'd been doing my shows since the CBC days, letting the music speak for itself, straight, undiluted. This played to Judy's talent. At rehearsals, her voice had none of the quavers that sometimes bugged her. She made the songs soar. I couldn't believe how smooth everything felt.

Then we flew west, the whole gang—Judy, her three trunks of stuff, the two writers, Mort Lindsey, the boxes of orchestrations, Kay, her farting dog—all on a plane to Los Angeles where things got less smooth in a hurry.

CBS wanted me to shoot the show in a studio at Television City. Nothing unusual about that. CBS had bought the show and CBS owned Television City. But I hated their studios. Television City looked like a Russian tire factory and must have been designed by an architect who had never seen a live TV show. He hadn't allowed for flies in the studios, space for sets to be raised and lowered between numbers down below. I wanted to shoot in NBC's Burbank studios where at least they'd heard of flies. CBS got furious. Shoot in the *competition's* building? We took turns screaming and yelling. Freddie and David yelled loudest.

We shot in Studio Four at NBC in Burbank.

The issue of the guest stars was next. CBS said we had to deliver two stars for the show from a list of ten names they had chosen.

Pardon me, wasn't this the *Judy Garland* show? CBS had doubts about whether Judy would draw enough of an audience by herself. The names they came up with were A-list. Fred Astaire, Gene Kelly, Sammy Davis. Like that. Fields and Begelman countered with Frank Sinatra and Dean Martin. For them, that was the easy part.

The hard part was persuading Sinatra to rehearse. Sinatra's idea of doing television was to show up and sing. But the casual approach wouldn't cut it for the precise and polished show we had in mind. All that special material.

I phoned Sinatra at his place in Palm Springs.

"Mr. Sinatra," I said. "This is really important for Judy. It's her first television special. She's very nervous. I know you're doing this as a favor." I'd learned how to do the show business dance well by then, the buck and wing, the patter, the wheedle, the sell. "This show will decide which way Judy's career is headed. A big TV star or just struggling along with her faithful fans. Sure, there are thousands of them, perhaps hundreds of thousands, but the TV special represents Judy's last chance to break through to a mass audience. Millions will see the show."

I was laying it on thick, and Frank knew it, but I had become a genuine Judy fan.

"So everything depends on this hour," I said on the phone. "It's got to be as perfect as everybody's rehearsing can make it. Judy's rehearsing. The band's rehearsing. *Yours?* It can be any time you want. Day or night."

Very long pause from the other end of the line.

"What time you want me there, kid?"

"Judy's not good during the day. Wednesday night? About seven?"

"You got it."

"Oh, and Frank, bring Dean, will ya?"

Big laugh from the other end of the line.

On Wednesday night, we set up Studio Four to make Sinatra feel at home. Romanoffs was his favorite Beverly Hills restaurant, so a very nervous Judy hired a Romanoffs bartender for the evening, laid out a buffet of specialties from Romanoffs' menu with Frank's Jack Daniel's on the bar. Sinatra walked in—on time, with Dean Martin—and he looked around as if to say, hey, these cats know how to treat a guy.

We rehearsed all of the special numbers. Frank was wonderful with Judy. Warm, affectionate, he let her shine. The trio number "You're Nobody 'Til Somebody Loves You" was dynamite. Judy relaxed and started to enjoy herself. Frank contributed and so did Dean. Kay Thompson helped with the staging, and the rehearsal was cooking.

Word spread around town that Studio Four was the hip place to hang out. Judy Garland was making a comeback, Sinatra was singing his ass off, the band was swinging. All the band members knew Sinatra had a fabulous ear and they enjoyed him. Dozens of movie people came by to catch the excitement. I think they envied what they found. A live TV show like we were working on got the adrenaline pumping faster than a movie shoot did. The studio was popping with energy and creativity, and when one of the visiting celebrities spoke to me during a break, I thought he was carried away in the thrill of the moment.

Tony Curtis draped his arm over my shoulders. "You do nice work, kid," he said. "When are you gonna make a movie?"

I laughed.

"Not so different from what you do here," he continued. "Movies, television, it's all just cameras."

"But I've never shot a foot of film," I said.

"What's the big deal? Just think about it," Tony persisted. "I've already shot one movie with a TV guy." He meant *The Great Impostor*, a movie directed by my friend Bob Mulligan, a live TV director, also from New York.

Tony was a genuine movie star. He had made such films as *The Sweet Smell of Success, Some Like It Hot, The Defiant Ones*. He was at the height of his career.

Tony had a specific movie in mind for me to direct. He'd just formed his own production company and signed a deal for the company to make movies for Universal. Okay, so he may have been looking for a young TV director he could get cheap, but I was happy to be asked.

The property Tony intended to shoot was *40 Pounds of Trouble*, a remake of a 1934 film called *Little Miss Marker*. It was from a Damon Runyon story about a gambler who gets stuck with a three- or four-year-old girl as an IOU for a gambling debt. Marion Hargrove had reworked the screenplay into a Curtis vehicle, Tony playing the manager of a Nevada hotel-casino who finds himself with the little kid on his hands. Tony sent me the script. It wasn't *The Sweet Smell of Success* or *Some Like It Hot*, but I thought it could work and, after all, what did I know about movies?

Sure, I would think about it.

Meanwhile, I got the Garland special ready. It opened with Judy singing "Just in Time" and "When You're Smiling" in front of a set that Gary Smith designed, nothing much more than a huge wall of light bulbs spelling out Judy's name. The effect was stunning, and the rest of the show barreled along from there.

We went to air at nine o'clock on Sunday night, February 25. CBS hadn't made it easy on us. They'd scheduled us opposite *Bonanza*, the second-highest-rated show on television. No sweat. Our audience share blew away *Bonanza*. Later, the show got nominated for four Emmys. Judy had a hit. It was another comeback. The last seventeen minutes of the show were the most exciting live television I'd ever staged.

But when it was suggested that she do a weekly show, I didn't think she could handle it. Danny Kaye, Andy Williams, people with stamina, yes. But Judy on a weekly show? Not a chance. She was wonderful but she was too fragile. And that's what I told Hunt Stromberg, the West Coast chief of CBS, and Judy's agents, David and Freddie: a few specials, yes, a weekly show, no.

They ignored my advice, and *The Judy Garland Show* began to air on a Sunday night near the end of September. George Schlatter was producing, a good man who'd done Dinah Shore's show and had worked for years in Vegas. The director was a TV veteran on the West Coast named Bill Hobin. The shows had started taping at CBS in Los Angeles in late June, but after five were completed, the CBS brass decided something was wrong. That's the way it worked with television network executives. They said Judy was too nervous. Hyper, hugging and touching people all the time. They just decided some amorphous, indefinable, inexplicable quality was lacking, and somebody had to take the fall for the problem. In this case, the fall guy was George Schlatter. CBS dismissed George (who bounced back five years later producing the hottest TV show of the late 1960s, *Rowan and Martin's Laugh-In*).

In mid-August of that year Dixie and I were at her uncle's cottage on a remote lake in the Haliburton Highlands of Ontario. The cottage had no electricity, no telephone, just a dock and a silence that was broken only by the occasional cry of a loon. I was sitting on the dock one hot afternoon reading a book. I began to wonder why a motorboat out on the lake seemed to be pointed straight for our cottage, why it was coming closer and closer.

A few yards from the dock, the old fellow in the boat cut his motor.

"Know where I can find a fella named Jewison?" he called.

"That's me."

"In that case, you're the one I got the telegram for."

"Yeah?"

"Says there's an emergency," the man said, holding up the telegram. "You're supposed to phone Judy Garland right away."

It took me almost an hour to go by boat and car to the nearest town, Minden, and find the only pay phone in the place. The telegram was from my agent, Larry Auerbach, at William Morris in New York. The number was for an exchange in San Francisco where Judy was apparently doing a concert. I didn't have enough quarters and dimes to dial long-distance. I stood in the sweltering heat of the booth in the middle of Ontario cottage country begging the operator at the Fairmont Hotel in San Francisco to accept a collect call.

Finally, Judy picked up the phone in her suite.

"Oh, Norman," she cried, plaintively, her voice shaky. "I need you! They're talking about canceling my show."

"I'm on my way, Judy," I said.

I told Dixie we would have to leave right away, that I just couldn't refuse. I had to try to help Judy.

"There are other directors they could get," Dixie snapped. She had little patience with temperamental divas. "This was supposed to be our quiet holiday in the wilds of Haliburton." The boys and our beautiful one-year-old American-born daughter, Jennifer, were enjoying the summer holiday in Canada. The boys and Jenny were with my parents at Lake Simcoe.

At the time, I was deeply depressed about a Broadway show called *Here's Love*. I had just been replaced as director by the show's producer, Stuart Ostrow. Apparently Meredith Willson, fresh from his success with *The Music Man*, felt I didn't have enough respect for him or his wife or his work.

I had worked so hard on this musical adaptation of *Miracle on 34th Street*. Weeks with Meredith in his home in Bel Air. Writing and rewriting. Encouraging him and trying to cope with his gigantic ego and manipulative wife. He really was Harold Hill, the Music Man. A guy who arrives in a corny Midwest small-town square with a razor-sharp edge and an inflated opinion of his talent.

At the beginning we had a close father-son relationship, but this was to change. We got into rehearsal at the St. James Theater in New York. I had cast Janis Paige, a leggy blond Broadway singer and dancer, as the mother, and Craig Stevens, TV's Peter Gunn, as the father. Laurence Naismith, a gifted British character actor, would play Kris Kringle. The multi-talented choreographer Michael Kidd was my real support, and the first four or five weeks of rehearsal were exciting. I was back with singers and dancers and rehearsal pianists. Musical arrangers and set designers. It was all very heady. I was directing my first big Broadway musical!

I wasn't accustomed, however, to the playwright and his wife and the producers sitting in on the rehearsals. At the end of which they would call me over. Everyone had a critical opinion. I found myself protecting the performers and suggesting that maybe Meredith should be back in his apartment writing and improving the score and the script.

One weekend, Dixie and I went up to Michael Kidd's home in

Poughkeepsie, about two hours from Manhattan. We worked all weekend on the problems facing us, and on Sunday afternoon Michael, who had his pilot's license, suggested he could fly us back to the city in his single-engine plane. We took off around four o'clock and flew south, following the Hudson River. As we approached the city, the weather started to close in. A light rain began to fall, and that and the low clouds forced us to fly lower and lower.

"How we doin', Mike?" I shouted nervously from the copilot's seat. Dixie was very quiet in a rear seat, staring straight ahead. She was pale.

"Don't worry, we're okay. Just have to stay under this low ceiling. As long as we can see the river, we know where we are, right?"

I nodded. "Sure." I was chewing gum because I couldn't smoke in the plane. I realized my jaws were working overtime.

"There's the George Washington Bridge," I shouted. "Jesus, it came right out of the fog. Do you see it?"

Michael was concentrating on what somebody was telling him through his earphones.

The rain was now pounding the windshield as we dropped lower. I looked at the altimeter and it registered eight hundred feet. My jaws were moving faster than Rod Steiger's in *In the Heat of the Night*.

"There's the old George Washington Bridge. The *bridge!*" I was shouting more loudly now. "Do you see it?"

Michael laughed and said, "Yeah. We'll just go under it."

As we zoomed under the bridge, I could see people in the cars. We were only a couple of hundred feet about the river. "Is this legal?" I screamed.

Man, was Michael Kidd cool! He skillfully landed a few minutes later. In an hour Dixie and I were safe in our own apartment at Sixty-first and Madison that we'd leased from the actress Alexis Smith for the duration of rehearsal.

The following week I was asked to leave the show. Apparently, when my suggestion to Meredith's wife that she not attend rehearsals and give her notes and opinions was passed on to Meredith, he told Stuart Ostrow to fire me.

"It's like taking Mickey Mantle outta the ball game," said Joe

Harris, our production manager backstage as I stood in total shock before a white-faced Ostrow.

It was the first time I had felt the deep sting and humiliation of rejection since I'd been an actor years before in London. I think Ostrow thought I was going to punch him out. My hands were trembling and I could hardly speak.

I called Charlie Baker at William Morris. He told me not to leave the theater. "Don't walk out! Then they can accuse you of quitting!" Larry Auerbach, my trusted friend and personal agent, came to the theater and met with Ostrow. Larry said I would still get my share of the gross because we were due to open within two weeks in Detroit.

"It's your show, kid. No matter who they bring in," said Charlie. "You gotta understand. This can be a terrible business."

I didn't understand. I was devastated. I walked home from the theater, defeated and exhausted. I was close to tears. The show, I thought. What will happen to the show?

They offered Michael Kidd the directorship of the show, but he turned them down. Stuart Ostrow, the producer, took over as director. Maybe he had it planned that way all along. That's why I'd left New York and headed for the Canadian wilds to lick my wounds.

And now Judy Garland was facing a similar blow. CBS was threatening to cancel after viewing the first four taped hours. I knew it would be a difficult task, but I promised that, somehow, I would get her series renewed. After producing several shows with exciting guest talent like Barbra Streisand, Ethel Merman, and Andy Williams, we managed to get CBS to commit to twenty-six one-hour programs. Although I had fought the idea of a weekly show with Judy, I ended up producing the first ten shows. In the process, I managed to bury my own rejection in my work.

5

The Girl Who Wouldn't Cry

Norman, you've ruined that child for life.

—*Boaty Boatwright*

After the Garland special, I could have taken my pick of new television projects. Or I could direct my first movie. I figured Tony Curtis's reasoning might have been that, with me, he was getting a talented young director cheap. The cheap part was true but I didn't care. It was going to be my first picture and I was glad for the chance. I also knew that Hollywood was reaching out for writers and directors in New York television. Let's get Paddy Chayevsky to write a script! Let's get Sidney Lumet to direct! New York TV was where the fresh, innovative work was going on, and all the young directors—Bob Mulligan, John Frankenheimer, Franklin Schaffner—were heading west.

Our move to California from New York was necessary if I was going to direct a movie. I had been in Los Angeles before doing three or four television specials. *The Danny Kaye Show* with Louis Armstrong. *The Jimmy Durante Special.* Pat Boone and, of course, Judy Garland.

I had brought Dixie and the kids out twice and we stayed in a bungalow at the venerable Chateau Marmont on Sunset Boulevard. The kids loved the pool and the constant sunshine. But Dixie and I always felt disconnected from Los Angeles. We had become real New Yorkers and, like most easterners, referred to California as "La La Land." A place that seemed totally artificial and divorced from reality. There was something hedonistic about the place.

I rented a furnished bungalow in the valley with a pool and we put our furniture in storage—just in case we had to leave if the movie didn't make it.

Tony Curtis introduced me to the forty or fifty people on the set at Universal Studios in Studio City, California. His words came out with an exaggerated spin. "This man is Nor-man Jew-i-son," Tony said. "He may look like your pa-per boy. He may look like a ki-id. But he's the di-rec-tor on the movie we're gonna make. And you can take it from me, he knows what he's do-ing."

Tony was wrong about the last part. I didn't have a clue what I was doing. Live TV had been my route into the business and live TV had precious little to do with making Hollywood movies. For a weekly TV show, with only five or six days to prepare, I had to break down the script and plan all the camera angles before the performers arrived on the scene. It was a race against time. Perry Lafferty, the senior producer I had worked for at CBS, used to watch me grow more and more frustrated when I couldn't get something just right at rehearsal and he'd say, "You want it good, Jewison, or you want it Wednesday?"

The answer was always the same: "Wednesday." The show had to go on when it was scheduled to go on. Compared to that, the making of a movie was leisurely.

Cameras made a huge difference. In television I worked with three or four cameras at once, and each had four lenses that the cameraman could switch, or "rack over," in a matter of seconds. When we were on air, live, for a weekly show, I was in the control booth wired up to the three or four cameramen, dolly grips, crane operators, and sound-boom men. I talked and shouted at them for the whole hour.

"Camera one, okay, in close, now dissolve to camera two...camera one, I'm coming back to you in twenty seconds, get the close-up ready, rack it over...all right, three, move in, go to three...one..." It was bedlam in the control booth. But I had zoom lenses, multiple cameras, total control over the sound and editing. I felt like an orchestra conductor, in charge of everything on the screen.

For the movies, at least at Universal in the early 1960s, there was just the one camera. On each scene, you shot from one angle, then moved the camera and shot again. And kept moving and shooting, till you had it right. It was the same with lenses. If I wanted one part of the scene shot with a different lens, I had to stop the film, change lenses, start again.

I knew nothing about shooting film.

It was early April 1962, and I was about to start directing *40 Pounds of Trouble* starring Tony, Suzanne Pleshette, and Phil Silvers.

What I felt from the crew when Tony put his arm around my shoulders and introduced me to the people on the set at Universal was hostility. Waves of it. It sure didn't help when Tony took me by the hand and started to walk me around the set on that first morning. As the entire crew watched and enjoyed themselves, Tony explained to them that I was this young man from Canada, by way of New York, and that I had never directed a motion picture. "Now, Norman, this is the camera and this is the mike boom." He was talking to me as if I were a child. Everyone was laughing. "Over here, Norman, we have the dolly and this is the klieg light."

New York television directors may have been the flavor of the month in Hollywood, but that didn't mean the working guys in the studio had to embrace us interlopers. Right then, I knew I had my work cut out for me. I had to make a movie. First, though, I had to make friends on the set.

The first person I tackled was the most important guy in the whole antagonistic crew. He was Joe MacDonald, director of photography. I needed him on my side. What won him over, paradoxically, was my own ignorance.

For an early scene, I drew up an elaborate floor plan. Calculated

The kid director at the Ed Sullivan Theater, New York, 1958.

My mother standing outside Jewison's Dry Goods and Post Office, Toronto, late 1930s.

Camping with the Cub Scouts at Highland Creek. Reid Scott on the left, with me and my dog, Spooky, 1934.

(above) The indomitable Gracie Fields introduces me to live TV with the assistance of Bill Davis at the CBC, Toronto, 1957.
(below, left) With Julie Andrews, *The Broadway of Lerner and Loewe*, Ziegfield Theater, New York, 1959.
(below, right) Working with the brilliant Luther Henderson.

Trying to direct Frank Sinatra, to the amusement of Dean Martin, *The Judy Garland Show*, Los Angeles, 1961.

Setting up a shot with the cameramen to show Judy's best side,
The Judy Garland Show, Los Angeles, 1961.

"Just taste it, Doris!" Taking a break on the set of the romantic comedy *The Thrill of It All,* 1963.

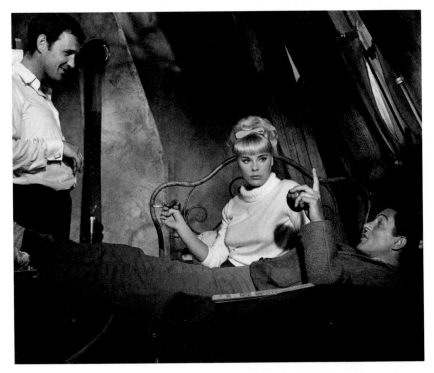

"I won't take this lying down!" Dick Van Dyke and Elke Sommer in *The Art of Love,* 1965.

"What do you mean, you never cry?" Directing Claire Wilcox in
40 Pounds of Trouble, 1962.

I have always had a thing for coffins. On the set of *Gaily, Gaily,* 1969.

the camera angles. Covered the details. I showed my sketches and ideas to Joe. He was a lanky guy in his fifties, had vast experience as a cinematographer, an Irish Catholic (which meant the crew he hired were likewise Irish Catholics). He gave my sketches a stare I would call mournful.

"You're doing too much planning," Joe said at last.

He proceeded to remind me that we had one camera, we shot the scene from one angle, set up the scene for another angle, moved the camera, shot again. Television went fast; movies went slowly. For TV, a director needed quick reflexes; for movies, a director needed the patience of Job.

"In movies," Joe MacDonald said to me, "you have to do the same thing again and again. Leave yourself room to try different things. Don't pre-plan so much. Things change in movies. Even the weather."

To make this movie, I realized I had to learn a whole new way of doing things. And this realization, my embracing this realization, was what broke the ice with Joe and the rest of the crew. In a perverse way, it started to make them happy that I seemed to be under-qualified, that I was asking for help. It made them happiest of all that I worked hard at learning their business. Over the first two weeks of the shoot, I took crash courses in lighting, set design, sound. I talked to carpenters, grips, gaffers. I asked everybody—the film editor, the prop man, the set decorator—questions. The ice, already broken, began to thaw. People filled the gaps in my understanding. They smiled at me.

I sat in the kitchen in Joe MacDonald's house in the San Fernando Valley and listened to his every word.

I knew I was getting through when the most censorious guy of all, the last holdout, Tommy Shaw, acknowledged my existence. He was the first assistant director, a large man, Irish naturally, with a voice that rattled the set. I earned his scorn, which was towering, on the first day, when we were starting to shoot the first scene. It was a simple scene, Larry Storch talking on the telephone. He was a New York comedian with a smallish role as the sidekick for the Tony Curtis character. Larry picks up the phone and speaks into it. Piece of cake, but I was nervous.

Everybody was in place, waiting for me to signal a start to filming. Tommy Shaw hollered for silence on the set. The bells rang. Red lights went on over all the doors. Everybody froze. It was suddenly very quiet. I was fascinated. Tommy called out, "Roll camera!" I watched the operator turn on the switch. "Roll sound!" he shouted. The sound man hollered back, "Speed!" Tommy yelled, "Slate it!" The slate board smacked shut. The big Mitchell camera began to roll film. All forty or fifty people in the cast and crew looked to me for the signal. I was mesmerized. The sound effects man was waiting to ring the phone. I sat there and stared. Tommy Shaw jabbed me in the back. "Say it," he told me. "Say it." And I couldn't lift my voice to more than a bashful mumble.

"Uh, yeah, go ahead," I said, barely audible.

Shaw's face turned purple. Didn't I *know* the word was "Action"? Where did they find this incompetent, ridiculous director? For the next several days, the guy came as close as someone in an AD's position could to giving me the cold shoulder.

But I wore him down with my quizzing, my seeking after information, my idiotic questions, my smiles. He stopped avoiding me. And I knew for sure he had chosen to take my side on the morning we were shooting a marginally more complicated scene. I had staged the scene and coaxed some good performances in the rehearsal. He was watching, and I nodded that we were ready to shoot. He hesitated. Our eyes locked. "Now," I said sternly. "I want to shoot now!"

He stepped forward. He raised his hand, imperious, in a command for everybody to shut up.

"Quiet on the set for MR. JEWISON," he bellowed.

He couldn't have articulated my name with more volume and clarity if he had been announcing me at Buckingham Palace (which, being Irish, he wouldn't do, but you get my point), and from that day on, we remained the best of friends.

Working on *40 Pounds*, I discovered in myself a willingness to go to any lengths to get what I wanted for a scene. I discovered that despite my training in the instant gratification of weekly television, I did have patience, an almost bulldog-like stick-to-it attitude, no matter how long it took. This strange aptitude first surfaced with Claire Wilcox, the child actress who played Penny, the forty-pound girl of the title.

Claire's problem on the movie, my problem really, was that she couldn't cry. She may have been the perfect kid who *never* cried. All I asked was that she give me a rush of tears in one scene. She couldn't, and I turned into a monster to make the kid weep.

It was Boaty Boatwright's fault.

Boaty was the first person I met on the Universal lot, a beautiful blonde from Greenville, South Carolina. Her accent was so Southern and syrupy she made Scarlett O'Hara sound like she grew up in Brooklyn. Boaty worked in Universal's casting department. She came to my movie with amazing credentials. It was Boaty who cast the three children in *To Kill a Mockingbird*. A person could base a whole career on a fantastic piece of work like that: the three kids didn't miss a step in the movie, and one of them, Mary Badham, won an Oscar nomination. I had hoped Boaty would pull the same casting coup in *40 Pounds*. Instead, she brought me the only kid in the world who couldn't cry.

Claire's flaw came to light in a scene near the end of the movie where Penny and Tony's character are supposed to be saying a tearful goodbye. The script called for Claire to run to Tony and sob on his shoulder. Claire could handle the run. Not the sob.

"Please, honey," I said to her, "we need tears to make the scene work."

We tried more takes. Claire's cheeks stayed dry. It was an outdoor scene, and we were losing the light. I told everybody on the set to hold their places. I took Claire into a limousine at the side of the set.

"Honey, I have very sad news for you," I said. I paused. "I'm very sorry to have to tell you this." I paused again. "But your dog has died."

I gazed down at Claire, my face drawn in pretend sorrow. And I watched with rising satisfaction as tears popped into Claire's eyes. It was no flood, but it was wet, and it looked like it might slide down her little cheeks.

I threw open the limo door and raced Claire to her mark. "Action!"

I shouted. Tony spoke his line, Claire clung to his shoulder, and something that would pass for tears dampened her cheeks.

"Print it!" I yelled.

"Claire." I kneeled beside the kid and held her tight in my arms. "A miracle has happened. They just called. Your doggy is still alive."

Boaty Boatwright couldn't believe what I'd done. "Norman," she said, "you've ruined that child for life."

I don't know everything that happened to Claire Wilcox in the years after the movie. But I do know that she became a successful agent herself, with ICM, legendary for her skills with artists, almost as famous as her smooth-talking colleague, Sam Cohn.

As far as Boaty Boatwright goes, she became my great friend, and when she switched from casting movies to representing people who make them, I hired her as one of my agents.

One person who never gave me grief on the movie was Tony Curtis. Tony was wonderful. He had a way of working that was different from most other actors. Tony loved the camera. But, with him, the reverse was also true. The camera also loved Tony Curtis. "The camera is my friend," Tony told me. This simple belief gave his work a distinctive quality. Tony never worried about the camera. He never got uptight, never lost control. He was always totally cool.

He was also generous. In one scene, Tony's character and the character played by Suzanne Pleshette, the female lead, are having an intimate conversation. I wanted to shoot Suzanne's face over Tony's shoulder. Without my saying a word, Tony shifted his shoulder to give the camera a direct line to Suzanne.

Tony's obliging attitude wasn't unheard of. Just rare. There are too many actors who try to upstage other actors. One type is the actor who checks out the camera, then positions himself to block out part of another actor's face. Or—this one's a lulu—the actor who speaks his lines to a distant spot instead of to the actor he's supposed to be addressing. Why? So he gets his noble profile on camera. For a director, it's embarrassing and frustrating to remind an actor half a dozen times to look at the other actor, to get his goddamned shoulder out of the way. I never had to say a word to Tony. He worked loose.

Here's how loose. After the shoot, he sent me a note of thanks for the "patience" I showed during "a difficult period in [Tony's] life." While we were making *40 Pounds*, Tony's marriage broke up.

He and Janet Leigh had been together for eleven years and had two great daughters. On his previous picture, *Taras Bulba*, which was shot in Argentina, Tony had fallen in love with his leading lady, a young German actress named Christine Kaufmann. That's another cliché in the business, the location romance with the younger woman (twenty years younger in this case), but Tony decided it was for keeps. He left Janet and later married Christine (a marriage that lasted four years). The major turmoil in the breakup came during *40 Pounds*. But it didn't show up in Tony's performance, not in our sunny little comedy. He thought I showed patience. Maybe so. But mostly, I think, Tony was such a professional, such a fine actor, his performance didn't show the strain.

I was enthusiastic about my work on the movie. That's me, an enthusiast. I try to make my enthusiasm contagious. Especially on a comedy, I try to get everybody on the set pumped up about the work we've come together to do. I try to make my sets busy, happy places. But just because I was enthusiastic about *40 Pounds of Trouble* didn't mean I couldn't be realistic, and realistically I knew there were only two sequences in the film that excited me as pieces of movie-making.

One was Phil Silvers's entrance into the gambling casino. Phil played Uncle Bernie, the irascible mob boss from Chicago who owns the casino. At one point in the story, he comes from Chicago to the casino in Nevada. There was nothing much in the script about the scene, just the simple indication "Bernie arrives from Chicago." We went on location for part of the shoot, to a real Nevada casino, Harrah's Club in Lake Tahoe. When I saw the place, the craziness of all these people in one cavernous room losing their money to slot machines and roulette wheels and blackjack tables, I knew I had to capture the frenzy of the casino action in the movie. Phil Silvers's entrance, I decided, would do the job.

The night before we shot the scene, I was asleep in the peaceful lakeside bungalow I'd been assigned by Bill Harrah, the guy who owned Harrah's Club. The phone rang.

"Norman, wake up," a man's voice said. "It's Freddie Fields. We got a problem."

"Freddie? What time is it?"

"Two-fifteen. Phil's wife just phoned me. She's hysterical," Freddie said. He sounded hysterical himself. He was Phil Silvers's agent. "Phil's at the crap table in Harrah's, and he's down fifty grand."

"What are you talking about?"

"Phil's a compulsive gambler, Norman. He can't help himself. Phil in this place, it's like an alcoholic loose in a liquor store."

"He's an addict? Why didn't somebody tell me before I brought him here?"

"You gotta do something, Norman."

"Why me?"

"You're the director," Freddie said, and hung up.

I got out of bed and harangued a pit boss into cutting off Phil's credit. That made Phil done for the night. It also made him a very angry actor.

Next morning, we shot in the casino where Phil had so recently dropped his bundle. He was right in character, pissed-off Uncle Bernie. He strode through the casino entrance and stormed down a quarter-mile of slot machines, past roulette tables, a bar, hundreds of gamblers. The camera went ahead of him the whole way. It was a difficult scene for Joe MacDonald to light because the ceilings in Harrah's happened to be awfully damn low. But he got Uncle Bernie's every step.

"Jesus, Norman," my production manager complained a couple of days earlier, "the bloody number of extras we'll have to bring into the casino, this shot's gonna be expensive."

"No extras," I said. "That's the point."

"No extras? You mean we use the real people in the place? But they'll keep looking at the camera. Spoil the credibility."

"Give everybody five silver dollars. Then wait and see."

Not one person in the casino gave the camera a glance. They didn't *see* the camera, that was how intent they were on losing their money. The only trouble I had with the scene was dragging my own people back from the tables. Between set-ups, they'd drift over to try their luck. Our set designer ended up having to mortgage his house. It was as if a disease was rampant in there, and that's what we caught in the scene, the gambling virus.

The other sequence that excited me was the Disneyland episode. It also rated only a line or two in the script. The plot premise that brought Disneyland into the story was this: Tony's character isn't supposed to step into California where his ex-wife lives. If he does and he's caught, his alimony payments get jacked up. But Tony promises Penny a Disneyland treat. He keeps his promise. At the park, the ex-wife's lawyer and private detectives spot Tony. They try to serve him the court papers. He runs. A chase is on through Disneyland.

The logistics were crazy. We had to set up the camera in fifty different locations. The chase started in a tree fort, raced across a swinging foot bridge, on and off a steamboat, through an Indian village, down a set of railroad tracks, in and out of a tunnel, on to a bumping-car track, on and off a train. There was virtually no dialogue, just "Hey, wait a minute!" and "Stop that mushroom!" Stop that mushroom? You had to be there. It was a sight gag, Tony briefly disguised in a giant mushroom costume. I packed in every joke element I could think of, including a dozen Keystone Kops. I loved Mack Sennett's stuff when I was a kid. The Kops moment in *40 Pounds* was my modest Sennett homage.

The entire chase, beginning to end, tree fort to railroad station, lasted nine minutes on the screen. The nine minutes took a week to shoot, longer to edit. The work was tough, but I felt exhilarated. I knew they were the best nine minutes of the movie. And I wondered what it would be like to feel this good about a whole film.

It was a question I wouldn't be able to answer until I directed four more movies.

Later I needed Tony back in the studio to loop some lines. He had left for Munich where Christine lived. He hated to fly. It would take weeks if he returned to Hollywood by train and ship. So I flew to him.

I supervised the looping at Geiselgasteig Bavaria Film Studios and used my spare time to look around.

When *40 Pounds of Trouble* was finished some two months later, I wanted desperately to show it to someone. Good or bad, I had directed my first movie. It was scored, dubbed, and ready for release to the world. I was filled with anxiety. This was before there were test screenings or computer analysis and demographics. All you had was a poster, a trailer, and hopefully a great publicity agent.

Dixie and I were living in a little rented house off Laurel Canyon in the valley. I invited my parents, Perce and Dorothy, to fly down from Toronto for a visit with their grandchildren. But secretly, I wanted to show them what I had done.

Two days after they arrived, I booked the Hitchcock screening room at the studio and ordered a limo to pick us up and take us for an evening screening. Dixie cooked a wonderful dinner of roast pork with crackling, applesauce, roast potatoes, and a berry pie. We finished dinner by 7:30. The babysitter arrived and so did the limo.

My parents were a little shocked when they saw the long black limousine. "Why are we going in a Cadillac with a chauffeur?" my father asked. I tried to reassure him. "The studio sent over the car. It's a courtesy." He looked at me, worried. "I'm not paying for it, Dad," I assured him. They both seemed uncomfortable. I looked at Dixie and shrugged. She rolled her eyes. I thought to myself they had probably never been in a limo before. In Toronto they were only used for weddings or funerals.

We arrived at Universal Studios in about twelve minutes. My dad said, "We could have walked!" The screening room was large, about two hundred seats. It was empty. "Is there nobody coming to see your movie?" my mother asked nervously. "It's a private screening, Mom. It's just for us." The four of us sat in the middle of the theater. I reached for the phone on the console. "Okay, Charlie, roll it whenever you're ready." "Right, Mr. Jewison" came the immediate reply.

The lights dimmed, the curtain parted, and my film began. "There's no newsreel?" my dad asked loudly. "Shhh, it's a private screening," my mother whispered. They watched the opening credits. When my name came up as director, I looked over at them. Their faces acknowledged nothing. They just sat and stared at the screen. They did not move, laugh, cry, or react in any way for almost two hours. The film ended and the lights came up.

There was silence. Dixie and I exchanged glances. Finally, my mother stood up and gave a tremendous burp. She struck her chest and apologized. "It must have been that roast pork we had for dinner." Then my dad turned and looked at me. "The little girl took her part very well," he said. "When she left him, it was very sad."

That was it! What did I expect? Applause?

6

Sinking Fast Isn't Funny

If there is nobuddy, there is no suicide.

—*Pierre Olaf*

Signing the contract to direct the Tony Curtis picture for Universal meant that I agreed to the standard clause that would indenture me exclusively to the studio for the next seven years. The Hollywood studios from the very beginning were always keen on contracting talent. The talent agencies peddled the flesh and the studios provided the market. The entire system was based on the exploitation of talent.

"Don't worry about it," my agents at William Morris said. "Just go in there and do a great job and let us handle the deal-making."

Since Alfred Hitchcock, Cary Grant, Doris Day, Rock Hudson, and Tony Curtis were all signed with Universal, I felt I was in good company. But my exclusive contract would become a serious problem in the years to come.

I've always thought that every story, every picture has to have a raison d'être. My next film, *The Thrill of It All*, was a satire of commercials and, in particular, of commercial television. I had a genuine hatred for commercials and their interruptions of the television shows I had been producing for CBS. In the U.S. in live television, directors were expected to interrupt their shows and direct commercials, live, in the middle of their programs. In hindsight, this was not altogether unreasonable, but I hated them so much I refused to comply. Another director was always assigned to do the commercials for my segment, and when he slid his chair into the booth, I crowded him for time and space. Many could not understand why I would pass up the added fees, which were sometimes higher than what I received for the show itself.

In *The Thrill of It All*, the ad agency characters were all buffoons, as *Thrill* was a comedy, a lighthearted vehicle for its star, Doris Day. I worked on the script with Carl Reiner. This was Carl's original idea, and we both wanted the film to satirize the commercialization of our beloved medium of television. Reiner was the writer-producer of the *Dick Van Dyke Show*, co-starring Mary Tyler Moore. He was anxious to use that as a stepping stone to theatrical movies. This was his first green-lit screenplay, and I was fortunate to work with such a gifted and generous man.

We both had children and had moved from New York to Los Angeles. His wife, Estelle, was a frustrated jazz singer and his very rebellious son Rob would later become a successful actor in *All in the Family* and an even more successful film director. I have always enjoyed the Reiner family. They were all creative, funny, and passionately devoted to every liberal cause in the chaos of American politics of the sixties.

Both Carl and I came from live television and were both natural rebels. We wanted to parody TV's product spokespeople and present the sponsors as one-note egomaniacs. Carl wrote a part for himself into the script parodying the *Sid Caesar Show*, in which both he and Howie Morris had appeared every week for years. A fictitious soap-suds company sponsors a self-important and rather pretentious drama series, "Happy Soap," with Carl himself playing the central character. In one scene, Carl is a Gestapo officer in a café, in another a playboy in a nightclub, in the third a cowboy in a saloon. In each episode, the Carl character throws a fit of over-the-top quivering anger, just as he did in the *Sid Caesar* sketches, face twitching, maniacal, until the woman he is mad at throws a cup of coffee in his face.

Doris's character, the perfect wife with two adorable children, gets a job doing live television commercials for "Happy Soap." Audiences love her, and the commercials bring her fame and fortune. But this is the sixties, so she doesn't buy into the success. She comes back to her husband and declares, "I want to be a doctor's wife again."

Thrill was scheduled to be the second of my seven-film package. Ed Muhl, the head of Universal, liked some of the zaniness of *40 Pounds of Trouble* and wanted to try me on another comedy, with another big star. I was to have lunch with Doris Day.

"Impress Doris," Muhl told me, "and you'll shoot her next movie."

He wasn't quite accurate about that. The person I had to impress wasn't Doris. It was her husband. His name was Marty Melcher, and he had two roles in her life, spouse and personal manager. He joined us at lunch in the Universal commissary.

"I like your work, Norm," Melcher said right off the bat. He was loud, taking over the room as soon as he arrived. He had on a slick Cy Devore suit. I was in my jeans and tennis shoes.

"That's great," I said. "But there isn't a whole lot of it, you know. Just the one movie."

Melcher gave a dismissive wave of his hand, the one with the big cigar in it. "I said I like your work and I mean it."

Doris was very blond and peppy, though she looked her age, which was thirty-eight. She had been in music and movies since her midteens and played exclusively fresh and wholesome types, the model for the American woman back then. Despite her film success, she had remained warm and direct. She was friendly and interested.

"Tell me about yourself, Norman," she said. "Where are you living?"

I told her we had rented a little house in the valley.

"You married?" she asked.

"Married, yeah. My wife's name is Dixie. We have three little kids, two boys and a girl."

"You been working with a lot of stars, Norm," Melcher said. "Harry Belafonte, Jackie Gleason, Danny Kaye, Judy Garland. I like that. You seem to be able to handle directing stars."

Obviously Melcher had taken the trouble to find out about my television work.

"What kind of background do you come from, Norman?" Doris asked. "Was it spiritual?"

"Spiritual? Well, it was Canadian. I grew up in Toronto. Don't know how spiritual that is, but we're all considered trustworthy—if a little dull. I think I remember you coming through town when you sang with Les Brown's orchestra."

"Sinatra give you much trouble, kid?" Melcher asked. "You handle Frankie okay?"

Doris excused herself to speak to someone at another table, and Melcher leaned over to me. It wasn't just Melcher's suit that was slick. Most things about him were slick. Even his hair was combed straight back from his forehead, slicked down flat over his scalp.

"Don't worry about Doris on this movie," he said. "All you gotta do is keep telling her she looks great. Remember that, she looks *great*. You won't have any trouble."

Melcher got a producer's credit on all his wife's movies. He didn't do any actual producing, but he collected a $50,000 fee on each picture. Universal went along with it because Doris's movies made so much money. Melcher had once worked at a talent agency called Century Artists, and he had been married to a Century client, Patti Andrews of Patti, Maxene, and LaVerne, the singing Andrews Sisters. Doris came along as a client, and Melcher dropped Patti in a flash for a more promising meal ticket. He wasn't a subtle guy.

The real producer of *Thrill*, the one who did the work, was the guy who had turned things around for Doris. His name was Ross Hunter, and a few years earlier, he'd convinced Doris—which meant Melcher too—to star in a romantic comedy called *Pillow Talk*. Until then, Doris had played only girls. Fresh and wholesome types. "I knew her before she was a virgin" was Oscar Levant's crack about that period in Doris's career.

She didn't think she could handle the part of the sexy, sophisticated interior decorator who was the central character in *Pillow Talk*. Ross told Doris he'd get her Jean Louis for the movie. Jean Louis was the fashion designer who put Lana Turner in clingy sweaters, Rita Hayworth in the slinky strapless gown for *Gilda*. For *Pillow Talk*, he dressed Doris in smart, fashionable, womanly outfits. Nobody was going to mistake her for Lana or Rita, but she did affect a tasteful sexuality. She entered her post-virgin career. This was the Doris Day whose new romantic comedies made her Hollywood's number one box office attraction. Ross Hunter intended to keep the streak going with *The Thrill of It All*.

Ross Hunter loved everything about Hollywood. He loved the studios. Loved the star system. He was so savvy about how the business worked that all the movies he made for Universal showed a profit— tear-jerkers, thrillers, romantic comedies. Ross was gay, and he and the man he lived with, a businessman named Jack Mapes, were two of the most elegant guys in town. They threw bridge parties. People would kill to get an invitation to those parties. Not me—I didn't play cards much—but Rock Hudson and Claire Trevor were regulars.

Melcher had been right about one thing: his wife's looks. They were Doris's weak point, not her looks per se, but the way she perceived them. Doris did not believe that she was an attractive woman. I thought she was beautiful. Millions of fans thought she was beautiful. Everybody she had ever worked with thought she was beautiful. Doris remained unconvinced.

I realized what I was dealing with the first minute I walked on the set. Russell Metty, the cinematographer for the movie, had lit the set with enormous ten-K lights.

"My god, Russ," I said, "what's with these lights?"

They were huge, the next thing to the enormous arc lights I first ran into on *Canadian Pacific*.

"Doris'll love it," Russ said.

"I don't know how she'll be able to open her eyes! She'll go blind!"

Russ motioned me over to the camera. "Take a look in here, Norman."

I bent over and stared into the camera's eyepiece. "What kind of a filter have you got in there? It's so soft."

"Doris'll love it," Russ said again.

Russ had worked with Stanley Kubrick and Orson Welles on two movies, had won an Oscar for his photography on *Spartacus*, and, more important for the moment, he had shot two earlier Doris Day movies. He knew what he was doing. The combination of strong lighting and soft filters would wash Doris clear of every wrinkle, every flaw, every blemish. She'd have the skin of a teenager.

"Yeah," I said, "Doris'll love it."

But she didn't. She seemed uneasy in the first scenes we shot on *Thrill*. She couldn't relax into the role and I suspected it was her anxiety about her looks. I tried a bit of reverse psychology.

"If you're worried about how you're going to look in the movie," I said to her, "why don't you take charge of everything?"

We were having the conversation in her trailer, just the two of us.

"What *are* you talking about, Norman?" Doris said.

"Do it yourself. You know what you want. Do your own makeup. Take charge of doing your gowns. Take charge of the lighting, the camera angles."

"Oh, Nor*man*."

"Who knows, take charge even of the directing."

"You're making fun of me."

"No, Doris, I'm taking you very seriously," I said. "What I'm trying to tell you is that all of us on the movie are dedicated to making you look great. You don't need to worry. Just let us take care of what we know how to do. Jean Louis, Russ Metty, me, the rest of the crew, we know our jobs. I want you to relax and concentrate on your job. Acting! Just give me a focused performance."

Doris responded the way I'd hoped. She got much less anxious about her looks. She started to have fun on the movie, which was the way it was supposed to be. She had terrific timing, a natural comedic rhythm. She had spent years singing with Les Brown's band, and she knew instinctively when to hit her lines and give them the right inflection. Rhythm and timing are vital for comedy, and Doris was better at them than just about anyone I have ever worked with.

Years later, when I was directing *Moonstruck*, I asked Julie Bovasso, who was both an actress and an acting teacher, to coach Cher on how to speak with an authentic Brooklyn Italian accent. That was tricky, to isolate an Italian accent to a specific place, Brooklyn. Julie did it by emphasizing the rhythms of that way of talking. Cher got it. Mostly, I think, because she was a singer. Doris was a singer and a great comic actress. The two went together.

Not that she was always on. No actor is.

The tenth day of the production, we had been waiting almost an hour for her to come out of her trailer.

"She won't come out," Tommy Shaw told me. He was first assistant director on the movie and the man I had worked with on *40 Pounds of Trouble*.

"She's been in makeup and hair since 6 a.m. and now I'm told she won't come out." Tommy looked defeated.

"Did you talk to her?" I asked.

"No, her dresser told my assistant she just wasn't coming out."

I thought it best to stall. "Give her another twenty minutes. I'm not quite ready anyway." As he turned to leave, I put my hand on his shoulder and whispered in his ear, "If she's not out in another twenty minutes, you go to her trailer. *You*, not your second assistant."

It was only my second movie and I was learning to be patient.

Twenty minutes passed and Tommy came back to tell me Doris still wouldn't come out. The studio heads were on the phone wanting to know what was wrong.

"Why don't you call Melcher? He's the producer and he *is* her husband. Why don't we let him handle it?" I suggested.

About half an hour later, Ross Hunter and Marty Melcher arrived, and we all stood on the set with worried looks, waiting. Russ Metty sat in his chair like a giant Buddha.

Finally, Hunter came up to me. "Norman," he said, "you're the director. It's your responsibility to keep this movie shooting."

With the entire crew watching, I started across the long walk to the end of the stage and Doris Day's trailer. I tapped on the door.

"Who is it?" a voice shouted.

"Tell Doris it's me—Norman," I whispered. We all waited nervously.

Suddenly the door opened and there was Doris, red-eyed, tears streaming down her face. "Oh, Norman!" and she fell into my arms, sobbing.

"What's wrong? What happened?" I held her gently. I knew everyone on the set was craning to see what was going on.

"It's Charlie, he's dead." Charlie was her small white poodle. "And it's all my fault. He choked on a bone. I gave him the lamb chop. I killed him!"

We sat together for another half-hour while I explained it wasn't her fault. Slowly, she stopped crying and returned to makeup. Half an hour later, she emerged, beautiful as ever. She had a deep love for animals but she was also a professional.

Doris was a serious person in one way, in the sense that she looked for answers to large questions. Religious questions. Spiritual questions, not the kind that came up during normal Hollywood conversations. The meaning of life, the meaning of death. She'd go down one road searching for answers. If that didn't satisfy her, she'd try another road. The one she was on during our movie was Christian Science. I think it turned out to be a dead end for her. But that didn't stop her from checking her road map for another route.

She was completely off alcohol. When I went over to her house in Beverly Hills for a meeting one day, the first thing I noticed was the soda fountain. The house was one-story, modest except for the enormous soda fountain. It was the genuine article, bins of ice cream, jars of chocolate, a row of spigots, a long marble counter, just like the soda fountain in Liggett's Drug Store when I was a kid in the Beach. I looked around for something stronger to drink. There seemed to be no liquor cabinet. I decided the soda fountain was supposed to make visitors not notice the absence of booze. The movie we were working on was a model Doris Day vehicle.

The only part of the movie Doris didn't appear in was one of fortuitous invention. It was a part I wanted people to remember when they left the theater. I wanted one big visual gag for the movie, kind of a signature piece, even if it was the signature of a guy directing only his second movie. I found the scene in a sequence that was just hinted at in the script. The idea came from a short news item in the *Los Angeles Times*: a suburban housewife wanted to surprise her husband by having a new swimming pool built in six days while he was away on a business trip. Of course, they tore down the carport to build the pool.

James Garner played Doris's doctor husband in *Thrill*. Casting him for the role was my idea, though Doris, Melcher, Ross Hunter, and a bunch of others had to sign off on him. Garner hadn't done much comedy in movies, but I loved his comic presence in *Maverick* on TV. He was a master at looking exasperated, put upon, fed up. That was what he had to project in the scene I planned for the first part of the big visual gag.

The scene began when Garner arrives home in his convertible. He drives into the garage. Except there is no garage. It's been replaced that day by a swimming pool as a surprise present to Doris from the Happy Soap Company. Garner doesn't know about the pool. He drives his convertible in to where the carport used to be, and off the edge, right into the pool.

It was a potentially funny scene, but it needed punching up. In real life, the convertible would submerge in a hurry. Sinking fast isn't funny. Sinking slowly, Garner sitting behind the steering wheel looking bewildered and indignant, the water line moving up his chest, his chin, the top of his head—that would be funny.

I got the special effects people to build a ramp in the pool just below the water's surface. Garner steered the convertible on to the ramp, which was rigged to a controlled lowering device. The ramp dropped slowly, the water rose gradually, Garner wore an expression like he was the captain of the *Titanic* going down with his ship, the doctor going down with his convertible. Great moment.

But it was just the prelude to an even bigger visual joke, which started the minute Garner hauls himself out of the pool. He's furious. He kicks the nearest object, which happens to be a large box of Happy Soap flakes. The contents spill into the pool. During the night, a rain storm passes over. The soap flakes billow into a mountain of suds.

Next morning, the soap suds loom over the house and cascade down the street. A crew from the city works department arrives to dismantle Suds Mountain. They balance the stuff on shovels, pile it into the backs of dump trucks.

The concept struck me as hilarious, the idea of characters confronting an avalanche of soap suds. What I hadn't anticipated was what would happen when we combined the suds with the hot lights of the studio. Waves of noxious fumes came off the suds. They washed over the set. People in the cast and crew coughed and choked. A couple of them threw up. One guy fainted. I reorganized the shooting schedule to allow almost everybody to take oxygen breaks. The only people who had to be on the set for every second of the shoot were me and the camera crew. I was okay, but the camera operator kept toppling off his seat. I called a break and gave him a chance to catch some pure air. We started once more. "Action!" The poor guy collapsed again. "Cut!" I sent an assistant director to a sporting goods store. When he came back, we went at the shot one more time. This time, the camera operator was wearing a scuba mask.

We got the scene.

The Thrill of It All scored big at the box office. It may have been the most profitable of the Doris Day romantic comedies. Doris herself loved *Thrill*. "It's probably my favorite of all the films I made," she once told my dear friend, the late Jay Scott of the *Globe and Mail*. I knew that Melcher liked it because he invited me to come right back and direct another of his wife's movies.

Lew Wasserman, who ran the studio, agreed with Melcher. The way the system worked, I had little choice. I had signed on to do seven movies, and I could either make the movies they assigned me or sit at home. I had much too much energy to sit it out.

Send Me No Flowers was a farce. It wasn't about anything that interested me, but it did offer some fun.

Doris still played a maturely sexy character, but the plot, rather than containing realistic elements as in *The Thrill of It All*, was nutty and screwball. I'd majored in farce in my earliest work in the theater.

The sketches I wrote, directed, and often acted in at university leaned on broad and exaggerated material. So did much of the work I did for *Spring Thaw*, a popular annual comedy revue in Toronto that I had written for and performed in before joining CBC Television. Farce and I were old friends.

Send Me No Flowers had begun life as a Broadway comedy. Julius Epstein, best known as one of the brothers who wrote the screenplay for *Casablanca*, adapted it for the screen. The story was about a married man who's a raving hypochondriac. He devours pills, checks his temperature hourly, studies the obituaries. One day, through a mistaken diagnosis, he and his doctor become convinced that he's contracted a fatal disease. The next obituary will be his own. He's concerned for his beautiful wife, who knows nothing about the alleged disease. He wants her to have a short widowhood, to marry a swell new husband, and he sets out to find the right man to scoop her up after he's gone. The wife gets the mistaken notion that her husband is fooling around with some other woman. More errors pile on. The pace of the mistakes quickens. Then, in a sudden puff of revelation, all becomes clear to husband and wife. The slate is wiped clean. Clinch. The end.

The trick in getting this sort of material to work is in the casting. Farce was delicate stuff, it was fragile. We couldn't afford to cast an actor who didn't have the right rhythms for outrageous lines. In *Send Me No Flowers*, Doris as the wife was a given. So was Rock Hudson as the hypochondriac husband. I had no control over those two pieces of casting. Where I did exert some control was in choosing the supporting cast, all of whom were people from the Broadway theater. I needed actors who knew how to play a part in a broad, comic way without tipping into idiocy. In *The Thrill of It All*, I had surrounded Doris with fine character actors off the Broadway stage—Arlene Francis, Edward Andrews, Elliott Reid. I did the same in *Send Me No Flowers*. I cast Tony Randall, Hal March, Ed Andrews again, and Paul Lynde as the hysterically funny salesman of cemetery plots. There wasn't a dud in the entire cast.

Doris showed me a different side of her acting in this movie, or rather, two new sides. One was her on-screen vulnerability. Not much of it was called for in a farce, but in a couple of scenes, she needed to project a wounded quality, and each time I asked it of her, she delivered. The other was a deft way with physical comedy that I hadn't entirely expected, so I kept inventing new, funny situations for her. In one, she turned a simple act, bringing in a morning delivery of eggs from the back porch, into a tour de force of small calamities. First, she locks herself out of the house. Then she catches her nightgown in the door. Then she drops the eggs. She carried it off beautifully.

Doris and I had become comfortable with each other. But working with Doris meant once again brushing up against her husband, Marty Melcher. This time Marty billed himself as the movie's *executive* producer and again collected his $50,000 fee for performing no visible service. I neither liked nor trusted Melcher and stayed out of his way as much as possible. But what I didn't know at the time—more important, what Doris didn't know—was that Melcher was even more of a con artist than I or anyone else dreamed.

That came out four years later, in 1968, when Melcher died. His death was a bizarre story all by itself. Melcher, following Doris's example, became a devout Christian Scientist and accepted the religion's dogma that doctors were unnecessary in a true believer's life. He fell ill. He refused medical treatment and died from complications of an enlarged heart. With Melcher in the cemetery, Doris discovered to her horror that the millions she had earned in movies had vanished and that she owed the federal government millions more in back taxes. It seemed that Melcher and his Los Angeles lawyer had placed Doris's fortune—and the savings of many other Hollywood friends of mine—in something called federal land grant bonds, then claimed income tax deductions on the bonds. The government disallowed the deductions and pursued Doris—and the other Hollywood unfortunates—for unpaid taxes and penalties. Doris sued the lawyer and in 1974 recovered $22.8 million, the largest award in a California civil suit up to that time, but a mere tenth of what she had earned.

Rock Hudson, the hypochondriac husband in *Send Me No Flowers*, had a nice touch with farce. More important, he had authentic star quality. He lit up the screen just by appearing on it. That probably surprised Rock more than anyone else. He was extraordinarily self-effacing.

I liked Rock, and Dixie and I often went out to dinner with him, usually to his favorite restaurant, Chasen's. Rock was good company. He had a wonderful sense of humor and he laughed a lot. He would give you the impression that he thought you were the wittiest person in the world. His date was often a tall, lovely woman named Flo Allen, a tennis pro who got into the agency business. Years later I found out that Rock had director approval on the film. Flo Allen told me she assured him that I was not only talented but had a sense of humor. She later signed Rock and represented him for more than twenty-five years.

Everybody in the movie industry knew Rock was gay, but nobody wanted to let the public in on this open secret. Today, performers like Elton John and Ellen DeGeneres proudly celebrate their gayness, and their careers continue to flourish. Back then, little more than thirty-five years ago, the thinking was that an openly gay actor would be hounded off the screen. And Rock was too good a money-earner for the studios to allow that to happen. That's why Universal always protected Rock from the media.

Rock proved himself, in the end, to be incredibly brave. When he got AIDS, instead of retreating into a shell, he emerged as the first actor, and probably the first public figure of any kind, to acknowledge his homosexuality. It was his stand that in large part paved the way for gay performers in film and television to be comfortable in public with their sexual orientation. His revelation also exposed AIDS for the deadly disease it was for so many talented young homosexuals. I had great respect for Rock Hudson's courage and honesty.

Send Me No Flowers showed good pacing. It was tight and had no wasted motion, and there were some directorial touches that pleased me. But it wasn't my movie. It reflected none of my ideas. It was the studio's movie. The studio picked the project, hired the screenwriter, selected the crew, cast the lead actors, and reserved the final cut on the movie. I was just a director who worked for the studio. I'd made three light comedies at Universal, and I was fed up with being a hired hand. I wanted the creative freedom to make my own movies.

But it was not yet over. I passed on a couple of scripts they pushed at me. One was *Goodbye Charlie*, a Tony Curtis movie adapted from a George Axelrod play. Vincente Minnelli, Liza's father, ended up directing it, and it bombed. The second was a movie version of Helen Gurley Brown's bestseller, *Sex and the Single Girl*. Richard Quine took it over and had a moderate success. I refused to do them because both were light comedies.

Then I agreed to make *The Art of Love*, the fourth under my contract and, once again, a light comedy. But there was a saving grace: I was reunited with Carl Reiner from *The Thrill of It All*.

Carl's original script for the new movie turned on the assumption that, when an artist dies, the value of his paintings doubles, triples, quadruples, skyrockets. The artist in the story was a young American living and painting in Paris and not selling a thing. He shares a flat over a *boulangerie* with another young American, in Paris to write the great novel. The difference between the two young guys is that whereas the artist works hard and is anxiety-ridden over his failure, the writer is unconcerned about his writing, blithe and a bit of a con man.

One night, in despair and somewhat drunk, the artist, encouraged by the would-be novelist who's also in his cups, signs a mock suicide note and falls into the Seine. He lands on a barge moving upriver. Meanwhile, the writer, believing his roommate has truly perished in the river, peddles his paintings at newly inflated prices to a dealer who suddenly sees value in the work. When the painter returns from his inadvertent trip on the barge, the writer persuades him to stay out of sight, pretend he's dead, and keep on painting pictures to sell at a huge profit. There's just one flaw in the scheme: the Paris cops wonder if the writer has actually murdered the painter, whose body has, of course, never surfaced. A certain Inspector Carnot gets on the case, and many frantic complications ensue.

Carl and I thought this was the funniest thing since Buster Keaton, and we planned dozens of sight gags to go with Carl's riotous dialogue. We cast two great young comic actors as our leads. For the artist, we got Dick Van Dyke, who was very hot in television at the time with *The Dick Van Dyke Show*. He was a marvelous comedian, kind of a latter-day Stan Laurel, lanky and rubbery, likeable, a master of the double take. We cast Jim Garner as the writer. With these two, Carl and I were certain we couldn't miss.

We had great fun making the movie. Even when things went wrong, we kept on laughing. We went to Paris for two weeks to do location work—or rather, as I'll explain shortly, a *few* of us went to Paris—and I shot scenes with the French actors we hired. One was a man named Pierre Olaf who played the policeman, Inspector Carnot. Pierre talked like Peter Sellers playing Inspector Clouseau, except that Pierre's humorous brand of English wasn't an act. That became unmistakably clear on the day Pierre had to speak the line "If there is no body, there is no suicide."

We were down on the bank of the Seine. The camera and sound were ready, and I gave Pierre the signal, "Action."

"If there is nobuddy," Pierre said, "there is no suicide."

"No, no, Pierre," I said. "It's No Body. Two words. Like a corpse. B-o-d-y. But there isn't one. Get it?"

Pierre nodded, and we started again.

"If there is nobuddy, there is no suicide."

"Pierre," I said, "it's *body*. If there is *no body*."

"If there is nobuddy, there is no suicide."

"Pierre, no!"

"If there is nobuddy..."

We tried twenty takes to get the scene. Then I gave up. Pierre would never speak the line if we tried one hundred and twenty takes.

But I was still laughing at the end of the day.

A bigger problem was simply getting to Paris for those couple of weeks of shooting. Carl had as usual written a script that had wonderful movement. By that, I mean he never wrote himself to a point where he had to have two characters talk to each other through a long scene in order to bring the audience up to date on the plot. A writer needed craftsmanship to avoid that kind of jam, and Carl had it. But he'd also written a script that took place entirely in Paris, and I was supposed to shoot the whole thing on sets at Universal. I had to show, for example, a character falling into the Seine without leaving a back lot in Hollywood.

I begged the producer for the money for a location shoot in Paris. The producer was Ross Hunter, and I learned that one way Ross made so much money for Universal was by staying under budget. He said the budget didn't allow for work in Paris. I begged and pleaded. He gave in just a little. He sent me to Paris with one principal actor, Dick Van Dyke. Another actor, Elke Sommer, who played the artist's love interest, lived in Europe. That gave me two actors on location, and I shot them in every scene from the script that featured the two in Paris exteriors. I also shot the French actors, and I shot scenes that gave us Parisian flavor. That was the real Eiffel Tower in the movie and the real Arc de Triomphe. Then I went back to Los Angeles and shot every-thing else on the Universal lot.

And I kept on laughing.

I laughed especially hard on the day I arrived on the set and found it full of flowers and fruit. I was sure they were Ross Hunter's idea. Ross was a detail man, and he insisted that the sets for his movies have real flowers in the vases and real fruit in the bowls. On a Doris Day movie, she would enter her character's apartment, and she would be surrounded by lovely fresh smells. So I wasn't entirely surprised when I walked onto the set for *The Art of Love* and found blooming flowers and shiny fruit.

"Ross ordered these?" I said to the set decorator.

"Fresh this morning, Norman."

"The scene, I don't know if Ross realizes this, takes place in a bordello."

"Oh."

"I'm not an expert on bordellos," I said, "but I don't think the madam checks every day to make sure the flowers and fruit are fresh. I'm not even sure they *have* flowers and fruit in a bordello."

The set decorator removed the vegetation.

The madam at this bordello was played by Ethel Merman, another Broadway performer. As with the theater people I used in the earlier movies, Ethel worked with more discipline than most actors who grew up in movies. But Ethel Merman was not my first choice for the madam of the brothel. Ross and I had desperately wanted to cast the legendary Mae West.

It took days to set up a meeting with her. Scripts were messengered to her Hollywood apartment off Fountain Avenue. The date and time were changed many times. Finally, we had a 4 p.m. appointment. When we arrived, the door was opened by a black giant in a white jacket. He looked like a bodyguard but spoke like a butler, with a gentle and almost formal voice. "I presume you are the gentlemen from Universal Pictures."

We nodded and smiled. He ushered us into the living room of the spacious Art Deco apartment. Everything was white—or was once white and was now a faded cream. White satin sofa and chairs, white satin lampshades, heavy white satin drapes, white carpet, and a white grand piano. The late afternoon sun dappled the room. I felt like I was on a 1930s movie set.

"Miss West will see you shortly," said the black giant as he disappeared through a door, shutting it firmly. We sat there. Ross rolled his eyes. I giggled nervously and Ross nudged me. On the wall facing us was a life-sized oil painting of a statuesque nude Mae West. Hanging onto one of the drapes in the painting was a monkey, gazing at her lovely breasts.

The door suddenly opened and the butler stood to one side as Miss Mae West sashayed into the room. She was wearing a huge blonde wig with the traditional curls, full makeup, and a pair of long diamond earrings. She had on a full-length, low-cut white satin dress. The white high-heeled shoes could do little for her height: Mae West was only five feet tall.

She had our screenplay under her arm and fixed us both with a sexy, come-hither look that certainly belied her age—she had to be over seventy. She put one hand on her hip and said in that wonderful, husky voice of hers: "Which one of you is the director?"

I immediately raised my hand. "I am, Miss West." She quickly moved to the sofa and sat close beside me.

"I read your screenplay and made a few changes. The part of the madam needs to be expanded."

I was amazed. She had underlined every speech in every scene and had rewritten or expanded them. For nearly an hour, the two of us read through the scenes. When I read some of her lines with my best Mae West impersonation, she giggled with delight.

At the end of our session she described how important it was for her millions of fans to see her in a starring role and indicated to us both that the entire script would need to be rewritten to meet her approval.

We were ushered out, disappointed. But I was exhilarated by her energy, humor, and total confidence in herself. She was as big off-screen as she was on. Mae West will always be one of my most favorite movie stars.

I shot *The Art of Love* through most of the late spring of 1964, and it remained fun all the way. The material cracked me up, even though I'd already spent months with it. That was how much Carl and I loved our own jokes. When Jim Garner's writer character is on trial for the murder of his missing painter friend, the Dick Van Dyke character, we put Madame LaFarge in the courtroom, an ancient, frightening crone cackling over her knitting. Carl and I thought this was hilarious. And when the jury is sent from the courtroom to reach a verdict, we showed them filing out of the court and then filing straight back in without a pause. Great sight gag, we told ourselves, and we kept on laughing like that until the movie was wrapped.

The Art of Love premiered at a theater in Los Angeles. Carl and his wife, Estelle, picked up Dixie and me in a limo, and we drank champagne all the way to the theater. We drank and we laughed and we slapped one another on the back.

We sat down in the theater, the lights dimmed, and the movie began. The familiar scenes unfolded on the screen, and Carl and I laughed all over again. But fairly soon, we couldn't help noticing that no one else in the theater was laughing. There was the occasional titter from one side, a giggle in the back, a single guffaw up in the balcony. The rest was silence.

"Carl," I whispered, "what's going on?"

"Nothing. Norman, that's the trouble, *nothing's* going on in here. *Nobody* thinks it's funny."

When it was over, we all went back to our house, and Carl and I talked late into the night thinking of reasons for the movie's failure. We blamed television. TV had made audiences tougher to entertain. They were used to getting laughs for free. That was the explanation, we told each other. The audience could laugh at Dick Van Dyke at home once a week on *The Dick Van Dyke Show*. So, the same audience would think, why pay to see him in a movie where he might not be as funny?

Later, long after Carl and Estelle had left, I realized something more fundamental was wrong. It was the movie's basic premise. The idea that a painter's work inflates in value after his death may work marvelously for Picasso and Matisse. But a painter like our Dick Van Dyke character remains as obscure in death as he had been in life, and his paintings are just as worthless. The bottom fell out of our plot. And the audience knew it (as did the reviewers the next day). I had directed my first bomb.

The first house that Dixie and I had lived in after we were married was a little place in Toronto on Bingham Avenue, just north of Kingston Road in the Beach. I had been directing and producing at CBC-TV, and I remember coming home some nights after a show, lying on the floor in the kitchen and pressing my face into the linoleum. A visitor arrived at the house one night. He looked down at me, then asked Dixie, "What's Norman doing on the floor?"

"Don't worry," Dixie said, stepping over me. "He'll get over it."

I'd been depressed and was looking for relief from that depression in the smooth, cool linoleum. I had always felt let down after I'd finished shooting a show, but I wasn't prepared for the horrendous funk I fell into in the fall of 1964 after the failure of *The Art of Love*. I was wretched. Here I was, I told myself miserably, not just still directing light studio comedies but directing a light studio comedy that nobody laughed at. I had directed four of them in a row, and I wanted to dig into something with meaning and conflict and substance. I felt that film was a more reflective and personal form of expression than television. Although it did not have the mass audience of TV, it was free from commercial interruption. It had the large screen, sensitive sound, and was taken more seriously by critics here and abroad. The best films, in my opinion, were almost all foreign. British, French, Italian, and Russian cinema were flourishing in the sixties.

I was impressed with Stanley Kubrick's work. He was already the "enfant terrible" of Hollywood in the early sixties. I was deeply moved by *Paths of Glory* in 1957, and *Spartacus* and *Lolita*. I was so exhilarated by *Dr. Strangelove* in 1963 I felt that my life was being wasted on these commercial comedies where everyone ended up happy and went to the seashore. That's not what really happens. Most people have lives that have little to do with the Hollywood movies I was being offered. The opportunity to make important films was passing me by. I felt I had something to say about the world around me, but I was trapped in the Hollywood system of long-term contracts. I was suffocating from the commercial restriction of any free creative thought. How the hell does Kubrick do it? I wondered. How can I break out of this place? He switched studios, why can't I?

Universal wasn't offering me the kind of film I wanted to do. The studio had categorized me as a light-comedy director and that was that.

Then two events turned everything around.

One was a letter that I never received. It was a letter from Universal telling me that the studio was picking up the option it held on my services as a director. Universal had locked me up for seven movies at the time of *40 Pounds of Trouble*, but the contract required the studio's business department to notify me by registered mail of its intention each year within a month of a certain date. The date and the month for 1964 had gone by in early October. The creative department had called about another comedy, but nothing from the business people.

I made an appointment with Abe Lastfogel in the middle of October. Abe was the head of the William Morris Agency in Los Angeles. (William Morris had continued to represent me since my CBS days in New York. Larry Auerbach, my original New York agent, still advised me but had turned me over to Stan Kamen and the West

Coast picture department.) Abe was a diminutive man, not much over five feet, who had a wife, Frances, built big and round like Sophie Tucker. The Lastfogels made an odd couple, and people cracked jokes about their appearance. It never occurred to me to make a joke about Abe. I thought he was a wonderful man and a wise agent.

Once before, in 1959, I had gone to Abe and told him of my disenchantment with commercial television. That I couldn't go on. Abe had comforted me by telling me that just the day before, Freddie Zinnemann, the famous director, had sat in the same chair with the same story about his career. "Take some time off for yourself," Abe told me. "Your marriage to Dixie okay?" he asked. I nodded. "The kids are okay?" Again I nodded. "You're not in any trouble financially. No addiction problems?" I shook my head. "Then listen to me." He'd leaned forward in his dark leather chair. The desk came up high on his chest. The bright California sun slanted through the closed venetian blinds of his large, paneled Beverly Hills office. He'd paused and looked over his glasses and pointed with a tiny hand. "The gold will always follow you. Remember that. Just keep working and follow the dictates of your heart. Forget about the money or what's commercial. We'll represent you and the gold will always follow because you're talented." Then Abe had got up. The meeting was over. Surprisingly I'd felt a lot better. No wonder Abe was a legend in this business.

Now I was consulting Abe again. He and his wife treated their clients as though they were their children. He was protective and understanding and patient, just the way a parent is supposed to be with his kids, except that Abe was collecting ten percent from his children. I didn't begrudge the ten percent. I still don't. No matter what it costs, a creative person needs someone who's always on his side, someone who will go to the studios or to the producers and shout and scream on the creative person's behalf. The only difference with Abe Lastfogel was that he never needed to shout and scream. He had accumulated such respect that he could go to the studio and say very quietly, "My client is upset," and the studio would listen.

Abe told me that the lack of notice within the required month freed me from the Universal contract. But to be safe, we should allow another month to elapse before we brought the whole thing to Universal's attention. Lie low, Abe cautioned me, don't answer the phone or go down to the studio, just disappear for a month. And at the end of that time, Abe would send a registered letter to Universal letting the studio know that I now considered myself a free agent. That was Abe's advice.

I took it.

Canada has no Abe Lastfogels, not even a few great shouters and screamers. Canadian actors and writers and directors need people to pound the table for them and say, "This is intolerable! I'm taking my client out of this movie immediately! I'm not allowing him to be treated in this outrageous manner!" A good agent gets respect for his client. He gets money for the client too. Jim Carrey would still be doing bar mitzvahs in Toronto if he hadn't hired a powerful American agent, a man who had one obsession, and that was to get Jim $20 million for his next movie.

Robertson Davies, the great novelist, was a neighbor of mine in the Caledon Hills north of Toronto back in the 1980s. One day, he came over to my house in despair. He asked me to look at a contract that an agent had persuaded him to sign a few years earlier. The contract sold the movie rights for Rob's popular novel *Fifth Business* to a film producer in perpetuity. In *perpetuity*? That was insane. Under the contract, it didn't matter when the company made a movie out of Rob's book. It didn't matter whether the company ever made a movie at all. Regardless of what the company did or didn't do, it owned the movie rights forever. Rob needed a good agent.

I kept my head down, and a month later, about ten days into November, just about the time when the notice from Universal was two months overdue, the second event occurred, the second event that turned things around for me. It was a phone call from Stan Kamen at William Morris.

"I've got a movie that's perfect for you, Norman," he said. "It's called *The Cincinnati Kid.*"

7

Making the Jigsaw
Pieces Fit

Shooter: Look, you're just cheating yourself, don't you understand? You'll be the loser, no one else but yourself. You've ruined the puzzle now. That doesn't go in there.

Melba (banging her fist on the puzzle piece): It does now.

—*The Cincinnati Kid*

At first, I told Stan Kamen that my answer was no.

"Sam Peckinpah started directing *Cincinnati Kid*," Stan said, "but now the producer's interested in having you take it over."

"I can't do that, Stan. I can't take a job away from another director."

"You don't get it, Norman," Stan said. "Sam's been fired already."

Peckinpah had established himself as a gifted director, but he was also known in the business as a hard drinker and a loose cannon. His loose cannon side had taken over on the first week of shooting *The Cincinnati Kid*. There was a minor scene in the script where a character played by Rip Torn is in bed with a nude hooker. Sam spent six hours shooting the scene. Some people on the set told Marty Ransohoff, the producer, that Sam was producing footage that could incur an X-rating. Also, Sam had insisted on shooting the movie in black and white—a very odd choice, I thought, for a story centered on red and black playing cards.

The Cincinnati Kid was adapted from Richard Jessup's short novel of the same title. It's about an epic confrontation over a high-stakes poker game between two professional card players, one a seasoned veteran and the other a rising young challenger. For me, the movie was about winning and losing. Winning is more important in the U.S. than in any other country in the world. I remember vividly when, at the 2002 Winter Olympics in Salt Lake City, the American women's hockey team was on the front page of every large American newspaper and on all the late-night TV shows. The team members were the reigning Olympic champions and expected to win the gold again. When they lost the gold to the Canadian team, they virtually vanished from the media—news of the event was relegated to page seven. Winning is a ticket to validation. The winner is venerated, the loser dismissed with contempt. And America has an image of the winner. He looks just like Steve McQueen, just like the Cincinnati Kid.

Marty Ransohoff, who was producing the movie for MGM, was a tough, bottom-line operator at the best of times, and these were the worst of times. He was paying the cast and crew of *Kid* to sit at home while he found a new director. The delay would end up costing him more than half a million. So Marty was mad, but I couldn't complain—not yet anyway—because he gave me three weeks to rework Ring Lardner Jr.'s script to my own satisfaction.

I found the Peckinpah script turgid and melodramatic. It needed an injection of lightness, of wit and irony. For that, I turned to another screenwriter—Terry Southern. Terry's career covered not much more than a decade. He had written or co-written the screenplays for *Dr. Strangelove*, *Barbarella*, and *Easy Rider*, all before 1970. His movie work and his 1959 novel, *The Magic Christian*, sparkled with hip, ironic outrage, and for a while, he was known as the leading avant-garde satirist in Hollywood.

I met Terry a few days after I started on *The Cincinnati Kid*. Terry had just finished work on another piece of outrageous movie-making, *The Loved One*. We were introduced by Hal Ashby, who was even cooler than Terry. Hal would emerge as one of the great American movie directors of the 1970s, making films like *Bound for Glory, Coming Home, Harold and Maude,* and my favorite, *Being There.*

When Hal and I became friends in the fall of 1964, he was still an assistant film editor to Bob Swink, who cut most of William Wyler's films. He was also the first real sixties guy I knew—tall, thin, wearing beads and sandals, smoking pot, his white-blond hair and beard long and scraggly. Our shared sense of humor brought us together. I was on the MGM lot just beginning to cope with the reorganization of *The Cincinnati Kid.* Hal was in an editing room working on *The Loved One* for Antony Gibbs, the British editor. I heard him laughing and wondered what was so funny. He invited me in to take a look. *The Loved One* was adapted from Evelyn Waugh's darkly comic novel about America's take on funerals, cemeteries, and the undertaking business. Terry Southern's screenplay and Tony Richardson's direction made the movie even more hilarious than the book.

I began stopping by Hal's editing room at the end of the day, watching the changes, smoking a little of Hal's pot and joining him in helpless laughter. The sicker the movie got, the harder we laughed. And despite the laughter and the pot, it became obvious to me that he was meticulous and fiercely passionate about his craft. Hal had an incredible memory for film footage. His old Moviola was surrounded by hundreds of feet of film in bins or hanging in clips from lines strung between the walls, but he knew precisely what shots were on each clip. I loved the smell of the exposed film and the tape used then to splice every cut. The pungent aroma was always mixed with the smell of cigarettes, coffee, and marijuana. I offered him the job of editor on *The Cincinnati Kid.*

It was a significant moment for me, hiring my own editor. On the four comedies I made at Universal, the studio had assigned an editor to me. I had little control over the first edit and even less over the final product. As a free agent making a movie for an independent producer, I now had the authority to choose my own editor and to work closely with him on the edit. I wanted someone who would look at a scene and see the same possibilities in it that I saw. Hal filled the bill. In fact, he kept on filling the bill as an editor and friend on three more of my movies.

Terry Southern was exactly the right fit too. I didn't want his whole bag of tricks, just some of his salty touch, and in early December, he and I settled into my office at MGM for writing sessions that lasted every day for a month. Because we were pressured for time, I hired another writer, Chuck Eastman, to rework the love scenes. Romance was Chuck's writing specialty, and when he was done, Terry and I folded his love scenes into the more plot-central material we were writing. The first two acts of the story were essentially a lead-up to the climactic poker game, which became the third and final act. What Terry and I had to do was loosen the overall approach to the story's events, sketch the principal characters in brighter colors, and build a sense of New Orleans's seamy gambling life. Then, once the players were sitting at the poker table in the hotel suite, we could let the game take over the story.

We had plenty of characters to work with: the Cincinnati Kid himself, a young poker player who wants to prove himself against "the Man"; the Man, otherwise known as Lancey Howard, a wise and confident old pro, played by Edward G. Robinson; Shooter, the dealer, played by Karl Malden; Shooter's sexy young wife, Melba, played by Ann-Margret; the Kid's girlfriend, Christian, played by Tuesday Weld; and Slade, the spoiled scion of a rich New Orleans family, played by Rip Torn.

Terry and I got into the habit of reading scenes aloud to each other, me playing the Karl Malden part and Terry playing Ann-Margret, or me as Steve McQueen and Terry as Edward G. Robinson. Sometimes this drove us into hysterics, but more often than not it led to some major decisions being made about the characters. Slade, for instance. We made him more villainous because the story lacked a conventional bad guy. (Lancey Howard was simply a veteran card player, neither good nor evil.) By the time we got finished with Slade, he spat out threats, flung insults, cheated on his wife, and blackmailed the Karl Malden character. When Rip Torn got into the part—Rip has a deeply sardonic sense of humor—he went at it with tremendous relish. He was relaxed and truly enjoyed himself.

For similar reasons, we rewrote the role of Melba, the Ann-Margret character. We wanted to inject some sexual tension into an already tense atmosphere, and we wanted to expand the role of this hot young singer-actress to keep her from disappearing from the screen for long periods of time. Melba became our seductress, our bad girl. We developed scenes that led to her seduction of the Kid during a rest break near the end of the card game.

To show the audience what sort of woman Melba was, Terry came up with a scene in which Melba is trimming a jigsaw puzzle piece in order to force it into place in the puzzle. "Do you have to cheat at *everything*, Melba?" her husband asks. This image of Melba trimming the jigsaw piece apparently stayed with many people. Thirty-four years later, in the middle of President Clinton's 1998 Monica Lewinsky crisis, I picked up the *New York Times* and read in Maureen Dowd's column: "Like Ann-Margret in *The Cincinnati Kid*, using her nail file to saw down jigsaw puzzle pieces to make them fit, White House aides are jamming messy Monica facts into a plausible picture."

One of the film's best lines comes at the end of the film. The end itself turned normal film conventions upside down. I knew that the audience would anticipate that the Kid, the good-looking young guy, would win the final poker hand. But, to the shock of everyone, the Kid loses. Lancey, the type who always loses in the movies, wins. He says, after the Kid makes his last and fatal play, "Gets down to that's what it's all about, doesn't it, Kid, making the wrong move at the right time?" Then, a few moments later, when the game is over and every-one is settling up, Lancey lights a cigar, leans forward, and looks into McQueen's baby blues: "You're good, Kid, but as long as I'm around, you're second best. You might as well learn to live with it."

I thought there was great truth in those lines, and they resonated on two levels: as the old pro Lancey Howard addressing the Cincinnati Kid, and as Edward G. Robinson, an old-time movie star whose star-dom was on the wane, addressing Steve McQueen, whose stardom was on the rise.

Once filming began, I got my first, but far from last, taste of Marty Ransohoff's hot temper. It was on my second day of principal photography in mid-January. The schedule called for me to shoot in New Orleans first. I'd do the scenes that used exteriors and interiors distinctive to the city, then return to the MGM lot to shoot the bulk of the interiors, particularly the poker scenes. As soon as I reached New Orleans, I knew I wanted to expand a sequence that would run behind the opening credits. We'd shoot the Cincinnati Kid walking past a traditional New Orleans funeral. The scene wasn't in the script but I went ahead anyway. The camera followed a funeral procession into a graveyard, the small band playing a stately, mournful dirge. Then, the funeral over, the camera rode high above the cemetery wall in an exhilarating crane shot as the band blasted into "Didn't He Ramble" and the mourners broke apart and began jiving. I thought it was colorful, original, and atmospheric, but when Ransohoff saw the footage back in Hollywood, he fired off a furious telegram warning me about wasting time and money on scenes that hadn't appeared in the script he'd approved.

Then I shot another scene that wasn't in the script. I needed a scene that reflected the Kid's mood just before the big game. The Kid is lonely because his girlfriend is out of town, and he's apprehensive about going up against Lancey Howard. He walks through the French Quarter of the city alone. It's a rainy night, and the Kid stops to look through the door of a bar where a woman is singing a slow, sad blues song. All of those things—the night, the rain, the singer—added complications.

We found a fabulous blues piano player and singer. Sweet Emma Barrett was about eighty years old and all but toothless, so short her hands had to reach up to the keys. She performed a blues song she had written herself:

> The river's in mourning
> The ships are all standing still
> The river's in mourning
> And the ships are standing still
> The girl that he loved
> She's gone over the hill.

A somber Steve McQueen walked through a burst of rain created by the special effects crew. He paused at the door to the bar. Sweet Emma Barrett sang her blues. And we had our scene.

Ransohoff whipped off another telegram: "Shoot the script. Stop improvising. You're behind schedule. Return to L.A. at once!" I shot off my own telegram pointing out that I was just a single day behind and that I'd have no trouble making up the time. I added, "If I have to come back to L.A. now, I'll leave the picture!" No reply. But it wasn't my telegram that shut him up. It was John Calley, the associate producer on the movie. (He went on to have a long, distinguished movie career, eventually becoming CEO of Sony Pictures.) John had been paying closer attention to the dailies from New Orleans than his boss had. His advice to Ransohoff was, essentially, "Jewison's shooting good stuff, so let's leave him alone."

Steve McQueen became my more immediate problem. Shortly after I took over *Kid*, he and I got together at his house way up in Mandeville Canyon in West L.A. He lived with his wife, Neile, and their two small children in a remote spot, which seemed to suit his personality. He was guarded, distant, and suspicious. I didn't mind an actor feeling me out in order to judge the approach I intended to take to the character he was hired to play. But Steve went far beyond that. He was testing me to determine whether he'd admit me to his private club.

"When the moon is full, does your husband get a little weird?" I asked Neile in a joking way when Steve was out of the room.

"Are you kidding?" she said. "He's a warlock!"

After I learned more about Steve's background, the "screw you" attitude made more sense. He'd had an incredibly tough childhood. His father deserted the family when Steve was a baby, and his mother wasn't much better. During drinking jags, she farmed Steve out to various relatives. His schooling was hit and miss. He spent time in Boys' Republic, a home for juvenile delinquents in Chino, California. He joined the Marine Corps and got thrown in the brig. Eventually, he landed in Greenwich Village, where he made a living at a variety of jobs, including driving a cab, before he drifted into acting. Hilly

Elkins, one of the great New York agent-managers, took over Steve's career and got him the starring role in the TV western *Wanted: Dead or Alive*, which paved the way to such movies as *The Magnificent Seven* and *The Great Escape*.

By 1964 Steve wasn't an actor, he was a movie star. He had a large Roman head and pale blue eyes that never blinked. He photographed beautifully. But his star quality came from his believability on the screen. I believed Steve on camera more than I believed actors with more technique. If you put Steve on an empty stage with a chair and a soliloquy to read, he wouldn't hold the audience. That took acting. A Laurence Olivier. But if I asked Steve to walk across a room for the camera, he would be natural and immensely appealing. Olivier would act the walk of the character. Steve would simply walk. It would be so real the audience would believe in him more than they would believe in Olivier.

Many top Hollywood movie stars were never great talented actors in the theatrical sense. Yet they had a personal charisma and magnetism in front of the camera that made them unique. It was the look, the large expressive eyes, the walk, the body language, and the charm that made some people movie stars and others just actors. Movie stars are always the same no matter what movie they are in. We always feel comfortable when they are on the screen. John Wayne, Humphrey Bogart, Cary Grant, Jimmy Stewart, Gary Cooper, Gregory Peck—all of them were personally more important than the characters they portrayed.

At the same time, perhaps as a result of his lack of formal training, Steve was the least giving of actors. He often didn't look at the other actor in a scene until he'd finished delivering his own lines, then he'd look away when the other actor began speaking to him. This wasn't an upstaging trick with him. He wasn't looking away in order to get his profile on camera. Steve was comfortable enough with the camera to avoid that sort of gimmick. It was simply the way he worked. He was a selfish actor and it was rough on fellow actors.

In the early scenes we shot, Steve was holding back, not really taking my direction. At the end of one shooting day, we sat down together on the curb of a New Orleans street, the thirty-nine-year-old director and the thirty-four-year-old star.

"Steve," I said. "I don't know what you want from me. Maybe you're looking for a father figure. God knows I can't be that. But I'll tell you what I can be. How about we think of me as your older brother, the one who went to college? I'm the educated older brother and I will always look out for you."

I was just winging it, but this seemed to get his attention. He apparently liked the idea of his director as an older brother.

"You and I are totally different," I went on. "You work with your hands. You can take engines apart, and you're fascinated with speed, you're great with a motorcycle. I can't do any of the things you do. But I'm the older brother, and I'm the guy who's always around taking care of your best interests."

Steve nodded, and our little chat seemed to place our relationship on a stronger footing. But we didn't finally get over the hump until we'd negotiated the matter of the dailies. Steve wanted to watch the rushes of his work at the end of each day. I didn't want him to see them.

"Why do you want to watch them, Steve?" I asked. "You want to check if I'm doing my job? You want to watch yourself? What I think is that the actor should concentrate strictly on his acting. Watching the dailies can throw the actor off. You should forget the dailies. You should rely on your director for guidance. A certain amount of trust is needed on this movie."

"You trying to twist my melon, man?" Steve said.

That was the way Steve talked. Sometimes he was so hip I had no idea what he was saying.

"I'm not doing anything to your melon," I said. "I'm asking you to trust me."

Steve gave in on the dailies, saying he'd rely on me as his "older brother" to tell him if anything was wrong. Three weeks later, I asked Hal Ashby to put together a sequence of Steve's scenes from the footage we'd shot up to that point. We ran the scenes for him, and afterwards, though he didn't say much, I knew he liked what he saw.

He never brought up the matter of the dailies again, and I sensed that I'd been admitted to the very small circle of people Steve McQueen trusted.

As for Edward G. Robinson, he and I had come to a meeting of the minds before shooting on the movie began. I was nervous about working with Robinson. I'd grown up watching his 1930s gangster films, and now I was directing him in my own movie. I was in awe of his strong persona. One of the first things I had to tell him was why Terry Southern and I had cut several of his scenes from the original script. In two or three scenes Lancey Howard and Shooter reminisced about Lancey's past triumphs at poker tables around the world. Terry and I thought the scenes slowed the movie down and we took them out. Edward G. Robinson wasn't amused.

"But don't you see, Mr. Robinson," I said at our first meeting, "when you're the king, the Man, the best damn poker player in the world, you don't need to talk about what you've done in the past. Only has-beens talk about the past. Lancey is thinking about the future, about his next game and his next win, about the way he's going to gut the Cincinnati Kid."

"Yeah, yeah, go on," Robinson said in that deep voice familiar from a dozen matinees of my youth.

"And look at your entrance in the movie. Lancey arrives in New Orleans by train. He steps onto the platform and a blast of steam comes from under the locomotive. Lancey emerges through the steam like Mephistopheles. The music hits on the soundtrack, and we get a close-up. He's a figure of mystery. Important. That's how Lancey Howard comes into the movie."

"That's good," Robinson said. "Yeah, I like it, kid. That's very good."

"Thanks," I said, feeling every muscle in my body relax.

"Look, why don't you and your wife come to my place for dinner," Robinson said. "I'll arrange it. We'll have dinner, and I'll show you some of my pictures."

Dixie and I visited his house in Beverly Hills several times. I stopped calling him "Mr. Robinson" and graduated to "Eddie." The "some of my pictures" included works by Picasso, Chagall, and Van Gogh. A large Renoir hung over the mantelpiece in the living room. Eddie Robinson, we discovered, owned one of the finest collections of Impressionist and later French paintings in private hands. He was a cultivated man, a generous host, and a gifted actor.

He certainly wasn't a man to be rattled by Steve McQueen on the set. After his first experience with Steve's look-anywhere-but-into-the-eyes-of-my-co-actor form of acting, Eddie said to me, "Don't worry about anything. I can take care of myself." And he did. His Lancey played brilliantly off Steve's Kid, and at the end of the movie, I could hear real triumph in Eddie's voice when he recited the famous line to Steve: "You're good, Kid, but as long as I'm around, you're second best."

We returned to Hollywood from New Orleans, to the MGM lot, and prepared to shoot the most demanding part of the movie. Motion pictures are all about movement, so shooting a static activity like a card game wasn't going to be easy. The drama would have to emerge in small touches, in the flip of a card, the turn of a hand, the contact between two pairs of eyes.

The script spelled out the logistics of the epic game. It began with five players and two dealers who alternated. The players were the Kid and Lancey, plus Yeller (Cab Calloway), Pig (Jack Weston), and Doc (Milton Sokal). The alternating dealers were Shooter (Karl Malden) and Ladyfingers (Joan Blondell). We also populated the hotel suite with a small group of spectators. Some of them served specific plot purposes, but their main job was to serve as a Greek chorus, commenting to one another about the moves at the poker table, speculating on bets, and keeping the audience in the theater informed about the possible strategies of the players.

The audience also had to be able to quickly tell the characters apart around the table. Casting got us over a big part of this hurdle. Cab Calloway as Yeller was the black player. Jack Weston as Pig was the overweight player with the fat stogie. Joan Blondell as Ladyfingers was the only woman at the table. Milton Selzer as Doc Sokal wasn't physically distinctive, so we invented idiosyncrasies for him—the hand fiddling with an elastic band, calculating the odds in a small note-book. A percentage player. Shooter, Lancey, and the Kid had already been fixed in the audience's mind by this point in the movie.

A much more difficult filming problem became apparent as the game began. Which direction should the card players look in their close-ups? The players were sitting at a round table. Somewhere at the table, for filming purposes, there had to be a center. We decided our center would be the character who was dealing the cards, either Shooter or Ladyfingers. If the dealer was our center, then, in close-ups, the players on the right side of the camera had to be looking camera left, and the players on the left side of the camera had to be looking camera right. That seemed clear enough, but in order to have room on the set for the camera to shoot the close-ups, we had to take the table out. This meant we were left with no immediate point of ref-erence. If Pig is making eye contact with Lancey, which way should Jack Weston look? Left or right?

"Jack should be looking to the right," I said on the set.

"No," Phil Lathrop, my director of photography, countered. "Definitely left."

"Right, looking right," I insisted.

"It should be left when he looks at Eddie," the script supervisor said, "and right when he turns to Steve."

"I still think it's right."

These arguments were replayed on every close-up until I finally decided the script assistant would have the last word. He was a smart young man, paid to keep track of every shot in the script and relate it to the actual filming of the lines. I appointed him in charge of all questions of eye contact. If he was wrong, we found out three days later when Hal had cut the film and matched the close-ups. If Hal had two characters, in their separate close-ups, obviously looking away from each other, we knew the script assistant had done it backwards. Fortunately for my sanity, he rarely made a mistake.

No one wanted to waste time on arguments given the physical con-ditions on the set. Poker games traditionally take place in smoke-filled rooms, and our game was no exception. These were the days before someone in the movie business had a eureka moment and thought of using a neutron haze made with glycerol and water. Our fake smoke was probably as bad as the real thing. When people needed to stun bees, they burned kerosene and puffed it into the hive. That's bee smoke, and it's what we used. It was the only effect that would look good on film.

Day after day, we worked in an atmosphere laced with this heavy smoke. It was far worse than the soap suds on *The Thrill of It All*. That was a breath of spring air compared to the thick, choking smoke of *Cincinnati Kid*. Everybody developed rasping coughs and terrible colds. Worst of all was the diarrhea. People kept bolting from the set to the bathroom. Yet it never occurred to any of us to refuse to work in such ghastly conditions. Nobody rebelled or mutinied. We were either crazy or totally devoted to the movie. Maybe a bit of both.

I had to cope with one other hazard that was peculiar to me, the Marty Ransohoff visits. His office was handy to the set, and he liked to drop by and see how I was spending his money. It drove me nuts to have the producer looming behind me as I tried to direct the actors in their scenes. It was like the math teacher in high school peeking over your shoulder when you were writing the algebra exam. In self-defense, I created an early warning system. A secretary in Marty's office would alert us when he headed for the set. That was my signal to hide. The first time it happened, I ducked into a fake elevator.

"Why aren't you shooting?" I heard Ransohoff's booming voice. "Where's the director? Where's Jewison?"

"He's, ah, in the bathroom," someone lied.

A few minutes later, Ransohoff roared again, "When's the scene gonna be shot? What's keeping Jewison?"

"We've, ah, had a problem lately with people getting the runs." Ransohoff left. Steve McQueen walked over to the elevator, tapped on the door, and whispered, "You can come out now, man."

Steve had a big grin on his face. He knew that he was supposed to be the difficult person on the set, the rebel, Peck's Bad Boy, as I often called him. Now here was his director in effect defying the producer. Steve liked that. It strengthened our relationship in a way I couldn't have predicted.

As for Ransohoff and his visits to the set, John Calley, his assistant producer, once again came to my rescue. He heard about my problem and advised Marty to stick to the producing and let me handle the directing. Ransohoff ended his forays to the set, and I got on with filming the poker game.

The deeper we got into the game, the more I began to feel confident that I could make it dramatic. The photography and editing were key. I counted on the creative talents of Phil Lathrop and Hal Ashby to help me pull it off. And we did.

Phil, an experienced cinematographer and impeccable craftsman, was a man of mildly eccentric habits for Hollywood in the sixties. He came to work every day dressed in a shirt and tie, looking like D.W. Griffith in old photographs from the silent days. In his pants pocket he carried a roll of bills fat enough to choke a horse. When Phil paid his share of lunch, he hauled out the enormous wad and laboriously peeled off the bills. It was Phil who created the movie's distinctive visual look.

The Cincinnati Kid's muted tone was produced by removing the primary colors from every scene in the film except in places where Phil wanted to emphasize something. He left the primary colors alone in shots of the playing cards so that the reds of the hearts and diamonds and the blacks of the clubs and spades would pop out of their muted surroundings. The effect was dynamic, and it guaranteed that the audience would have no trouble reading the cards and following the nuances of the poker game. Ann-Margret's dress appeared bright red in the scene at the cock fight—the crimson blood of the fighting cocks reflected back in the dress worn by the scarlet woman. And then there was the cat, which I imagine some people have puzzled over. It kept its natural bright yellow simply because we ran out of time to spray it down to a less vivid shade.

I always felt that the muted colors would give the movie a period feel. I pegged the game as taking place just before World War II, a time that seemed somehow more congenial to professional poker playing. Our production designers, Edward Carfagno and George W. Davis, and our set dressers, Henry Grace and Hugh Hunt, were meticulous about achieving a consistent look for the period. Our budget limited our shooting of street scenes, which required vintage automobiles. To achieve the look we were after, we relied heavily on costumes, sets, and props. And of course on Phil's soft lighting of the sets.

Phil and I had to become especially inventive in working out camera angles for the card game. We had to make it as visually interesting as possible to hold the audience's interest. In the first hand, we shot the play at the table entirely from behind Shooter, the dealer. It was an uncomplicated, businesslike shot that established for the audience the positions of the players and the mood and style of their poker playing. For the second game, we felt free to energize the action by swinging the camera from player to player as each man constructed his hand and made his bets. A little further along in the game, we reached the hand that ends with Pig folding and leaving the table, and here we got much busier with the camera set-ups. At the beginning of the hand, the camera stayed close on Shooter's hands as he pulled the cards from the deck and dealt them (a shot that was made possible only through the inhuman number of hours that Karl Malden practiced shuffling and dealing). Then we set up, in succession, a group shot from over Yeller's (Cab Calloway's) shoulder; a shot of Lancey from Pig's side; a shot of Pig (Jack Weston) and Shooter (Karl Malden) in the same frame; and finally a series of close-ups, Pig, then the Kid, then Lancey. Through all this the camera was tracking the action and reaction of the players as Lancey suckers Pig into betting his entire roll. Pig storms out of the game and out of the hotel suite.

"Man doesn't have much luck," Lancey says.

"He never did," the Kid answers.

Most of the brisk pacing of this sequence was created later in Hal's editing room, but it was the resourcefulness of Phil's camera and the footage exposed that gave Hal and me the material we needed.

It was exacting, thrilling work, but the final hand was looming closer and I had a problem. From the day Terry and I had begun working on the script, I'd worried about that last stud-poker hand. The game the Kid and Lancey were playing was one card down and four up. The four cards up had to lead everyone at the table, in the hotel room and in the movie theater—everyone except the Man—to assume, incorrectly, that the Kid was in the process of gutting the mighty Lancey. In Richard Jessup's novel, the hand that the Kid drew was a full house against Lancey's straight flush to the queen. But the novel wasn't our bible. And for all I knew—and I didn't know much because I wasn't a card player—there might be a better choice of cards. I became obsessive about finding the perfect hand. I quizzed every poker player I knew until I got to Joe Schoenfeld, one of my William Morris agents.

"Straight flush," Joe said, echoing the Jessup novel. "Lancey's got the jack to fill out a straight flush. The eight, nine, ten, and queen are on the table, and the jack's in the hole."

Joe understood poker. He considered himself something of a philosopher of the game. But more importantly, he understood drama.

"The odds on a player holding a straight flush are about five thousand to one," he said. "Only two kinds of player imagine they can make a straight flush, a beginner or a man who is desperate. Nobody's going to think Lancey can fill to the straight flush. He must be bluffing. And if he bets a conservative amount at first, then everybody will be certain he's bluffing. The Kid, if he's sitting there knowing he's got a full house in his own hands, will feel completely confident and he'll play into Lancey's bluff. He won't be able to help himself."

And that was the way we shot the hand.

The editing of the last game with its passage of time required some pickup shots. Hal and our editing assistant, Bill Sawyer, came up with some ideas, and among us we managed to shoot for two days without any of the cast. Just the camera moving onto the Tiffany lamp over the table. Tight insert shots of cards hitting the green felt. Cigarette smoke swirling around lace curtains.

Editing is probably the most important element of the filmmaker's art, followed by the writing, the photography, and the acting. Pudovkin, the famous Russian filmmaker, is quoted as saying that editing is the only original and unique art form in film. I think that's true. Writing comes from literature, acting comes from the theater, and cinematography comes from photography. Editing is unique to film. You can see things from different points of view. This creates a new experience for the viewer.

Pudovkin gives the example of a guy hanging a picture. Suddenly you see his feet slip. You see the chair move. You see his hand go down, the picture falls off the wall. In that split second, a guy falls off a chair, and you see it in a way that's unique through editing.

Some TV commercials are brilliant pieces of editing. Telling a story in thirty seconds. No content. Yet the visual poetry sometimes leaves the viewer breathless.

Hal Ashby was, without doubt, the most committed editor I ever worked with. Over the course of my next three films, which I did with Hal, we would bond as close as brothers. In 1969 I would have the opportunity to produce *The Landlord*, a script we developed and made possible for Hal to direct. He would of course move on to become one of the finest directors in (contemporary) American film.

On my first four movies, I felt a professional commitment to make the films as well as I could given the circumstances. But they were studio assignments. On *The Cincinnati Kid*, *I* was in control and it made a difference in my attitude to the work. There was a passion and an involvement in the movie that consumed me fourteen hours a day for more than three months of shooting. All of which didn't mean that I was completely free of MGM and Marty Ransohoff's contributions, not even at the end.

My contract for the movie gave me what is called first cut to third public preview. That meant *Kid* was shown to preview audiences in and around Los Angeles three times. After each preview, I was permitted to go back to the editing room with Hal. We'd then make the changes that I thought were necessary and justified by the audience reaction. It wasn't as good as final cut, but it was the next best thing. If I didn't have the movie in the precise shape I wanted after a third preview, then I never would. And with *Kid*, I knew we had accomplished what we had aimed for all those months ago.

But still Ransohoff took my cut and made a cut of his own that affected the ending in a way that, I think, reduced its power. In the ending, as I structured it, the Kid, after losing the game to Lancey Howard, staggers out into the back alley in New Orleans and slumps against the wall. The shoeshine boy, who lost to the Kid pitching quarters in the first scene of the movie, challenges him again. "Come on, Cincinnati, get up." The Kid rises and pitches his last coin. This time he loses. "You're just not ready for me yet," the boy jeers. The camera comes in close on the Kid. He's stripped of everything. He's lost to Lancey. He's lost his girlfriend. And now he's lost his last quarter to the shoeshine boy. He's beaten. He's cleaned out. And for ten seconds, at the end of the movie, the camera freezes on the Kid. Then the credits roll.

Ransohoff took out the ten-second pause. Now, ten seconds may seem insignificant. But in this American movie, the man who looks like the winner loses, and I wanted the audience to reflect on this astounding twist of fortune. I wanted them to devote ten seconds to examining the new face of the loser in America. Ransohoff took away those ten seconds.

Worse was to come. In the version of the movie that was shown in Europe, the entire ending was changed. I couldn't blame Ransohoff for this. It was done at the insistence of the powerful MGM executive who was in charge of distribution of the studio's movies in foreign markets. He wanted a happy ending for *The Cincinnati Kid*. Unfortunately, I had shot a somewhat happy ending but had ditched it in a saner moment. In it, when the Kid emerges from the hotel, he encounters, not the shoeshine boy, but Christian, his girlfriend. She forgives him. The Kid loses the poker game but not his girl. The executive was insistent that American movie stars should never lose. Nobody likes a downbeat ending.

Even with that silly finale, *The Cincinnati Kid* was a big success in Europe. One cinema in Amsterdam ran it for a year. The movie attracted good audiences and favorable reviews throughout Europe and North America. It won no prizes, though, and in that failure, I was disappointed on Eddie Robinson's behalf. His portrayal of Lancey

Howard was his best work in the later part of his career, and he merited at least an Academy Award nomination.

But none of the disappointments, not Eddie's Oscar shutout or Ransohoff's hijacking of the ten seconds, could overshadow the sheer joy I felt making *The Cincinnati Kid*. It remains one of my favorites because it is the one that made me feel like I had finally become a filmmaker.

8

The Canadian Pinko

Has Arrived

What would the Russians be doing on
United States of America island, with
so many animosities and hatreds
between these two countries? It is
too funny an idea, is it not? We are
of course Norwegians!

—*Lieutenant Rozanov, The Russians Are*
Coming, The Russians Are Coming

"Dear Lars, This would make a hell of a funny movie for you to
direct," began a letter I received from Jerry Lieder in 1963.

Jerry was a friend from my CBS days in New York. He was a CBS
program executive working under Mike Dann, the New York network
program director. And "Lars" was Jerry's nickname for me after an
infamous trip to Paris that the two of us had taken three years
previously.

At the time, I'd been interested in directing a dramatic show. Jerry
knew this, and one day he walked into my office and handed me a
script for a TV drama based on a Stefan Zweig short story. Ingrid
Bergman was slated to play the female lead.

"Do you want to direct?" he asked.

"Absolutely," I said. Who wouldn't?

Ingrid Bergman's sad, beautiful face had filled the movie screens of
my adolescence. She was a screen goddess. I couldn't quite imagine

myself directing the same woman Alfred Hitchcock had directed in *Notorious*, but I sure wasn't going to pass up the opportunity.

There was just one catch. Miss Bergman hadn't actually agreed to do Jerry's show. He and I had to meet her in Paris to discuss it.

Nothing I can't handle, I thought. We flew to Paris and took a taxi to her apartment. A tall, gloomy Swedish fellow opened the door and introduced himself as Dr. Lars Schmidt, Bergman's husband. He led us into the living room where the still lovely actress sat on the sofa with a copy of the TV script in her hand. Like her stone-faced husband, she wasn't smiling. She was wearing a large pair of horn-rimmed glasses and no makeup. At forty-eight, she still exuded that Nordic, sensual beauty.

After we were introduced, I began to talk about the character Miss Bergman would be playing. She cut me off. She had underlined each scene in the script in which she would appear *and* she had counted how many lines she had. *That* was what concerned *her*. Then she abruptly ended the conversation and told us we could deal with Lars in any further negotiations.

In ten minutes flat we were out the door. It was obvious that, according to Lars, her doctor and now agent-manager, there would be no further negotiations. The part wasn't big enough for a star of her stature. I felt like the little kid who had come close to getting his idol's autograph but had missed out at the last minute. Jerry started to laugh at the look on my face. And from that moment on, just to rub it in a little and remind me of the guy who epitomized the whole deflating experience, he called me "Lars."

The book Jerry sent me in 1963 was *The Off-Islanders* by Nathaniel Benchley. The novel didn't particularly grab me, but it did have a unique idea that jumped out at me. A Russian sub accidentally runs aground on an island off the New England coast. The locals fear the worst. They're convinced the Russians are invading and it's the beginning of World War III. The Russian seamen are just as terrified as the Americans. They think the Americans will blow them out of the water. All they want is a tow off the sandbar so that they can get back to sea.

I thought it could make for a fantastic political satire. A film that could point out the absurdity of international conflict and the need for co-existence. The timing seemed perfect. Memories of the 1962 Cuban missile crisis were still fresh in everyone's minds. The Cold War was at its peak. I took out an option on the novel for $2,500 and made an appointment to see Charlie Baker, one of my agents.

Charlie was a senior agent at the William Morris Agency and looked after the agency's theatrical clients. An intelligent man of impeccable taste, he was revered on Broadway for his trustworthiness and good advice. (The later infamous New York and Hollywood agent Sue Mengers was his secretary. Charlie trained her well.)

"Nathaniel Benchley, hmmm, I don't know the man," Charlie said. "Of course I knew his father." (Robert Benchley was the great *New Yorker* writer.)

My first big hurdle, I told Charlie, was finding the right writer to put together the screenplay. The Mirisch Corporation and United Artists, who were interested in financing my film, would require an established screenwriter.

"I am aware of just one person who possesses the ability to write a screenplay from such material."

"Really?" I said. "Who?"

"William Rose."

I didn't know much about him. He had written two English comedies in the fifties—*Genevieve* and *The Ladykillers*. And I seemed to remember that he was an American who lived somewhere in England.

"My dear boy," Charlie said. "I'll arrange a meeting between the two of you."

Within a week, Charlie phoned. "Next Tuesday evening at eight o'clock you are to proceed to a restaurant called Les Bras d'Or on the Left Bank."

"In Paris?" I gasped.

"In Paris. You will wear a red rose. Walk to the third booth on the restaurant's right side. William Rose will be waiting to dine with you."

Charlie loved intrigue and I went along with his little game. When I arrived at the restaurant, a tall, good-looking man, also with a rose in his lapel, was sipping wine in the third booth. We introduced ourselves, laughed at the situation, and shook hands. I sat down, he poured me a glass of wine, and we began a friendship that would last until Bill's death in 1987.

About ten years older than me, Bill had grown up in Missouri and joined the Black Watch Regiment in Canada at the very beginning of the war. He was shipped overseas and never went back. After the war, he became a screenwriter and settled in England. He absolutely loathed Hollywood, which helped explain why he rarely worked in American movies.

When the main course arrived, so did Charlie Baker, much to our surprise. He sat down, ordered a second bottle of wine, and helped himself.

"I came to Paris, not as you might speculate to preside over the alliance of a rising young director and an established writer looking for a fresh challenge. I came not to be with two of my favorite clients from whom a brilliant film will emerge. I came to Paris, my dear boys, to purchase a new pair of gloves and go to the opera."

With that, he finished his glass of wine, stood up, straightened his elegant jacket, and left the restaurant.

During dinner Bill agreed to write the screenplay for my Cold War comedy. He agreed with me that the story, though a comedy, could make a strong political statement. But only if we never mentioned communism or capitalism. Five or six months later, though, not a word had landed on my desk. No script, not even a treatment. We'd had many telephone conversations, but I was beginning to worry. Charlie did mention that Bill was a little slow with the writing. The Mirisch brothers, who had already paid a large writing fee, were even more worried. Did he have writer's block? Perhaps a bit of prodding in person was called for.

Bill and his wife, Tanya, lived in a pleasant old house on Jersey in the Channel Islands. Soon after my arrival, Bill sat me down in his office and talked about how he worked. He subscribed to Elaine May's theory of screenwriting. It was all about structure. The structure had to be so seamless that the audience wouldn't see it.

"I work every moment of the story out in my head before I even think about writing," he said.

And his first crack at the writing wasn't on the script itself. First, he told me, he made notes on index cards, one card per scene. He pinned the cards to a wall in his office and when he looked at the cards, the whole movie was laid out before him. Only then did he start writing the script.

I noticed that there weren't many cards on the wall.

"I never write anything that can't actually be done," Bill continued. And then he remembered a scene we had improvised on the phone. The Russian sailors tie up two Americans, a New York writer and a buxom female phone operator, back to back. Left alone in a second-floor room, the pair decides to escape. They spin themselves in a half-circle inside the ropes so they are facing each other, then hop their way down a steep flight of stairs. Was this even possible? Bill wondered.

I could see where this was leading. Bill called Tanya and asked her to tie the two of us together with a rope. For almost an hour, we bounced around the Rose living room, becoming increasingly hysterical, until Bill was satisfied that what we had imagined the two characters doing in the movie was possible in real life. It would be even funnier if the woman was someone like Tessie O'Shea, a large English comedienne with an enormous bosom.

My adventures with rope in the Rose household continued that night. I was staying in their guest bedroom over the stable, which was home to a donkey. A long cord hung down from the bedroom ceiling.

"About the cord," Bill explained when he showed me up to my room. "There seems to be a serial killer loose on the island. He's killed two or three people. I don't think there's any real danger, but just in case, you can pull the rope and ring the bell if you think the murderer's striking again. Everybody for miles round will come running. But don't pull it unless you're absolutely certain."

He's got to be kidding, I thought. But Bill seemed quite serious and Tanya showed me some grisly newspaper clippings.

I fell asleep, but woke up to a thumping noise somewhere below me. I sat up in a panic, looking for the rope. I could smell the faint trace of manure. Oh right, I thought, it's only the donkey. I fell back asleep, only to sit up again with a start a little while later. I'd heard a sound like a woman screaming somewhere nearby. Then it stopped. Perhaps I'd imagined it. Back down I fell. I slept, then I thought I heard another scream. Back up. Back down.

In the morning, I dragged myself to breakfast.

"I almost pulled the rope three or four times last night," I moaned. "I swear I heard a woman scream."

"Oh, that's not a woman," smiled Bill. "That was Gerald's panther."

"Gerald's what?"

"His black panther. Sounds almost human, doesn't it?"

It turned out that the Roses' neighbor was Gerald Durrell, the famous naturalist, writer, and owner of his own private zoo, whom we later went to visit.

It was a pleasant few days. Bill was a great conversationalist, and one of the things I noticed about him over the years was how much he enjoyed taking a woman's point of view in discussions at dinner parties. In *The Russians Are Coming, The Russians Are Coming*, he thought the only sane character was Elspeth Whittaker. He loved women. It was mentioned to me that at one point he'd had a romantic affair with Katharine Hepburn in Italy. This was long before he married Tanya. Bill and Dixie got along famously, and he drew a beautiful sketch of our daughter, Jennifer. It still hangs in our house, a memento of the man who loved women.

Two months passed and no word from Bill. I called him and told him I'd bet Harold Mirisch that I would have a script in two weeks or I would owe Harold $1,000 and my kids would not get any presents at Christmas. Bill's screenplay reached my office on December 15. He'd typed it on his portable typewriter without a typo or a white-out in its ninety pages. And it read as well as it looked. It was funny and original. It had only one flaw—the ending.

The story's action takes place over the course of one Sunday in late summer, from before dawn when the Russian sub runs aground until late afternoon when there is a final showdown between the islanders and the Soviet seamen. In the hours between, paranoia escalates on both sides. What was lacking in the ending was a moment of enlightenment, a catalyst that makes both groups realize that they have more in common than they realize.

When I asked Bill to change the ending, I knew he might have problems with my request. He was part of a generation of screenwriters, actors, and directors who had witnessed the McCarthy era firsthand. He was still an American, and despite the fact that he seldom worked in his homeland, he didn't want his script to give anybody the idea that he was soft on communism. That sounds crazy today, but in 1964, we were only ten years away from a time when screenwriters—Ring Lardner Jr. being one—had served time in jail for their alleged communist sympathies.

Bill got to work on the ending and produced a brilliant solution. While the islanders and seamen are facing off in the harbor, a little boy climbs up into the church belfry for a better view of the action. He slips from his perch, slides down the roof, and is caught by his pants on a drain spout high above the ground. Both sides forget their stand-off and form a human pyramid to rescue him. The boy is saved and the rescuers are united. The Cold War is momentarily forgotten as Russians and Americans celebrate the saving of a child's life. In the meantime, the most hard-line member of the townspeople has summoned a couple of jet fighters to blow up the sub. Elspeth, the voice of reason, persuades the islanders to form a convoy of their own boats to escort the submarine out of the harbor. The sub glides out to sea, the jets are ordered back to base because they don't want to hit any American civilians, and the story ends on a note of universality.

"Start pinning those cards on your wall," I told Bill after reading his ending. "How about this for a title?" I suggested tentatively, "'The Russians Are Coming.'"

There was a long pause. Then Bill laughed. "Great—but twice!"

On June 21, 1965, more than two years after our dinner in the Paris restaurant, the final draft of the script for *The Russians Are Coming,*

The Russians Are Coming was complete. It was well worth the wait. Good films always start with the writing. There's a certain amount of improvisation that occurs when shooting begins, but if you don't start with a strong script, you usually run into trouble.

"How are you going to get a submarine?" asked Walter Mirisch.

The Mirisch Corporation, run by Harold and his two brothers, produced films for United Artists. They were like a mini-studio. Harold made the deals, Walter produced, and Marvin took care of the books (money). Unlike Marty Ransohoff, Harold was known for giving his filmmakers the creative freedom they needed to make wonderful movies like *The Great Escape, Some Like It Hot,* and *The Pink Panther.* Since I was producing and directing this one by myself, the Mirisches made sure I had a strong production team. They gave me a tough production manager, Jim Henderling, and Bob Relyea, an experienced production executive, both of whom were already working for the Mirisches.

Today, of course, you can probably buy an old Soviet sub on the Internet. But when we told the United States Navy in 1965 why we wanted to borrow one of their submarines, their response was a frosty no. According to them, the whole premise for the movie was ridiculous: "A Russian submarine couldn't run aground without our knowing about it," they sniffed.

"But that's not true," I said. "What about the Soviet sub that sailed into San Francisco harbor with a desperately ill seaman onboard? You didn't even know it was there! It was in all the papers."

The answer was still no. The Canadian Navy offered a World War II German sub but that wouldn't work either. The U.S. Navy wouldn't allow a foreign sub within twelve miles of the coast. So our only option was to build one. The Mirisches agreed and arranged a meeting with Arthur Krim, the president of United Artists. When I pleaded with Krim that I needed another $150,000 of his money to build a submarine because the U.S. Navy wouldn't cooperate, he reluctantly agreed. He loved the theme of détente, and Arnold Picker, UA chairman of the board, was also a strong supporter of the project. So they took a collective deep breath and told me, "Norman, you go make *your* picture and you build *your* submarine."

Robert Boyle, our brilliant production designer, headed up a team that built a 180-foot submarine out of Styrofoam and plywood. Bob located an old conning tower from a film called *Morituri* at the Fox studios. We found a gun dealer in San Diego who had two naval guns and some heavy machine guns from a World War II sub. We put the tower on our hull. Painted black and equipped with real guns, the sub looked amazingly authentic. They fit four ninety-horsepower motors beneath the hull so that we could actually sail it into the harbor at Fort Bragg, where we shot the film.

Bob Boyle was also responsible for turning Fort Bragg, north of San Francisco, into a New England town complete with the requisite white church and steeple. He attached East Coast–looking house fronts onto the town's houses, scattered piles of lobster traps, put up authentic-sounding street signs, and replaced California license plates with Massachusetts ones. In fact, he did such a good job of transforming Mendocino County into Cape Cod that when Henry Luce, the editorial chairman of Time Life, saw the film he complimented me. "Wonderful film," he said. "You've captured Cape Cod, but you shot it on Grape Island, didn't you? I recognized it. You can't fool me."

I was too embarrassed to admit the truth, so I said, "No, I shot it a little farther west, sir."

The entire town got caught up in shooting the film. We hired many of them as extras, and every night they would pile into the local theater with their kids to watch the rushes. They recognized many of the actors up on the screen from film or television, but there was actually only one bona fide movie star in *Russians*. When we were casting it, this was a big problem for United Artists.

Originally I wanted Jack Lemmon to play the male lead in the film, the role of Manhattan playwright Walt Whittaker. When he turned me down, I asked my old friend Carl Reiner. He loved the screenplay and was delighted to play the part. After *The Thrill of It All* he had continued writing and producing the television hit *The Dick Van Dyke Show*, which was based on his own life as a young husband and father who wrote comedy. A similar role in *Russians* was a natural for him. The studio only agreed to cast him, though, when I got Academy Award winner Eva Marie Saint to play opposite him as his wife.

Like Carl, Alan Arkin wasn't on the studio's A list either. They wanted a star to play Lieutenant Rozanov, and Alan had never even appeared in a film. He was a brilliant stage actor. I had seen him in *Luv*, a Mike Nichols play on Broadway and thought he had a marvelous everyman quality about him. I also knew he could do dialects. "What if I get him to do a screen test?" I asked. United Artists agreed reluctantly, and then I had to convince this established, Tony Award–winning actor to do one. He finally agreed and did a very funny improvisation of a Russian agent pretending to be a member of the Bolshoi. After seeing the test, the studio agreed, again reluctantly, to let Alan play the role that later won him a Golden Globe and an Academy Award best actor nomination.

Throughout the film, the Russians speak Russian to one another or mangled English to the Americans, so I arranged for Alan to work with a Russian-speaking translator at the UN in New York. In the film, he was so convincing that moviegoers thought he was Russian. Even Russians who saw the film believed he was Russian. Alan's Russian was that good.

Another actor we cast who hadn't done much work in film was Jonathan Winters as Officer Norman "We've got to get organized" Jones. Like Carl and Alan, he was brilliant at improvising. During the filming, when we were all holed up in Fort Bragg, Jonathan decided this was the perfect time to give up drinking. For some reason, he thought woodworking might keep his mind off the booze, so we bought him some woodworking tools and a large block of wood. The assistants could always find him by following a trail of wood chips. After six weeks of whittling, he proudly produced an egg.

For the four months that we were isolated in that little town, miles from any major city, we all helped one another cope with being away from family and friends. Jonathan provided the daily entertainment, a different character each day. Some days he was Ma Fricker, a sassy old grandmother. Other days he was a forest ranger. We never knew who would turn up.

My family did, in fact, come to stay with me for ten days. My location manager had rented an old frame house overlooking the Pacific for me. Dixie bravely packed luggage, our three kids, and Deecho, our huge white Alsatian, into a tiny Cessna and flew up from San Francisco. The kids ran marine flags and signals up the towering flagpole on the front lawn and explored the empty beaches and nooks and crannies of the rugged coastline. It was a great week and a bit.

All of us who work making movies are constantly separated from our families. Like the military, we travel to distant locations for months at a time. It's hard on relationships. There are a lot of divorces and broken homes in this line of work. It's a business that requires everyone's concentration six days a week and often fifteen or sixteen hours every day. There are many lonely nights for everyone and many location romances—though few that find any permanence.

Over the years, my children always visited location shoots when they were not in school. This is probably why they all ended up in the business. They were put to work in wardrobe or props. They were trained in various departments and expected to help, along with the rest of the crew, in making every set-up as quick as possible. By the time they finished high school, the film business was something they knew a lot about.

Back home after the shoot, Dixie and I were invited by David and Dawn Wolper to their waterfront home in Newport, a wealthy enclave in the heart of conservative Orange County, some forty miles south of L.A. David was a successful television producer, who later became famous for producing the stunning TV series *Roots*. It was New Year's Eve and we were celebrating the arrival of 1966.

We drove down late in the afternoon. Dawn, a tall, athletic-looking California beauty, met us at the door with the news that John Wayne, Claire Trevor, and Edgar Bergen would be coming to the party. After a quick swim in the ocean, we went back to the house to dress for dinner. I fell asleep in one of the guest bedrooms and was the last to shower.

The doorbell rang. John Wayne came in with his wife and immediately shouted for a drink. Hearing that familiar voice booming from the hallway, I scrambled out of the upstairs bathroom, pulling on my pants as I went. Just as I crossed the top of the stairs, David Wolper looked up and said to Wayne, "Have you met Norman Jewison? The film director?" I looked down the long flight of stairs, shirtless and clutching my pants. John Wayne stared back, swaying slightly and holding a large glass of whiskey. Before I could say anything, David said, "Norman has just directed *The Russians Are Coming*. He and Dixie are our guests for the weekend."

Wayne continued to stare at me, his face expressionless. I managed to murmur, "It's an honor to meet you, Mr. Wayne."

"What are ya?" he suddenly shouted. "One of those goddamn pinkos?"

Speechless, I smiled weakly and scampered into the bedroom to finish changing. I could hear him bellowing about commies taking over Hollywood. When I finally slunk downstairs to join the party, I realized I was the only guy with a beard. This was foreign territory, politically speaking. Every time I saw the six-foot-four Mr. Wayne headed my way, I managed to hide. Remember *True Grit*? That's what he looked like that night, and I'd heard that the drunker he got, the meaner he was.

He scared the hell out of me.

Before the film was released in May 1966, nearly every bus in New York carried bright red and yellow signs warning "The Russians Are Coming!" We had bumper stickers made up and tiny stickers that were plastered on public phones and in public washrooms. It was a bold, original ad campaign, which owed much of its success to the logo and opening titles for the film.

I wanted the opening titles to establish for the audience in the first few minutes that this was a comedy based on a serious political idea. To do this, we needed something fresh and original. Hal Ashby and I turned to Pablo Ferro, a young Puerto Rican commercial film editor working out of New York. Pablo was one of the first creative concept artists to work in the trailer and film title field. We tossed around all kinds of ideas, but it wasn't until we played the Red Army Chorus and "Yankee Doodle Dandy" contrapuntally that we all agreed the title sequence should be a battle of the Soviet and American flags.

At first United Artists opposed the use of the Soviet flag and Pablo's Russian-looking title logo with its reversed R's and hammer-and-sickle G's. (Remember, this was at the height of the Cold War. It wasn't only John Wayne who saw commies under every rock and behind every bush.) Freddy Goldberg and Gabe Sumner, who headed up UA's marketing department in New York, courageously decided to go ahead. The teaser ads popped up everywhere. In Orange County, a few tires were slashed on cars carrying the bumper stickers, and a few ads were defaced here and there by those who thought they were anti-American.

Arthur Krim arranged a special screening in Washington and invited Vice President Hubert Humphrey to be the guest of honor for the evening. Army and Navy brass, congressmen, senators, and foreign ambassadors attended, and afterwards an admiral walked up to me and asked, "How did you get the Air Force to cooperate and give you two jets?"

"It's because they knew I wasn't getting any cooperation from the Navy, sir," I said with great satisfaction.

The ambassadors from the Soviet Bloc were invited to the screening but most didn't come. However, when the Russian ambassador to the U.S. heard that the film was a comedy and that it didn't make the Russians out to be heavies, he asked United Artists if a print could be sent to the embassy. The print then made the rounds of Russian embassies from the U.K. to France and wound up at the Kremlin. By the time it was returned, the print was badly scratched and had obviously been watched numerous times. They loved it.

Later that year, after the film was chosen to open the Berlin Film Festival, I received a personal invitation to visit Moscow and attend a showing of *The Russians Are Coming* at the Soviet Filmmakers Union. It was an extraordinary invitation. None of the Americans I worked with on the film could have gone because at that time Americans were not allowed to travel behind the Iron Curtain. I was one of the first western directors to be invited to Moscow.

My trip was arranged by Ilya Lopert, the head of UA operations in Europe. Ilya was a Russian émigré who lived in a suite at the George V Hotel in Paris. He was a big man with large appetites. He loved women and gambling almost as much as he loved film and food. He took a personal interest in me and in *The Russians Are Coming*.

After I checked into the Dorchester Hotel in London on the first leg of my trip, Ilya told me that someone from the Russian embassy would contact me. That evening there was a soft tap on my door. A Russian in a baggy dark suit asked me for my passport. Ilya had told me to give it to him and I did. He disappeared into the night with it. The next day I called Canada House and asked them if I could go to Moscow. Sure, they sniffed, but you will never get a visa. There was another soft tap on my door that evening. My Russian friend had returned with my passport *and* a visa. The next day I caught the Aeroflot flight from Heathrow to Moscow.

At the Moscow airport, a young Customs officer pawed through my suitcase filled with the usual clothes and toiletries, plus Oscar Peterson jazz tapes, copies of *Time*, *Newsweek*, and *Esquire*, several bottles of perfume, and a few bottles of Jack Daniels, which I'd heard the Russians liked. He stopped at a copy of *Playboy* and accused me of smuggling in pornographic material. Next thing I knew Ilya was bellowing in Russian from the other side of the barrier. I imagined it was something along the lines of "How dare you search this man. He has been especially invited to your country by top members of the Politburo!" He was amazingly proficient at pushing officials around. His flowing cape and huge fur hat made him look like Sol Hurok, the old Russian New York impresario. After solving my *Playboy* problem, Ilya hustled me through the airport to a waiting black limo and off we went to the Ukrainia Hotel.

Everything was big in Russia. My hotel covered four square blocks. We were ushered into a gigantic suite lit by an equally gigantic crystal chandelier. Ilya had told me that everything we said inside the hotel

Me and my homemade Soviet sub, on the set of *The Russians Are Coming, The Russians Are Coming,* 1966.

A family outing on location. Left to right: Dixie, me, Kevin, Jenny, and Michael, 1966.

With Alan Arkin, playing a nervous Soviet naval officer in *The Russians Are Coming, The Russians Are Coming*.

Jack Weston desperately trying to see Edward G. Robinson's hold card. Creating drama in a game of stud poker, *The Cincinnati Kid*, 1965.

In my naval uniform, I hitchhiked through the American South in 1946.

A moment with Sidney Poitier, *In the Heat of the Night*, 1967.

Rehearsing with Rod Steiger—I'm playing Sidney.

Dixie joins me on location in Sparta, Illinois, for *In the Heat of the Night*, 1967.

With Governor Bill Clinton on the set of *A Soldier's Story*, 1984.

Denzel Washington entertains the crew at my expense, *A Soldier's Story,* 1984.

Directing the "Chess with Sex" scene in *The Thomas Crown Affair*, 1968.

would be recorded, so it was best to wait until we were outside to say anything we didn't want overheard. "You will have plenty of Russian contacts," he warned. "Don't trust anyone."

I had thought our screening in Berlin was a triumph. Willy Brandt, foreign minister at the time, had praised me and the film, a tractor had towed a large sign, "Die Russen kommen!" up and down the Berlin Wall, and everybody loved the idea of a comedy satire about American and Russian relations. But the screening in Moscow was everything a film director could hope for. The theater was bigger than Radio City Music Hall in New York. To sit in that enormous theater, jammed with over two thousand Russians, and watch their reaction to my movie was an amazing experience.

As the film ran, a Russian interpreter gave a simultaneous translation over the sound system. I had been told that if a Russian audience didn't like something, they would make a "chuh-chuh-chuh" sound, so throughout the screening, I prayed I wouldn't hear it. They laughed at the jokes in Russian that the Americans didn't get, and everything was fine until Theo Bikel, the Russian sub captain, threatens to blow up the town. You could feel the tension in the theater, then the "chuh-chuhing" began. I thought, "Oh God, they think they're being made to look like the villains again." But when the stand-off is broken by the little boy falling from the church belfry and the Russians help save him, the audience began a rhythmic clapping and many burst into tears. Directors Sergei Bondarchuk and Grigori Chukhrai were on their feet clapping and crying.

I was sitting next to Vladimir Posner, the Brooklyn-born editor of *Soviet Life.* "Why are they crying?" I asked.

"Because they didn't make it first," he replied.

I realized then that the film, although made primarily for an American audience, expressed the hopes and fears felt by people in both countries at that period in the Cold War. What the Russians of course couldn't believe, and were blown away by, was the fact that I had been allowed to make the film at all. Posner informed me the next day that I was now considered a friend of the Soviet Union.

Then three days later as I went through Customs and Immigration at JFK in New York, my little moment of détente nearly stopped me from returning home to my family.

"What were you doing in Russia?" demanded the Immigration officer, looking at my passport.

"I was there to screen a film."

"What film?"

"*The Russians Are Coming!*" I said, struggling to keep a straight face.

He paused. "You're a resident alien?" he asked.

"Yes, sir, here's my green card."

"Well, you're unacceptable," he said, returning my passport and card.

"Unacceptable? What are you talking about? I have a family in Los Angeles. I live there."

He shook his head. "You don't have a re-entry permit and you had no right to be behind the Iron Curtain without permission from the State Department."

"Look," I said. "I'm not an American citizen and I don't travel with an American passport. The Canadian government gave me permission to go, and I didn't know I needed a re-entry permit to get back into the States."

He shook his head again. "You're unacceptable."

After sitting and stewing in the airport lounge for a while, I decided enough was enough. It was 2 a.m. and I wanted to go home. I rapped on the glass and asked to speak to the supervisor. The officer shrugged and suggested I get the next plane to Montreal or Moscow. And then it occurred to me. Why not do what Jonathan Winters as Officer James does in *The Russians Are Coming*?

I drew myself up to my full height of five-foot-eight and said, "I want to make a phone call to Washington, to the vice president. I'm going to talk to him and then *you're* going to talk to him."

"You don't have the number," he snarled.

"I do have the number. I'm going to talk to Hubert Humphrey and then you're going to talk to him, because three weeks ago he saw the film I just screened in Russia. I'm sure the vice president will vouch for me."

The guy finally backed down and grudgingly said, "Okay, you can get on a plane and go to L.A., but you have to report to Immigration first thing Monday morning and I'm confiscating your green card, you pinko Canadian." He didn't actually say "you pinko Canadian," but that and a dozen other epithets hung in the air between us. For several years afterwards, I had trouble crossing the border. I was in the Big Black Book.

If *The Cincinnati Kid* was the film that made me feel like a filmmaker, *The Russians Are Coming* was the film that gave me a strong anti-establishment reputation. When it received a Best Picture nomination from the Academy, Billy Wilder invited me to sit at his table in the Mirisch commissary, where I had gone most days for lunch but had never been invited to eat at anyone's table. Kirk Douglas took out a full-page ad in the Hollywood trades endorsing the film. Sam Goldwyn's secretary phoned and told me I was invited to have lunch with the legendary boss himself. I had been on the lot for over two years but all I had ever seen of him was the black limo as it whooshed by on its way to the Goldwyn Building. Sam had his own butler, his own chef, and his own dining room. His secretary, who must have been at least seventy years old, waved me through with a casual "Mr. Goldwyn will see you now."

It was a modest room with a dark plank floor, Venetian blinds, leather chairs, and a huge wooden desk. Sam Goldwyn was shorter than I had expected—a giant in our business, but still a little guy. Bald, smiling, white shirt, narrow gray tie, gray suit with shortish sleeves.

"How much do you think *The Russians* will make?" he asked over the soup. We had moved to the elegant dining room with silver cutlery, damask tablecloth, and a waiter in a white jacket.

"I don't know, Mr. Goldwyn."

"I can tell you what it's gonna gross in North America," he said.

The movie had opened only a couple of weeks before, but the number he gave was accurate within five percent.

"Have you got a piece of the action, Norman?" he asked as he leaned toward me.

"I have a bit of the profits," I said.

"You're all right," he said. "A young Jewish kid from…where did you say you were from? Let me give you some advice. When the Mirisch brothers want to buy your twenty-five percent, don't sell. Don't ever sell your piece."

A week later Harold Mirisch called. Come to my office, he said. They were all there: Walter, Marvin, Harold. They told me how pleased they were with the movie. They thought it might even be a hit. Then Harold said, "Tell you what, Norman, you've got a small piece of *The Russians*."

I nodded.

"We'd be willing to buy it from you."

"You would? Now?" I asked.

They offered me $75,000 cash because, they said, they were willing to take a chance on me. Why wait to see if the movie makes it and why wait for maybe years before I would see any of that meager percentage?

I thanked them and left.

I never sold my piece of *The Russians Are Coming* and thirty-five years later, I still collect my checks from its TV reruns, videos, and DVDs, and I still think fondly of Sam Goldwyn.

The Canadian pinko had arrived.

9

In the Heat of the Night

That's maximum green, man!

—*Ray Charles*

"If Norman gets reincarnated," Boaty Boatwright once said, "he'll want to come back black and Jewish and blind."

Boaty had a point. I had felt I shared a bond with the real Jewish kids I went to school with. It had a lot to do with being treated as a minority, an outsider, a victim, and the feeling never left me for the rest of my life. The connection with black people came later, when I traveled through Mississippi, Louisiana, Alabama, and I couldn't escape the violence of it all, the injustice, the unfairness of segregation. That was the word I kept using to myself, "unfair." I thought I understood the trauma of being victimized, and even though I might have tended to romanticize my own experiences, I came to identify with blacks in a way that lasted long after my hitchhiking trip through the American South.

My first opportunity to say anything about racism in America was in my early television days in New York. *Tonight with Belafonte* in 1959 was sponsored by Revlon. I remember joining Harry at a meeting with Revlon founder and president Charlie Revson, where we sold him on the idea of putting one long commercial at the front of the hour and another at the end. Harry handled the white establishment with ease. His critics, who thought he was too close to "whitey," had no idea of the work he did behind the scenes in the struggle for civil rights. He was constantly on the phone, financing a protest in the South or pushing for change with congressmen and senators.

"We can't just use this TV special as a social vehicle for protest," I told Harry. "We have to entertain and captivate the audience and give them a solid hour of entertainment."

"Then why are you opening the show with chains?" he asked.

"They're going to be elegant white chains," I laughed.

The show began with Ronald Reagan, the spokesman for General Electric, announcing that their usual show was pre-empted for a special live program, *Tonight with Belafonte*. He was followed by a glamorous white Revlon model telling all the women watching that they could be lovely too if they used Revlon. Cut to the chains and an uninterrupted live broadcast of the first African-American TV special.

In 1966, when *In the Heat of the Night* came my way, I was ready to direct the movie. More than that, I felt that I *needed* to direct it.

In the Heat of the Night had first appeared in April 1965 as a crime novel written by John Ball. The screenplay had been started by Robert Allan Arthur and reworked by Stirling Silliphant. It was Silliphant's earliest rough draft of the screenplay that landed on my desk. Walter, the youngest of the Mirisch brothers, was the producer. I don't think anyone seriously expected me to make the movie—it was originally planned to be shot in the studio, not on location, and for very little money. I read the script out of curiosity and instantly connected with its story of racial conflict in the South.

It wasn't, then, an especially elegant piece of writing or plotting, but what it had going for it was, at its core, a compelling confrontation. A smart, sophisticated black homicide detective from Pasadena, California, named Virgil Tibbs has the bad luck to be passing through a racist Georgia town on the night when a prominent white business-man is murdered. The local police are convinced the detective is the guilty party, but once it becomes plain even to them that he's inno-cent, the black detective, Tibbs, stays on in the town long enough to solve the crime for the white police force. For the period, this was incendiary material, the notion that a black was in any way superior to whites. Blacks were still being lynched in the South in 1965, and laws barring black people from full citizenship remained on the books in many states south of the Mason-Dixon Line. In that atmosphere, a novel with a black character who was smarter than the white charac-ters, better informed, better dressed, and more sophisticated, seemed revolutionary. It had the potential to make a provocative and progres-sive statement about race in America.

Marty Baum was the first to spot the book's promise as a film. Baum was Sidney Poitier's manager, and he suggested to Walter Mirisch that Sidney would make a natural Virgil Tibbs. Sidney had won the Academy Award for best actor in a sweet little movie called *Lilies of the Field* just two years earlier. The first black actor to win, he became an inspiration for the next generation—Morgan Freeman, Sam Jackson, and Denzel Washington, to name but a few.

Walter bought the film rights to the novel and sold the package—the book with Sidney—to United Artists. Silliphant had just finished writing and producing a movie with Poitier and Anne Bancroft, *The Slender Thread*. When he wrote *Heat*, he had Sidney in mind for Tibbs, and the two of them had become friends. Before that, he had written a big chunk of what America watched on television every night, seventy-one scripts for *Route 66*, all of *The Naked City* episodes for 1962, plus many other dramatic shows. Silliphant had a great way with dialogue, and he put it to work on the script for *Heat*.

I still had my hands full finishing *The Russians Are Coming* when I launched my campaign to direct *In the Heat of the Night*.

"No, no, Norman, it's not for you," Walter Mirisch insisted. "We love the idea for the movie, but we're not going to spend much money on it, and we want it shot on the Goldwyn lot. Norman, the movie's too small for you at this stage of your career."

At Christmas that year, as most years when the children were growing up, I took the family on a ski vacation, all of us, Dixie, me, the three kids. We headed to Sun Valley in Idaho where the second youngest of our intrepid skiers, Michael, promptly broke his leg at the finish of a downhill race. While we were waiting for the doctor to fit Michael into a cast, Dixie and I happened to get into a conversation with the parents of another boy who had busted his leg earlier on the same hill. The parents were Bobby and Ethel Kennedy.

They invited us to a small New Year's Eve party at their private lodge. That was the night when a celebrated American mountain climber named Whittaker, on a dare, climbed up the fifty-foot river-stone fireplace in the Kennedy A-frame living room using his fingertips and toes to grip the edge of the stones. But what I most remember about the night was Bobby's reaction when I told him the story of *In the Heat of the Night*. His response was much more than polite interest. Bobby immediately picked up on the significance of the film.

"It's very important, Norman, that you make this movie," he said, tapping the air with his right hand in that familiar Kennedy gesture. "The time is right for a movie like this. Timing is everything in politics, in art, and in life itself. Now is the time to make *In the Heat of the Night*."

He later mailed me research material about the state of young black people in the South. Bobby had been senator from New York for a year by then, and he had made the politics of race a major issue in his platform. He believed in the urgency of establishing citizens' rights, in equal treatment under the law and, with his great enthusiasm and infectious optimism, he saw that this was inevitable despite the shocking images of unarmed civil rights protesters being beaten by white policemen. Even as the civil rights movement gained momentum, police in the South were attacking marchers with billy clubs and fire hoses. Television broadcasts were filled with horrific images of black protesters being attacked by dogs urged on by their handlers.

I didn't tell the Mirisches that while I could live with the tight budget, I had no intention of shooting the film on the Goldwyn lot.

The film cried out for filming on location. It needed the taut, sweaty atmosphere of a small town in the South. I kept my mouth shut about that for the time being and continued to make a pest of myself about my passion to direct the film.

Reluctantly, Walter finally agreed.

Stirling Silliphant and I made the decision that, through the script, we were going to give the movie a spare, controlled feel. We refrained from overloading on explanation and exposition. Just the reverse—we left some key elements hanging for a few scenes. We let several minutes of screen time go by, for instance, before we revealed that this character whom the audience has met early in the story, this black man, Virgil Tibbs, this murder suspect, is in fact a policeman himself. That kind of approach was a guiding principle all through the script—withhold information, strip the story to its essentials, build suspense.

The draft of the script that Stirling produced in early March of 1966 worked so many changes on the John Ball novel that the original plot was barely recognizable. Some of the changes were ones he and I had already kicked around. Some were Stirling's ingenious inventions. All represented enormous improvements in the story's dramatic content. Now the events took place in deepest Mississippi, not Georgia, and Tibbs came from Philadelphia, Pennsylvania, not Pasadena, California. These were simple changes, but they emphasized the north-south, black-white division in the story. The script pushed one character into the background, Sam Wood, the police officer through whom much of the story is related in Ball's book, and brought forward another, stronger character, Bill Gillespie, the police chief who is a relatively minor player in the book. This sharpened the black-white conflict by pitting two cops, Tibbs and Gillespie, against each other.

Stirling produced a tight, dramatic script. But it wasn't perfect. I put check marks beside the pieces of dialogue that I wanted Stirling to take another run at. Then I tried a psychological ploy on him. The forty-eight-year-old Stirling was the most experienced script writer I'd yet worked with, even more of a veteran of the business than Bill

Rose, and I judged that I ought to be diplomatic about blunt requests for rewrites.

"What's the little check mark I see on your script, Norman?" Stirling asked on the first day I put the ploy into action. "Right there on page 42, that check mark? What's it mean?"

"Oh, this check mark," I answered, all innocence. "Jesus, I don't remember. Never mind. It's beautiful, that speech."

Next day, Stirling phoned me first thing in the morning.

"That line you marked on page 42, Norman?" he said. "I got thinking about it last night, and it's too perfect for a movie. It's overwritten, just too pat. I've fixed it."

"Well, okay, Stirling, if you think so."

Or, with other lines I had my doubts about, I read them aloud as if I were Don Adams in *Get Smart*. I exaggerated the lines. Stirling winced and made changes.

By the first week in July, we had a script that I knew I could shoot.

George C. Scott was my first choice to play Chief Gillespie. Rod Steiger was my second choice. George wasn't available, so I sent the script to Rome, where Rod was working on the Russian film version of Napoleon with the Russian director Sergei Bondarchuk. He loved the part of Gillespie, and he'd be finished shooting the film in Italy by midsummer. That made Rod available, and I've often wondered whether *Heat* would have been as powerful if George C. Scott had played Gillespie. Probably not. Gillespie and Steiger were a perfect combo.

For the other, smaller roles I made the decision to go with unknown actors. Established actors often create expectations in the audience's mind. If an actor is known for playing heavies, then the audience anticipates that his character will turn out to be the murderer, the villain, the bad guy. In a mystery story like *Heat*, I didn't want the actors' histories in past movies to get between the audience and the story line. I looked for people who had little or no screen time.

The closest we came to a familiar face in the supporting cast was Warren Oates as Officer Sam Wood, but even he was in the early stages of his career. Besides, he met the other criterion I'd decided on, and that was to cast as many Southerners as possible. I wanted actors whose voices had Southern inflections. Oates came from Kentucky. Anthony James, the young actor who played the weird guy behind the counter in the diner, was from Myrtle Beach, South Carolina. *Heat* was his first movie. It was also the first for Quentin Dean, the actress we cast as Delores, the sexy teenager who tempts Sam by parading around her kitchen at night in the nude. Scott Wilson took the part of Harvey Oberst, the young pool room character whom Gillespie arrests, wrongly, for the murder. Wilson had very limited movie experience, though he went straight from *Heat* to *In Cold Blood*, in which he played one of the leads, one of the two killers. Ironically, the part of the other killer in *Cold Blood* was taken by Robert Blake, who had also read for the role of Harvey in *Heat*. Jon Voight, in his pre-star days, read for Harvey too. And both Ed Asner and Gavin MacLeod auditioned for Sam Wood, just four years before the two became stars on *The Mary Tyler Moore Show*.

If any of the actors stumbled on the nuances of a Mississippi accent, Meta Rebner came to the rescue. Officially, Miss Meta was the script supervisor; unofficially, she was the speech consultant. She came from Mississippi. She was elegant, precise, literate, and she had been William Faulkner's mistress. She always wore a dress and big floppy hat, and she had a sharp ear for intonations.

"We pronounce our 't' in the word 'gate,' Mr. Steiger," she said to Rod one day.

Rod had a line where he asked another policeman to fix the small swinging gate in the police station.

"I'm an actor!" Rod roared at Miss Meta. "I know something about accents!"

"Nevahtheless, we pronounce our 't's,'" Miss Meta said. "And kindly don't raise your voice to me, Mr. Steiger."

Miss Meta Rebner may have been soft-spoken, but she had a will of iron.

The one exception I made in casting was Lee Grant as the widow of Colbert, the murdered businessman. The accent didn't matter in the role since Mrs. Colbert came from Chicago. That was no problem, but Lee hardly met my other condition of being an unknown. In her very first movie, *The Detective*, in 1951, she won an Oscar nomination. Lee was a magnificent actress in films, on stage, on television, but that was not the only reason I hired her.

Fifteen years earlier, the House Un-American Activities Committee, the congressional group that went snooping for so-called communist sympathizers, had labeled Lee's husband a pinko. He was the playwright Arnold Manoff, and HUAC summoned Lee to testify about her own husband. Lee refused and the major movie studios and television networks immediately blacklisted her. By the mid-1960s, Lee was feeling her way back to work. She got a role in television on *Peyton Place* (and won an Emmy). I was thrilled when she agreed to play Mrs. Colbert in *Heat*, and Lee went at the role as if she were driven to make up for lost time.

The budget on the movie came to about $1.5 million. So we knew going in that there was very little room to maneuver. More than that, I had to prove to Walter Mirisch that I could make the movie for the same budget on location as I would if I shot in Los Angeles at the Goldwyn studios. In the end, I didn't shoot in the "real" South. Not exactly.

In the early summer of 1966, we went looking for locations, "we" being my production manager Jim Henderling, my unit manager Howard Joslin, and me. Among the three of us, we checked out at least 150 possible shooting sites in a huge piece of country that was bounded by Memphis in the south to Galena, Illinois, in the north, Paducah, Kentucky, in the east to Joplin, Missouri, in the west.

Then Sidney Poitier spoke up. Sidney said there was no goddamn way he'd go below the Mason-Dixon Line for the eight weeks we'd need to shoot the movie. Earlier in the year, Sidney and Harry Belafonte had flown to Mississippi to deliver money to a civil rights group led by the activist Stokely Carmichael. After they had been picked up at a small airfield in Greenville, a bunch of crackers followed their car. A car chase sequence in *Heat* is inspired by Sidney and Harry's real-life adventure in Mississippi.

Sidney had no desire to expose himself again to white Southern hospitality. This lopped several states and a few hundred thousand square miles off our search for a shooting location.

We ultimately settled on a town named Sparta in the southwest corner of Illinois close to the borders with Missouri and Kentucky. This place was as Southern as we could get without actually crossing into the Confederacy. It looked authentic—sleepy, semi-rural—and it brought with it some money-saving advantages. The cast and crew would stay at Augustine's Motor Lodge in a larger town west of Sparta called Belleville where the rates were a whole lot cheaper than at a tony place like the Palmer House up the road in Chicago. A second advantage was that the meteorology records for the region indicated that Sparta's autumn weather stayed steady and light on precipitation.

We moved in to begin the shoot on September 19, and for the next week, the skies pelted rain. Oh well, one out of two wasn't bad.

"It's a shame about the name," someone on the crew said to me just before we finally started filming. "Sparta."

"What's wrong with it?" I asked.

"In the book and the script, the town's called Wells."

"Then let's change the name in the script to Sparta."

Which is why, in the scene where Gillespie pulls up to the mayor's place of business in the town, we didn't have to touch up the big sign across the top of the building: "Sparta Equipment Co." And why we could photograph the town water tower without doing a paint job on the name. Anything to save a buck.

Haskell Wexler saved us many more bucks on the shoot. Haskell was my cinematographer, fresh off winning an Oscar a few months earlier for his work on *Who's Afraid of Virginia Woolf?*, which makes him the last man to get an Academy Award for black and white photography. We shared the same liberal political beliefs, the same independent feelings about the big movie studios. As a director of photography, Haskell had an extraordinary aesthetic sense, and he knew how to be resourceful, something that was crucial on *Heat*. We decided that the nature of the movie called for it to be shot in a semi-journalistic style. He caught that realistic approach precisely in his photography, and in our cash-strapped state, he managed the feat without frills in the way of equipment. No crane, no steadicam, no video assist, nothing except Haskell's improvisatory genius and skill with a hand-held camera. There was a scene—this was typical of Haskell's sense of invention under pressure—in which the Scott Wilson character, Harvey Oberst, is running through the woods chased by the police and their hounds. I wanted part of the scene shot from the point of view of the pursuing hound dogs. Haskell devised a platform made of two-by-fours, mounted the camera on it, and showed four grips how to hold it low to the ground as they ran behind Scott Wilson through the trees and brush. The shot worked like a dream.

To save even more money, Haskell used a forced development film technique. What this meant was that he shot scenes at a lower light level than the exposure in the film required, then forced the development of the negative to produce the picture. It was a method of working with less light. A way of trimming the budget and obtaining a gritty look. Scenes that would normally take Haskell an hour to light, he could organize in half the time. We worked faster and cheaper. The downside was that the technique could make the negative very dicey. Too much green could seep in and spoil the color. But Haskell produced a print with perfect color. Haskell was an artist who liked to live close to the edge.

Rod Steiger was an artist who liked to live in character. The actors and I spent a week rehearsing before the shoot began, and Rod used the time to work his way slowly and gradually, by tiny increments, into the character he was playing, to examine Gillespie objectively and then climb inside him subjectively. This was the Actors' Studio approach, the Method, and Rod was an Actors' Studio alumnus. He applied the Method to Gillespie, grew comfortable with the accent, with the clothes, the rumpled uniform, the shirt open at the neck, the cowboy boots with the pants tucked into the tops, and once he was tight in the character, Rod stayed inside Gillespie, in character, for the entire shoot. In front of the camera and away from it, all day, all night, he walked and talked and dressed like Bill Gillespie, police chief of Sparta, Mississippi.

My contribution to this process was pecan pie. I wanted Rod's gut hanging over his belt. I wanted him to look like the stereotype of every beefy, bigoted police chief in the South. All Rod needed to match the image was a few more pounds around the middle.

"That pecan pie sure looks good tonight," I said to Rod at dinner every evening. "I think I ought to have another piece."

"Why y'all bein' so nice to me, Norman? Why you always feedin' me?"

Pecan pie—and chewing gum. Stirling Silliphant had written gum into the script, Bill Gillespie chomping on gum all through the movie. Rod didn't think the gum was in character for the chief. He considered it an unnecessary cliché.

"Just chew on it the first few scenes," I said. "The gum works for me, but if you still don't like it after the first scenes, we'll drop the gum."

Rod gave it a chew, and after a day or two, he realized his chewing was a way of letting the audience know what was going on in Gillespie's head. When he chewed at a normal rate, Gillespie was in a settled state of mind. When he speeded up his chewing, Gillespie was thinking hard. And when he stopped chewing altogether, Gillespie had come to a conclusion and was letting the implications of the conclusion filter through his consciousness. A simple activity, chewing gum, turned into a smart dramatic device in Rod's hands.

Rod had serious trouble with only one line in the entire movie. The line came in what was probably *Heat*'s most electric scene. Gillespie and Tibbs have come to Endicott's house, Endicott who was the wealthy, aristocratic patriarch of the town, living in the big home on the hill, the symbol of a dying racist South. Tibbs wants to question him about the murder. When Endicott realizes the reason for the visit, realizes what this uppity black man is doing in his house, he steps up to Tibbs and slaps him across the face. Without a pause, Tibbs slaps Endicott right back. This was the first time in an American movie that a black man had slapped a white man back, and that fact added to the shock of the scene.

"Gillespie, you saw that?" a stunned Endicott says, Endicott as played by a fine New York theater actor named Larry Gates.

"I saw it," Gillespie answers, himself stunned, perhaps grudgingly admiring Tibbs for his ballsiness.

"What are you going to do about it?" Endicott demands.

"I don't know."

This was the line that drove Rod crazy. He tried it twenty different ways. He accented different words, varied the rhythms. Nothing he did with that short sentence made him happy.

"Rod," I said, "the reason you say 'I don't know' is because you really *don't* know what you're going to do. You're completely baffled. It's a situation you've never confronted before. It's beyond your wildest imagination. You don't know."

"I don't know?"

"You're at a crossroads."

"Ah, a crossroads."

We tried the scene again, and Rod said the line as if Gillespie, in this sudden, unexpected moment, has come to a turning point in his life. The black man slapped the white man. Now what? How is the chief of police supposed to react to something new and changing in his experience? He isn't yet sure. Rod spoke the line, and the instant of bewilderment Gillespie feels just hung in the air, perfectly ambiguous.

Sidney Poitier had both great performing technique and great screen presence. He was another actor whom the camera loved. In *Heat*, I got the impression he was taking another step in his acting, that he was getting inside the emotions of his character. He wasn't just *indicating* what Tibbs felt. He was *being* Tibbs. Partly this growth in Sidney as an actor seemed to be a product of working with Rod and absorbing Rod's Method technique.

From the beginning of shooting, Sidney felt that Rod was often guilty of overacting. He was afraid that when Rod got mad and slammed the door of the police car, shaking the whole frame, then bellowing his lines, the actor he was working with was out of control. Sidney took me aside more than once and whispered, "You going to let him do it like that?" I reassured Sidney that Rod knew exactly what he was doing and I always let him start high in the scene and then encouraged other interpretations.

But I knew that Sidney was working harder because Rod was challenging him constantly. This was a case where bare feelings of both actors were being exposed as they butted heads in almost every scene.

And partly it seemed a matter of the role. As Virgil Tibbs, Sidney was confronting racism once again. The result was that Sidney's scenes with Rod had more drama and power than the script had ever led me to expect.

For that matter, Sidney's scene at the police station with Lee Grant, who happened to be another Actors' Studio graduate, had the same strength and integrity. Lee as Mrs. Colbert is alone in the chief's office. No one has informed her of her husband's murder. Tibbs arrives and takes on the task of breaking it to Mrs. Colbert. The way Stirling Silliphant wrote the scene, Tibbs comes flat out with the terrible news. That was how real policemen handled it, fast and blunt, no agonizing. Tibbs takes the same approach. Then he must watch this woman as she struggles against the horror of what she has just heard. Tibbs must gauge how to react, must decide whether to take her hand, leave her alone, stand back, all the possibilities.

Lee said later that she wasn't satisfied with the way she herself played the scene, that she didn't break down as totally as she should have. I disagreed. I thought Lee gave the scene a moment of pure grief. And Sidney was just as nakedly honest. He wasn't the focus of the scene. He was on the periphery. His job was to react to Lee, and his reaction hit the same pitch of raw emotion. Then, as the scene moved to its climax, Lee as Mrs. Colbert finally reaches for Sidney's hand. She's resisted until this moment, choosing at first to hold herself in and keep her emotions to herself. But at last she feels the need for support. She extends her hand, and Tibbs encloses it in his. It remains a remarkably moving scene today, decades after we shot it, one in the handful of cinematic moments that I'll always cherish.

The scene where Sidney and Rod played most brilliantly off one another, a second exquisite cinematic moment, came near the end of the movie. I wanted a scene in which the two protagonists experience a measure of bonding, where they acknowledge one another as men. Stirling had written a scene that was something along those lines. It took place when the two are alone in Gillespie's house having a drink late at night, but Stirling's scene missed the sense of intimacy I was looking for. It felt flat and without edge. Still, we might have gone with the scene as written except that a heavy rain hit at the moment we started shooting. The rain made such a racket on the roof of the house that it was impossible to record the actors' voices. I halted filming until the storm let up, and during the lull, Rod, Sidney, Miss Meta, and I waited out the rain in a car. As we sat there, with the windows steaming up, the actors and I began to improvise new lines for the scene. We went back and forth with it, as Miss Meta scribbled down the dialogue in her notebook, and in our new version, the two men, Tibbs and Gillespie, get to talking about insomnia, about drinking, about women, about neither man being married.

"Don't you get a little lonely?" Gillespie asks Tibbs near the end of our improvised scene, two men talking man to man, not a white man to a black man, just a couple of troubled cops.

"No lonelier than you, man," Tibbs says after a pause.

"Oh now, don't get smart, black boy," Gillespie suddenly snaps, realizing he may have gone too far with this bonding stuff. "I don't need it. No pity, thank you. No thank *you.*"

It caught what we'd been groping for in the scene, that brief improvised dialogue, and when the rain let up and we climbed out of the car, that was the way we shot it.

Something Sparta lacked was a cotton field. I wanted one in the movie, the part of the landscape that had been central to my mental picture of the South ever since my hitchhiking tour years earlier, a cotton field populated with black farmhands bent over their work. Sparta didn't have one, and it didn't have a plantation house either, a home for our aristocratic Endicott character. But a town that my location scouts found, Dyersburg, Tennessee, had both, and that was where we went for a final week of shooting.

It took a large concession from Sidney to travel south of the

Mason-Dixon Line. He was nervous, and in fact, events almost made the work in Dyersburg as dangerous as he feared. Late one night at the beginning of the week, a bunch of locals descended on the Holiday Inn where the cast and crew were staying. The locals buzzed the place in their pickup trucks, roaring around the parking lot and banging on doors. I never found out what these men were up to, but Rod Steiger has always told the story that one of them was a young husband looking for his straying wife. He thought she might have taken up with somebody from the film crew, and he'd brought his friends to assist him in his search. All I knew at the time was that, up in the room where I'd been asleep, I woke to the sound of heavy pounding on doors all around me. Without switching on my light—I didn't intend to be anybody's target—I rang my first assistant's room and instructed him to round up a few of the biggest grips in the crew and to stand by for further instructions. The next person I called was Sidney.

"No problem in my room, Norman," Sidney whispered from his end of the line. "I got a gun under my pillow."

"A gun? Jesus, Sidney, I hope you don't use it!"

"Only if one of those crackers comes through the door."

I hung up and waited in the dark. There was more door banging, more shouting and swearing, and finally the sound of the engines of the pickup trucks roaring into life. The trucks pulled away from the Holiday Inn. I hadn't needed to summon the grips into defensive action, and Sidney hadn't been called on to whip the gun from under his pillow. But it had been a hot and tense autumn night in Tennessee.

We stuck it out in Dyersburg long enough to shoot the slapping scene with Tibbs and Endicott, which we filmed in a lovely old plantation home owned by a man with the quintessentially Southern name of Granger Ledford. In the same general area as the house, we found the cotton field of my memories.

I hired Quincy Jones to score the music for *Heat*. Although he had almost no movie experience, he was a superb jazz musician and composer. In the scene where Harvey Oberst, fleeing from the police and their dogs, begins running across a bridge over the Mississippi River to get out of the state, we used a 500-millimeter zoom shot of Scott in distant silhouette. Haskell timed the zoom in to a close-up with me singing a blues riff. Quincy later scored to the exact beat of my riff. It was an ingenious piece of photography and music welded together as the music synchronized perfectly with the movement of the lens.

After our first screening of the rough cut in Hal Ashby's cutting room, Quincy thought the film's opening needed a great blues song and suggested we hire two of his close friends, the songwriting team of Alan and Marilyn Bergman.

From my very first meeting with Quincy, Alan, and Marilyn, I felt part of an extended family. We all shared the same political attitudes, laughed at the same things, and knew the same people. The day "Q," as we called him, played the piano and Alan sang the lyrics to the title song, I knew it was going to be a hit. And when Quincy announced he was going to try to get Ray Charles to record it, I broke out in goosebumps. I've always loved being around musicians and songwriters, and my association with Quincy, Alan, and Marilyn has remained strong through the years. The Bergmans have written songs for many of my films, and Quincy has helped me with recordings and choosing the right artists.

Ray Charles was only three years older than Quincy, but he'd been a mentor to Quincy dating back to their days as young musicians in Seattle. Ray was already a star in the early sixties and we were lucky to have him. He came down to Goldwyn's screening room to sit through a rough cut of the movie, with Hal Ashby and me describing the visual moments on the screen, and to hear a run-through of the title song.

"That's maximum green, man!" Ray said about the song, meaning he liked it.

Then he said to Quincy, speaking of the Bergmans whom he'd never met, "They're brother and sister, right?"

"No, no, Ray, they're white."

"No, they ain't! Can't be, man, not with lyrics like that."

Ray recorded the song, backed by an orchestra that Quincy loaded with terrific jazz musicians: Roland Kirk on reeds, Ray Brown on bass, Bobby Scott on piano. And right off the top of the movie, first scene, an out-of-focus shot of a night train with Virgil Tibbs on board pulling into the darkened station in Sparta, Mississippi, the song, the lyrics, and Ray Charles's voice came together to put the audience smack in the middle of a Southern town where bad things seem bound to happen this night.

In addition to the title song, I told Quincy and the Bergmans that I also wanted specific songs for the music track. The movie has a scene in which Sam Wood is driving his police car late at night. He switches on the small portable radio hanging from his windshield visor. What kind of radio station would Sam choose? What style of song would he react to? What song would reflect Sam's character?

In movies, the music that comes from a radio or a TV set or a jukebox is called "source" music, and when I screened a first cut of *Heat* at the Goldwyn Studios for Quincy and the Bergmans, I explained to them that I didn't want established popular songs for the movie's source music. My reasoning was that the audience brings preconceived notions to familiar music, their own memories that the music triggers, and this familiarity has the effect of taking the audience out of the story on the screen. I wanted original source music, and for the scene in Sam Wood's police car, the Bergmans came back with a lyric they called "A Bow-Legged Polly and a Knock-Kneed Paul" ("Can't get together at all"). It was a bouncy country song, corny in an obvious way, close to the style Roger Miller was making popular in the 1960s. The way Glen Campbell sang the tune on the movie's soundtrack cut straight to the sense of Sam Wood as a bit of simpleton. It's what I wanted the audience to think.

In the same way, there was a scene in which the creepy counterman at the diner, the character who turns out to be the killer, drops his nickel in the jukebox. The Bergmans wrote a song called "A Fowl Owl" for the scene. It was a low-down, vampy, vaguely menacing tune ("Hey little lark/Get out of the dark/Fowl owl on the prowl"). It was a song that gave the audience a snapshot of a character who could mean trouble.

I decided to use music sparingly in *Heat*, behind carefully chosen scenes, and on the rest of the soundtrack, the non-music part, I wanted the same approach. I wanted the creak of Gillespie's office chair, the heavy breathing of Harvey Oberst running through the woods, the crunch of the gravel under Sam Wood's patrol car. I wanted sounds to match the movie's semi-journalistic approach. And that was what I got from the sound recordists on the shoot and from the technicians who did the rerecording and mixing back at the Goldwyn Studios. Goldwyn's sound department under Gordon Sawyer was the best in the business in those years.

Everybody in post-production brought the same level of passion to their work that had inspired the actors and crew on the shoot. The sound technicians, Quincy and the Bergmans with the music, Hal Ashby in his editing, all of them cared deeply about the movie. Maybe their attitude grew out of the civil rights struggle that was taking place in America in that period. Maybe that helped to explain why people working on the movie were so moved by it, why they respected it. I felt on a high all through the post-production.

Then we previewed the movie, and I fell off my high. The preview took place in San Francisco in the middle of May. We went into a theater on a Friday night, unadvertised and unannounced, and after the scheduled feature, the theater manager walked on stage and invited the audience to remain in their seats and watch another movie, one, he said simply, that starred Rod Steiger and Sidney Poitier. Most of the audience stayed, and I hunkered down in the back row with Hal Ashby. A scene came up early in the movie where Chief Gillespie tinkers with his air conditioner. The audience went into fits of laughter. The scene wasn't intended to be that funny, and I found the audience's laughter curious but, I supposed, acceptable. Then we came to the scene a little further along in which Gillespie wonders why Virgil Tibbs has so much cash in his wallet. He demands, "What do you do up there in Philadelphia to earn that kind of money?" And Tibbs answers, "I'm a police officer!" The audience went crazy. They laughed and they hooted and they cheered. That sort of reaction kept on coming all through the movie. I thought the audience must have completely missed the point of the film.

"I've ruined the movie," I said to Hal.

"You're wrong, man."

The two of us left the theater, and for hours, we walked through the San Francisco streets.

"The movie's a failure," I moaned. I felt devastated.

"You don't get it, man," Hal argued. "The audience was really into the film. Maybe they weren't exactly sure how to react because the movie was such a new experience for them. The movie's so different."

"They laughed," I said. "I can't believe they laughed so much."

"Not *at* the movie, man. *With* the movie. They were so knocked out by it, they had to react the only way they knew how in a dark theater. You have to expect some participation from an audience."

"I don't think so," I said. "I've blown it."

I had to wait a few weeks to find out that Hal was right. When the movie opened in June, right away it found a big audience who understood and loved it. By the end of the year, *Heat* had grossed $14 million at the box office, impressive for a movie about a risky subject that had cost less than $2 million to make. The critics gave it overwhelmingly favorable reviews. One exception was in my home town, where a reviewer dumped on it, though that may have been a Toronto thing, finding fault with the local guy who's left town to work south of the border. "What did Jewison know about the American South?" the *Toronto Star* complained.

The New York Film Critics Circle named *Heat* the best dramatic film of 1967. The prize-giving was held at Sardi's, and the person who presented *Heat*'s award in January of 1968 was the senator from New York, Bobby Kennedy.

"See, I told you, Norman," Bobby whispered to me. "Timing is everything. I told you the time was right."

In February, *Heat* received six Academy Awards nominations, including one for best director. But in early April, a few days before Oscar night, a national tragedy blotted the Oscars from everybody's mind: Martin Luther King Jr. had been assassinated.

The Academy postponed its ceremonies from the traditional Monday to the Wednesday after Reverend King's funeral in Atlanta, and a chartered plane of West Coast mourners flew east for the funeral. It was very quiet on board that plane. We were all overcome with a sense of hopelessness, a sense that the anger and bitterness in the country were so great, no one could save the future now. Quincy, Hal, and Haskell were there, as were Lena Horne and her composer-husband, Lenny Hayton; Marlon Brando; Cesar Chavez; and me.

In Atlanta, we joined the others in the long, sad, dusty post-funeral march from Ebenezer Baptist Church to Morehouse College, following the casket on a wagon pulled by a team of mules, marching arm in arm with Bobby and Ethel Kennedy, Harry Belafonte, Sammy Davis, and hundreds of civil rights activists. All the American political leaders were there except President Lyndon Johnson. Perhaps his advisers were afraid there would be another assassination. We walked for miles on that hot day in Georgia, linking arms, saluting the people on the sidelines. It seemed to me that Bobby Kennedy was at the center of our march, though he made no gesture to draw attention to himself. People lining the streets cheered as he went by. It seemed to be Bobby who carried everyone's hopes for the future in the terrible time after Martin Luther King's murder.

A few days later, at the Santa Monica Civic Auditorium, Gregory Peck opened the Academy Awards show on a properly somber note. He was the president of the Motion Picture Academy that year, and he said, "We must unite in compassion in order to survive." Then, for a few hours, we put aside our grief and celebrated the art of making movies. The people from *Heat* could start celebrating early because the very first award of the night was for best achievement in sound, and the Oscar went to the Goldwyn Sound Department for *In the Heat of the Night.* What was especially remarkable about that is that small pictures never win the sound award. But *Heat* seemed to be on a roll. Hal Ashby got the Oscar for best editing. The next Oscar was for best adapted screenplay, and it went to Stirling Silliphant for *Heat.* Best actor was won by Rod Steiger (who thanked everybody, including the Maharishi Mahesh Yogi, who was in that year).

I held my breath when it came to the best director Oscar. The nominees were Richard Brooks for *In Cold Blood,* Arthur Penn for *Bonnie and Clyde,* Stanley Kramer for *Guess Who's Coming to Dinner?* (written by my friend Bill Rose), Mike Nichols for *The Graduate,* and me. Dixie and I had great seats, eighteen rows back, handy for a victorious sprint to the stage. But I made no sprint that night. Mike Nichols won the award.

My instant reaction, sitting in the auditorium, was terrible disappointment. As I watched Mike accept his Oscar, I began to rationalize. Mike was better known than I was, a popular comic performer, a leading Broadway theater director, an Oscar nominee the previous year for *Who's Afraid of Virginia Woolf?* He was popular and, unlike me, he was an American. If I hadn't been so deep into my own movie, I would have known that the people from *The Graduate* expected to clean up that night. They expected to win best actor for Dustin Hoffman, best screenplay, best picture, best everything.

As things developed, it was the only award the movie won. The last Oscar of the evening, the big one, the award for best picture, went to *In the Heat of the Night.* Walter Mirisch accepted.

Suddenly, losing the best director Oscar didn't seem like such a big deal. That night ended, after all, on a note of triumph for all of us. We all felt that the success of the movie was more than what such things tend to be: it was a confirmation that America was ready for our message. That it was ready for Martin Luther King's message of hope and for Bobby Kennedy's message of reconciliation.

The year 1967 saw the publication of William Styron's Pulitzer Prize–winning novel *The Confessions of Nat Turner.* When I read it, I was determined to put the story on the screen. Turner, a black man who in 1831 led an armed rebellion against slavery in the American South, was a truly mythic figure. He was hanged on November 11, 1831, in Jerusalem, Southampton County, Virginia. It was said he was decapitated and the skin peeled from his body.

America in the late 1960s, however, was a time when the Black Power movement had captured a great deal of public support. Some important black intellectuals fiercely attacked Styron's novel, and militant groups began organizing protests to stop any film based on the book. But I was deeply moved by the novel and even more committed when I began my own research into Turner's life.

William Styron, in my opinion, had written the most important American novel of my lifetime. Many white Americans had never heard of Nat Turner. Sadly, I believe the majority of young black Americans also had no idea of the importance of Turner's armed rebellion. Styron was white and born in the South, and although his book made Turner an exciting character with deep religious and social convictions, it also included the story of his romantic relationship with a white woman, whom he later kills. This left Styron open to critics who condemned the novel for perpetrating the stereotype of the black man's desire for white women, the idea of which really motivated their actions.

I saw a different story. I saw a story that would treat Nat Turner as a black Gideon, filled with a deep religious fervor to fight injustice and the terrible evil of slavery. Nat Turner, to me, was a revolutionary hero. A visionary slave who sustained an armed rebellion against the U.S. government for days, fueling the abolitionist movement and putting slavery into the center of public thought at the time. This would be my film.

I couldn't understand why so many black leaders did not want a historic film about Turner. Didn't they know where I stood on the issue of racism in America? The Belafonte shows and *In the Heat of the Night* were, I felt, pretty good qualifications. I had my agents immediately contact David Wolper, a close friend and successful television producer who had acquired the film rights from Styron, to tell him of my interest. Wolper called me and we made a deal very quickly. David suggested I try to persuade Styron to write the screenplay. He turned us down. I came up with the idea of hiring the black playwright James Meredith to write the first draft. I met with Meredith and we began to work. But with tensions between the black and white communities at a fever pitch, I found myself caught up in an angry confrontation with people on both sides.

On a hot summer night at a trendy nightclub in Los Angeles, a fantastic debate took place. Who was responsible for setting this up, I can't remember—whether it was David or someone in the black activist movement. Styron flew in from New York. James Baldwin, the respected black poet, playwright, and author, acted as host and moderator. The actor and civil rights activist Ossie Davis, for whom I had the greatest respect, vehemently attacked the book and the projected film idea.

Styron had arrived at my house in Brentwood in the afternoon. He was a gentle and eloquent Southerner who displayed a sharp intellect and a keen thirst for Bloody Marys. He would need them. When we arrived in the evening, the nightclub resembled my setting for the cockfight in *The Cincinnati Kid*. It was filled with tobacco smoke, tobacco mixed with pot. It was unbearably hot. There were hundreds of sweaty faces, both black and white—people hanging from the rafters. Angela Davis and her group were there. Black Panthers from Oakland and press from television and the *Los Angeles Times*.

The attack on Styron revolved around his racial heritage: "What right has a white Southerner to interpret black history?" Ossie Davis, an eloquent Broadway actor, was formidable. Styron fought back by stating he had humanized Turner and had spent six years of hard work digging out the truth. People cheered and jeered. It went on for hours when Baldwin opened it for questions from the audience. At the end I was even more convinced that this story represented the epicenter of racial violence in the history of America.

I never got the opportunity to make this film. It's been the biggest disappointment of my career. I feel, somehow, that I let William Styron down. Sidney Lumet tried again in the seventies, but it was still considered too controversial, and the project was abandoned by 20th Century Fox, who had bought the film rights from Wolper. Maybe someday a passionate young black filmmaker will have the chance to put Nat Turner's story on the screen for future generations. After all, he was the first black revolutionary hero in America.

However, on February 10, 2004, a new documentary, *Nat Turner: A Troublesome Property*, was broadcast on PBS. Thirty-six years later the debate continues. Scholars and writers are still digging for answers about Nat. Was he a misguided fanatic? A hero or a villain? Maybe he is just being used by those who need him to be what they want him to be. A new book by the historian Scot French, *The Rebellious Slave: Nat*

Turner in American History, deals with the interesting theory that it's not simply a black-white divide, but it is ideological. How we mobilize history in our own world.

In the years following its Academy Award win, *In the Heat of the Night* came close to disappearing. I mean physically disappearing. Walter Mirisch happened to see a print of it in 1994, and the sight appalled him. The colors had separated. They were scratched and faded. The negative was damaged. The movie was headed toward disintegration. Walter spoke to a man named Michael Friend, whom the Academy of Motion Picture Arts and Sciences had employed to restore classic films. He and his technicians set to work on *Heat.* It was a painstaking process, a frame-by-frame restoration that would take years.

Finally in October 2000, a special screening of the restored print was shown at the Long Island Film Festival. It was a gala event attended by many members of the New York and national press. Walter Mirisch, Haskell Wexler, Rod Steiger, Quincy Jones, the Bergmans all attended. Sidney was busy marrying off one of his beautiful daughters and couldn't attend. At the press conference later we all reminisced about our experiences. It was the first time I realized that *In the Heat of the Night* had become a classic.

10

The American Dream

Thomas Crown: Do you play?

Vicki: Try me.

—*The Thomas Crown Affair*

It wasn't what I'd call a script. It was more like a legal brief. Then I found out that the man who wrote it, Alan Trustman, didn't write scripts for a living. He practiced law. He was an associate in an old Boston firm called Nutter, McClennen & Fish.

His brief ran to thirty pages. Long on description, short on dialogue. I was intrigued, not by the prose, but by the central event of the story line and the two principal characters. The story opens with the perfect bank robbery. The character who masterminds it is a young Boston brahmin named Thomas Crown. He's rich, handsome, Phi Beta Kappa, a member of the establishment who acts with a massive ego out of some kind of rebellious, anti-establishment urge. The character who sets out to catch him is Vicki Anderson, a beautiful investigator from the bank's insurance company.

Alan Trustman's agent, John Flaxman at William Morris in New York, sent me the project at the end of March 1966. In his covering letter, he gave me a week to get back to him. If I didn't, he said he would assume I had no interest in it. Talk about holding a gun to my head. He massaged me a little by writing that I was "the first person in the world to read the treatment." I met the deadline and began working with Alan. We worked together, on and off, for fifteen months. That's how long it took us to convert his brief into the script for *The Thomas Crown Affair*.

I think Alan saw himself as Thomas Crown (minus the criminal tendencies). He had the right lineage. His father was a senior partner at Nutter, McClennen & Fish, the fifth name on a letterhead of forty-six lawyers. Alan had some dash to him, and in the years after our movie was made, he let his rebel side take over. He quit the law, divorced his wife, changed his wardrobe, and moved to La La Land. He wrote scripts. He wasn't an experienced dramatist, but he knew how to come up with exciting concepts. He earned a co-writer credit on *Bullitt*, a very good crime-action movie, then slid to the B-movie level with *Lady Ice*, *Hit*, and *The Next Man*. His writing career petered out. But Alan was no dummy. He got into the stock market and made some good investments. In the years after we worked together, I regularly received two kinds of mail from Alan—scripts and investment opportunities. Although I never took him up on either kind of offer, he was a fascinating character.

From the start, I knew this movie would be a matter of style over content. The content was minimal, one character engineering a bank robbery followed by another character pursuing the first. But the robbery was ingenious and the characters were charismatic. We could accomplish a lot with a little. Alan's legal training and clever imagination gave him the tools to invent the flawless bank robbery, and together we fleshed out the two characters. Both were amoral—Thomas Crown robbed banks and Vicki Anderson wasn't above using sex to nab her man. We gave them great clothes and classy lifestyles. We had Thomas seduce an entirely seducible Vicki. We added polo games, a glider sequence, saunas for two, intimate dinners, a Rolls-Royce. Style over content.

Through 1966 and into the winter and spring of '67, whenever I wasn't shooting or editing *In the Heat of the Night*, I was pushing Alan to rework the *Thomas Crown* script. Mostly I wrote or telephoned, but two or three times, I flew to Boston for long sessions with Alan in a suite at the Ritz-Carlton. The script was evolving, but very slowly. As late as March 1967—we were scheduled to shoot in June—I was firing off memos to Alan about fundamental script problems. He needed to be more specific about Crown. Other than rob banks, what did Crown do for a living? And Vicki needed changing. Alan had given her a personality that was too flip. That would wear thin in a hurry. I also wanted a first meeting between Thomas and Vicki that was more interesting than what Alan had written.

For someone with no previous writing experience, Alan worked incredibly hard. He had just one bad habit. He insisted on showing the script to his friends and asking their opinions. One day toward the end of March, he came back from a ski holiday in Sun Valley and bombarded me with changes his skiing pals had suggested. He reminded me of Jules Styne, the songwriter who was famous for canvassing everybody about their thoughts on his Broadway tunes. "My god," I wrote to Alan. "You'll be getting like Julie Styne next, asking the caretaker at the theater what he thought of the big number!" Alan promised to stop taking bad advice, and by the end of April we had a script ready for shooting.

I made one change in the script that wasn't necessary. It reflected an idiosyncrasy of mine. In Alan's version, the loot is dropped off in a warehouse for Thomas Crown to pick up later. I changed the warehouse to a cemetery. I'd seen just the right one on my last trip to Boston. It was a relatively new cemetery with gently rolling hills and lots of space between the gravestones. It made an ideal setting for the first drop-off scene and the fake drop-off that provides the movie's climax.

I love cemeteries. Whenever I travel, I search them out. Most of my movies have a cemetery in them or a funeral or at least a body. *The Cincinnati Kid* opens with the New Orleans funeral march. *In the Heat of the Night* has a scene where the sexy teenager talks about making love on the cool marble of a tombstone. And *Gaily, Gaily*, my next film after *Thomas Crown*, ends at a funeral. My film crews kid me about it. "Here comes Jewison," they say. "There's gonna be a deadie in the movie." In *Moonstruck*, my directing credit appears over a shot of an old man laid out in his coffin—an inside joke appreciated by all.

My father probably had something to do with it. He had a friend who was an undertaker. Bill Sherrin ran the Sherrin Funeral Home on Kingston Road in the Beach, and Dad would sometimes ride in the hearse with Bill at night to keep him company when he went to pick up bodies. Back at the funeral home, the two men used to smoke cigars next to the corpse, Bill putting down his stogey long enough to do the embalming, Dad puffing away and taking in the details of the procedure—scenes right out of the hit HBO series *Six Feet Under*. Maybe everybody is fascinated with death. Next day, he'd tell me about it. Dad didn't find this interest in the serious business of tending to the dead morbid. Neither did I. Maybe it's a genetic thing.

Steve McQueen wanted to play Thomas Crown. He campaigned for the part. He begged me to cast him. But Steve was practically the last actor in Hollywood on my list to play Thomas Crown. The actor had to be elegant, at ease in a tailored suit, deft with a witty line.

My first choice was Sean Connery. Alan Trustman had him in mind when he was writing the script, and I agreed with his choice. But when I spoke to Sean, he said he needed some time off after shooting his latest James Bond movie. Scratch Sean Connery. I thought of other possibilities. Jean-Paul Belmondo? Too Gallic to play a Bostonian. Maybe Richard Burton. I thought of a couple of other actors. I didn't think of Steve McQueen.

Steve heard about the role from a bit-actor pal of his named Steve Terry. Terry had worked for me on *The Russians Are Coming* and had somehow learned about my new project. McQueen was interested enough in the part that he asked the Mirisch Corporation for a copy of the script in whatever stage it had reached. It wouldn't have been polite to turn down his request. Or smart either. In the two years since I had directed him in *The Cincinnati Kid*, Steve had become the number one box office attraction in the business. Even if you didn't want him in your movie, you didn't turn down his request for a script. Steve read the script and was determined to get the part.

He arrived at my house at 313 North Barrington, in Brentwood, on a Sunday afternoon. We sat in the garden and I spoke my piece first.

"This character wears suits, Steve," I said. "You've never worn a suit in a movie. Or in real life for that matter. The only time I've ever seen you with a tie on was for the poker game scenes in *Cincinnati Kid*. Thomas Crown is a Dartmouth graduate. You didn't get out of high school. You're wonderful on a movie screen, but this part doesn't seem like a natural fit at all."

Steve began his pitch, and as he spoke, a few truths dawned on me. This was an actor pleading for a role. It wasn't the actor's agent or his lawyer. It was the actor himself, in person. That had never happened to me before. And it only happened two more times: Anne Bancroft personally asked me to cast her as the Mother Superior in *Agnes of God* and Bonnie Hunt did the same for the part of the best friend in *Only You*. The point in all three cases, and especially Steve's, was that it wasn't about money or the deal or stardom. It was about the role. It was about that character. It was about the art of acting and his desire to play that specific character.

Steve must have connected with something in the persona of Thomas Crown. Maybe he wanted to play Crown because he had never before attempted to play a character who had such style and sophistication. Maybe he thought it was time to take on a new challenge. Whatever was going on in Steve's head, he thought he could handle the role. I was impressed by his passion and began to believe in him, too.

"Steve," I said that Sunday in the garden, "you've got the part."

Alan Trustman was upset.

"Steve McQueen!" he shouted into the phone. "He's all wrong!"

The irony was that Alan would go on to write *Bullitt*, another Steve McQueen movie.

I told Alan to leave Steve's acting to me. I was the director. I'd make Steve look and move like Thomas Crown. All Alan had to do as the writer was trim Steve's lines. Steve didn't make long speeches in his movies. He was a man of few words. Other actors might bitch if their lines were cut. Not Steve. He was so confident of his screen presence that he knew he could make an impact without saying much.

"Just turn Thomas Crown into a more laconic character," I told Alan. That would be easy, I thought. Alan didn't write much dialogue anyway.

Steve signed his contract for the movie. Just because he wanted the part didn't mean he would forgo his usual fee. Out of a total budget of $4 million, he got $750,000. Steve was a careful man with a dollar. Later on, when we were shooting the movie, there was a scene in which Thomas Crown checks his watch. Given the character's background, it had to be an expensive one. We brought in a dozen watches, but Steve rejected them all. Too chintzy. He wore his own watch in the scene, then had his agent bill us $250 as a rental fee for the watch.

Steve's contracts always contained clauses that were strictly McQueen. His dressing room, for instance, had to be outfitted with a set of 80-pound dumbbells and a set of 200-pound barbells. We had to ship Steve's fleet of motorcycles from California to Boston, where the movie was shot. And we had to pay for periodic trims by Jay Sebring, the hot men's hair stylist of the time. Sebring lived in L.A. Actually, the contract gave us a break in the barbering department by saying that, in a pinch, Steve would accept the services of a hair stylist who was "equally as good as Jay Sebring." (A year or so after the movie came out, Jay was one of the victims in the Charles Manson gang killings at Sharon Tate's home in L.A.) The FBI questioned me because I had visited Jay the week before on his Sausalito houseboat.

Faye Dunaway was my idea.

The casting director, Lynn Stallmaster, and I had compiled a list of about fifty actresses who might be right for the Vicki Anderson part. We were leaning toward European actresses, I suppose because we thought the English, French, and Italians had more flair and joie de vivre than the Americans. Julie Christie, Leslie Caron, Diane Cilento, Vanessa Redgrave, Virna Lisi, Françoise Dorléac (I can't imagine why we didn't include her sister, Catherine Deneuve), Anouk Aimée, and Samantha Eggar were all on the list.

I even corresponded with Brigitte Bardot's agent. Without consulting Bardot, the agent wrote back wondering why the movie's locale couldn't be switched to Paris. That piece of wrongheadedness—Boston was crucial to the story—should have tipped me off that I was chasing the wrong actress, but I tried again. This time, the agent wrote back that Bardot herself had considered the part, but thought it should be played by "an American without an accent." She was right, of course, and I abandoned the European list.

But not before I tested Camilla Sparv. That was Steve McQueen's idea. I wasn't sure who Camilla Sparv was. She turned out to be a lovely European actress, but not right for the part. Next I interviewed Sharon Tate. She was stunningly beautiful but too young. I considered Raquel Welch, Candice Bergen, and Suzanne Pleshette. Whoever it was, I knew if she wasn't on Steve's personal list of acceptable actresses, she would be a tough sell.

It was mid-May of 1967, just five weeks away from the beginning of the shoot. By then I had at least figured out the type of actress I had to find. I needed a beautiful woman who wouldn't be blown off the screen by Steve's star quality. I needed someone with acting chops. As I had learned on *Cincinnati Kid*, Steve wasn't a giving actor. The actress I chose had to possess enough confidence in her own talent to get past Steve's acting style. And she needed to be able to project inner strength. This was a movie about a power struggle, the bank robber versus the insurance investigator, the man versus the woman, the rebel (him) versus the establishment (her). The audience had to recognize that it was a fair battle, that the woman had a chance to win. Beauty, talent, and strength. What about Faye Dunaway?

Hardly anyone knew Faye at this point in her career. She had made three movies. Neither *The Happening* nor *Hurry Sundown* had any particular impact. *Bonnie and Clyde* hadn't been released yet. *Bonnie and Clyde* would make Faye a star and win her an Oscar nomination, but for now she remained relatively unknown. I had seen her in an off-Broadway play, *Hogan's Goat*, a couple of years earlier and thought she was very promising. Arthur Penn, *Bonnie and Clyde*'s director, was editing his movie in New York, and offered to show me some footage. I flew east to look at some of Faye's scenes in Arthur's editing room. She looked glorious. If she could stand up to Warren Beatty on the movie screen, I knew she could handle Steve McQueen. I had one tiny reservation. When she grinned, her teeth looked awfully big. We'd have to watch that in editing. Otherwise, Faye was my Vicki Anderson.

"Faye Dunaway?" Steve said. "Never heard of her."

"You will," I said. Steve didn't give me the argument I'd expected from him. We shared the top film agent at William Morris. A brilliant New Yorker with a law degree named Stan Kamen. I'm sure he knew that Faye was hot and told Steve that I was right.

In my pursuit of style over content, I took Haskell Wexler and Hal Ashby to Expo 67 in Montreal. We went in June, just before the shoot on the movie began in Boston. I had signed Haskell once again as my cinematographer and Hal functioned as editor, associate producer, casting consultant, script idea man, and all-round good companion. I wanted them to see a remarkable short documentary film put together for the Ontario pavilion by a Canadian filmmaker named Chris Chapman. The film, *A Place to Stand*, made the most amazing use of multi-image screen techniques that I'd ever seen. It deservedly won the 1967 Oscar for best live-action short.

Chapman's film was a cinematic portrait of Ontario. To tell the story of the province visually, he filled the screen with several images at once, sometimes repeating the same image many times—ninety minutes of images crammed into one strip of film, which ran a breathtaking seventeen and a half minutes. It was dazzling. And it worked because the eye, unlike the ear, is a selective organ. It sorts out and absorbs many different images, many different pieces of information, at the instant they appear. I thought we could use the same technique in our movie, not as a gimmick but as a legitimate editorial tool and stylistic storytelling device. Haskell and Hal agreed.

We used the multi-image technique in a spare but exciting way in the opening credits, just to give the audience a taste of the visuals to come. Then we used it more lavishly for the polo sequence. This is the part of the movie where Thomas Crown first becomes aware of Vicki Anderson. He is playing in the match and wonders who the glamorous stranger is, the one who seems to be aiming her movie camera at him. By splitting the polo action into many simultaneous images, we generated enormous cinematic energy. But probably the most effective use of the technique came in the run-up to the first bank robbery.

The genius of the robbery is Crown's use of five men who have never met before the robbery. Crown gives each man his instructions over the phone. They carry out their individual assignments, then immediately leave the scene, never to cross paths again. It would take too much screen time to show all of this to the audience in a conventional way. Using multi-images allowed us to speed up the narrative process by throwing many images of the robbers up on the screen at once. We showed them making their separate ways to the bank, carrying out Crown's instructions, then slipping away from the crime. We condensed what would have taken fifteen minutes of screen time into less than four minutes. It was and is today one of the best-edited films of the sixties.

The multi-image process became an identifying mark for the movie. Most of the critics, especially in Europe where film buffs seem to appreciate the style of a film more than they do in North America, loved the look of *The Thomas Crown Affair.* I just wish Pablo Ferro, the editor of the multi-images, had received more acclaim for his work. Pablo designed the titles for *The Russians Are Coming* and I commissioned him to take his art to another level on *Thomas Crown.* Chris Chapman had used separate negatives for each of his images and had three hundred pages of storyboard layouts, but we didn't have the time or money for that. So Pablo came up with a complex process that involved mattes, an animation camera, an optical printer, and a work schedule of twenty-hour days. His creativity on this film should have won him an Oscar. Unfortunately for him, 1968 was also the year of *2001: A Space Odyssey.* The Academy Award for best visual effects went to it.

Steve McQueen learned to play polo in six weeks. Mastering enough of a difficult sport to look convincing on a movie screen was an astounding physical feat. Especially for Steve who didn't like horses. He may have starred in a western series on television, but he never became comfortable around horses. He spent three weeks learning to play polo at the Marblehead polo grounds outside Boston. Jack Reddish, the first assistant on the movie, happened to be a top polo player. With Jack's help, Steve perfected one particular move, a back swing shot. It looked spectacular and we used it three or four times in the polo sequence. What the camera didn't show was the blood on Steve's hands. He gripped the wooden mallet and the horse's reins with such ferocity that his fingers and palms were scraped raw.

No matter how demanding and painful, it was still the physical side of Thomas Crown that came easiest to Steve. He was such a physical man. He liked the challenge of learning how to play polo, and the dune buggy scenes were pure bliss for him. We had three separate sequences of Steve roaring a dune buggy across the sand at Crane Beach on the Atlantic. This was a man who raced cars and motorcycles for fun in his spare time. He went nuts over that little red dune buggy. He poured thousands of his own dollars into overhauling it, juicing it up. Naturally the scenes of Steve behind the wheel were terrific. No stuntman required.

The only person who wasn't thrilled by the dune buggy scenes was Faye Dunaway. In one of the sequences, Vicki Anderson goes along for the ride. Faye was terrified to do the scene and I didn't blame her. I got Steve to promise to keep the speed under 60 mph. Not that that made much difference. Faye was convinced Steve was going to roll the buggy. She came back from the ride pale and shaky, but on the screen she is smiling and laughing in the passenger seat, her head thrown back, squealing with delight. It may have been her finest piece of acting in the whole film.

For Steve, the non-physical side of the Thomas Crown character was the hard part. He looked, as always, wonderful on the screen. His natural ease in front of the camera made him look equally at home in a suit or his usual jeans and sweater. But Steve needed direction in conveying the rest of Crown through gestures and his reading of the lines.

Early in the film we had to get across a sense of Crown as an authoritative businessman. We managed to accomplish that by shaping a scene where Steve had virtually no lines at all. The scene opens on Crown and his assistant sitting at a conference table with three other businessmen. Crown is selling a piece of prize commercial real estate to the three men. The deal closes, the businessmen look smug, and Crown speaks for the first time.

"You overpaid," he says, smiling, then walks out of the room.

In four words, Crown shows that he's a better businessman, the kind of guy who's always ahead of everyone else. And it was a line that Steve, the man of few words, handled with something like aplomb.

That was the way we dealt with Steve all through the film. We rehearsed his lines with him until they sounded like short pieces of improvisation. I trimmed three-sentence speeches to two and two-sentence speeches to one. And came up with little gestures or actions that would underline aspects of Crown's character. In the scene where Crown returns home after the first successful robbery, he pours himself a martini, lifts a cigar out of the humidor, sits back on the sofa, and laughs out loud. But there was something missing from the moment. It needed an extra gesture, a little something that would by itself define the character's mood. Maybe a quick twirl of his uplifted feet as he sits down? I'd been known to do that myself when something had gone my way. I suggested it to Steve. He tried it and it worked. The little twirl gave the scene the sense of giddiness that had been missing.

Steve took all of this direction, this concentration on the minutiae of his character, in good spirits. But he had his moments. Late one afternoon, we were waiting for the sun to drop in the sky. We wanted to shoot a scene at the beach with Steve and Faye just before sunset, at the magic hour. Haskell had his camera in place. The crew was waiting. The sun sank and the moment had arrived. But Steve was a mile down the beach doing wheelies in the dune buggy, totally self-absorbed, enjoying himself. By the time he got back, it was too late. We'd lost the light.

"What's up?" Steve asked, hopping out of the dune buggy totally unconcerned.

"It's too late. You cost us the scene, that's what!" I said. The crew was loading up the trucks. I was furious and felt humiliated.

The next morning I arrived on the set carrying a long seagull's feather I'd picked up on the beach. I stuck it in Steve's cap. He squinted at me. "What's that for?"

"On days when you wear the feather, you're the chief," I said. I took the feather out of Steve's cap and stuck it in mine. "But most days, I wear the feather, and that means I'm the goddamn chief!"

Steve had the grace to act embarrassed.

Where Steve looked absolutely convincing was in the romantic scenes. He and Faye had great on-screen chemistry. With Faye's beauty and the way she let her emotions play across her face, she matched Steve in sex appeal.

We shot them in a sauna, wrapped in a couple of towels. This was something new for the time. You couldn't use real steam because it would fog up the camera's lens. Haskell's inventiveness made the scene possible. He suggested dry ice (where was he when we were shooting the card game in *Cincinnati Kid*?). We sprayed Steve and Faye with a mixture of glycerin and warm water to simulate perspiration. Then Haskell shot them with a reddish filter that gave the feeling of heat. On screen, it looked as though the two lovers were talking and smooching in a real hundred-degree sauna. I made one key contribution to the scene: I was the guy who waved a piece of cardboard to waft the mist off the dry ice and across the lens.

The movie's major romantic scene takes place over a chessboard. Thomas and Vicki have arrived at his townhouse. They're in the library. The lights are low. The fireplace flickers. Vicki hovers over the chessboard.

"Do you play?" Crown asks.

"Try me," she answers.

After those two sentences, the script had a three-word description about what should follow: "Chess with sex." No dialogue, just a man and a woman, a chessboard, chess pieces, and a charge of sexual tension. We shot that scene for three days.

Steve and Faye radiate spontaneity in the scene, but in fact they were responding to my directions. I sat on the floor a couple of feet away, just under the camera, and coached them. Since there wasn't any dialogue, I could talk to them during the take.

"Faye, you're playing chess, but another game is going on... Without thinking, your right hand goes up your left arm and lightly caresses your throat... Steve, let your eyes follow Faye's hand... Faye, look up and catch Steve watching. You're embarrassed. You smile and look down... Faye, stroke the bishop. Use your fingertips... Steve, what's she doing? Masturbating the bishop? My god, she's throwing you off your game..."

And so on for six minutes of screen time.

"Check," Vicki says. The silence is broken.

Crown stands up, studies the board, confirms that he has lost. He roughly pulls Vicki to her feet.

"Let's play something else," he says.

They kiss. Not a brief, tender kiss. I was going for the all-time longest kiss in screen history. Two people pushing their lips together can make for a dull scene without some juice in the photography. What Haskell did was cover himself and the camera in a large black hood with only the lens peeking out. The hood blocked any reflections that might creep into the shot from what Haskell did next. He climbed onto an oversized skateboard. Two grips then pushed the board in 360-degree loops around the kissing couple. Round and round he went as the lovers embrace. Not a hint of bare skin, but the kiss was far sexier than a shot of two nudes. It lasted for eighty seconds of screen time. I wasn't sure whether I'd established a movie record for a kiss, but I did know we had created a highly sensual piece of film. If you can believe it, that kiss earned the movie a Mature Audience rating, and most newspapers would not reproduce our open-mouth kiss ad for the film.

All the scene needed was a great romantic musical score. For that, I chose Michel Legrand. I knew his work from European films—*The*

Umbrellas of Cherbourg was his—but *Thomas Crown* was his first significant American movie. Michel had a bottomless cache of melodic lines and he gave us one of his loveliest for the chess-with-sex scene. He opened, as the chess match begins, with a quick burst from a jazz tenor saxophone, then went into a downward swoosh from the strings that carried the line into the main theme. He called the melody "His Eyes, Her Eyes."

But this wasn't the piece that later turned into a standard in the repertoires of dozens of ballad singers. That came from the accompaniment to the glider sequence. The original script called for Crown to go skydiving as a release from his post-robbery tension. I changed the skydiving to glider-flying. I had two reasons. Gliding looked better. And with all the insurance hassles caused by skydiving, plus the stunt doubles that would be required, glider-flying was cheaper to shoot. The scene was simple, just a glider drifting and rolling against the blue sky (and, no, it wasn't Steve at the controls; there was a limit to how many sports I could ask him to learn for one movie). As we were shooting it, I knew it would need a particular kind of song behind it, something like the Beatles' "Strawberry Fields."

Michel produced a melody that was, like "Strawberry Fields," on the baroque side. Listening to the melody, one had the sense that it would go on forever, just like the flight of the glider. Alan and Marilyn Bergman picked up on this quality in their lyrics. The images they conceived were all circular: "Like a snowball down a mountain/Or a carnival balloon/Like a carousel that's turning/Running rings around the moon." The song was called "The Windmills of Your Mind" and I loved it.

Andy Williams and I had worked together on live television in New York. In my first year with CBS, as a summer replacement, I produced and directed Andy's first show. I wanted him to sing the song on the movie's soundtrack and release it as a single. If we were lucky, we'd have a hit song and a great tie-in with the movie. Michel and the Bergmans performed the song for Andy. He seemed puzzled by it. He liked the melody but not the lyrics. I couldn't believe it. I told him that the Bergmans were true poets. That the song was brilliant. Andy didn't get it. In the end, Noel Harrison sang the song. It became a hit and won an Oscar for best original song. Then of course Andy wanted to record it and so did twenty other top vocalists. The song became a classic standard and an annuity for its composers.

The Thomas Crown Affair touched on themes that have always fascinated me. Power struggles. Anti-establishment versus establishment. Betrayal. Still, as I kept reminding everybody, the movie was more about style than content, and that included the music, Haskell's photography, the use of multiple images, the sets, and the clothes. Theodora Van Runkle designed Faye's wardrobe, as she had done in *Bonnie and Clyde*. For *Thomas Crown*, Thea dressed Faye in the miniskirts of the era, sleeveless little dresses, backless little dresses and for the chess-with-sex scene, a dress that was both sleeveless *and* backless. The clothes were part of the movie's consistent look, feel, and mood.

That approach carried over into the story itself, particularly its ending. Thomas Crown is planning a second bank robbery. He keeps the target and the details of the robbery from Vicki, but reveals the spot where he'll turn up with the money. The cemetery. She betrays Crown by telling the police, and Vicki and the cops are waiting for him when his Rolls-Royce turns slowly into the cemetery. But the person who steps out of the Rolls isn't Crown. It's a Western Union delivery boy. He hands a telegram to Vicki.

"Left early," the telegram reads. "Please come with the money or you keep the car. All my love. Tommy."

The screen goes to a shot of Crown sitting on a plane to South America. Then returns to Vicki in the cemetery. She smiles, rips the telegram in pieces and looks up at the sky, frowning, then smiling, then in tears. The screen returns to Crown on the plane. He smiles. He knew Vicki would betray him.

Style over content.

When *Thomas Crown* was released in 1968, I was working on *Gaily, Gaily*, based on author and screenwriter Ben Hecht's memories of his days as a cub reporter in 1910 Chicago. It was a story about the America that emerged in the early 1900s. The Wobblies were in one corner, the Trotskyites in the other, and the robber barons were in full swing. We shot in Chicago, Milwaukee, and Galena, Illinois. Melina Mercouri played the madam of the famous brothel, Hume Cronyn was a corrupt city politician, and a young Beau Bridges was our star reporter. It was a film that dealt with innocence and corruption.

Gaily, Gaily was a sprawling, complicated production, and I was fortunate to find a tough young production manager and associate producer in Patrick Palmer. He would turn out to be my longest and most trusted associate for fourteen films and some twenty years. When we first met, he was a tough little guy with a crew cut, reddish blond hair, and a bulldog stance. We became the perfect good cop–bad cop combination when dealing with outsiders. He was a brilliant negotiator, and he had an innate ability with numbers. He could figure out what a movie would cost to make in less time than it took a team of expert accountants, and he was passionately committed to filmmaking. We became friends and partners.

Dixie and I had put down roots in California. We had a beautiful home in Brentwood, the requisite pool, a collection of bonsai plants, a huge brick barbecue. We held receptions. Dixie helped establish the first child-care center in Watts, where the 1965 riots had left more than thirty people dead and hundreds more injured.

I had been working for Bobby Kennedy's campaign for the presidency ever since our meeting in the Sun Valley hospital where our sons were being fitted for casts. I liked him instantly, and I liked what he stood for. He was a shy man, always in his brother's shadow, but I believed he was about to change the world. He promised hope.

Bobby was well on his way to the White House, having won the California primary on June 4, 1968. I was beginning to think that life was good.

That night, Dixie and I took Melina Mercouri for a quick dinner in a Chinese restaurant before heading down to John Frankenheimer's house in Malibu so we could introduce her to the next president of the United States. Bobby and Ethel were coming there around 10 p.m.

after a victory celebration. Melina, a green-eyed blonde with a deep, smoky voice, was, at that time, in exile from Greece where a military junta had taken over the government. Melina was one of the most committed political activists I have ever met. She was determined to see democracy restored in her country and spoke out at every opportunity against the military regime. She was married to expatriate American director Jules Dassin, who had directed her in the now-famous Greek film *Never on Sunday*. Dassin was himself a victim of the right. He had been on the Hollywood blacklist. Needless to say, Melina was anxious to meet Bobby.

We were sitting in a Chinese restaurant somewhere in Santa Monica, chatting about politics in America and in Europe. Suddenly the waiter ran down the narrow lane between the tables, yelling, "Kennedy is shot! Kennedy has been shot!"

We sat there, looking at him, not believing the words. Surely he was talking about JFK, surely, he must be mistaken. Dixie leaned across my arm saying, "Oh my god, Norman..." Melina stood, staring at the TV set. I remember running to the bar where the TV was. Moments before it had been droning on about the sports results of the day. Now it showed people in shock, silent, crying, a reporter at the scene describing the shooting. Even he talked as though he didn't believe what he was saying. Bobby Kennedy had been shot.

We left the restaurant in silence. There was nothing any one of us could say to make the moment bearable.

When we got back home, I sat outside in the garden, staring at the night sky, thinking that, for me, the American dream had crumbled. Bobby had been a beacon for all of us in the civil rights movement. His assassination meant that America was so violent a society, it could not abide its best. First John Kennedy, then Martin Luther King, now Bobby Kennedy.

I knew then that I had to escape or I would lose my sense of joy in making movies, the joy that drove me. If I lost that, I would be finished as a director. The opportunity came soon after with the offer to make *Fiddler on the Roof.*

11

The Spirit of Chagall

Sunrise, sunset,

Sunrise, sunset, swiftly fly the years

One season following another

Laden with happiness and tears

—*Tevye, Fiddler on the Roof*

I broke the news in the big, sprawling family room of our Barrington Avenue house; the boys perched on the arms of a chair, Jenny was lying on the floor surrounded by some of her toys, Dixie had just come in and was still lingering in the doorway, Deecho lay on his back, the length of the couch. Deecho was our white German shepherd, much beloved by everyone, except the Romeros down the street from us. Deecho had killed Cesar Romero's cat a while back and they still hadn't forgiven him—or us, for that matter.

"But we live in California," Kevin said, emphasizing the "live."

"We do, now," I said, "but we are going to *live* in England next month."

"You're not going to sell the house?" Kevin asked. Being the oldest, he was always the one with the serious questions. Selling the house would mean we were not coming back.

"We won't need a house in L.A. if we are living in London," I said, evasively. "We'll need a house in London, instead."

I explained that I had to be in London to make my next movie, that it would take two years, that England was where some of the best movies were being made—*Doctor Zhivago, Lawrence of Arabia,* the Bond films—that Pinewood Studios was the center of filmmaking. "I promise it will be very exciting."

They all looked at me. Not believing. No one spoke. Even Deecho stared at me balefully, suspiciously.

I didn't have to tell Dixie that the night Bobby Kennedy was assassinated I realized I had to get out of the United States to preserve what joy and hope I had about life. She knew. And she knew I wouldn't be able to make *Fiddler* without that. *Fiddler* was a musical, and even in its darkest moments, there was joy in the music and hope in the exodus. Martin Luther King had been murdered, Jack Kennedy was killed, Bobby—the man who had offered hope after the killings, sanity in the face of mindless violence—was dead; Nixon was president. Reagan was governor. I was losing my sense of humor.

It took a long time but I sold them all on the idea of the move, much as I used to sell stories to my friends at Kippendavie and Queen. I told them about the big ocean liner, the games on board, the cabins and berths, the adventurous seas, the wonders of London, Tower Bridge, the Queen, her guards, the pomp and circumstance of the grand old Court, the ghosts of the little princes in the Tower, Shakespeare and Marlowe for Kevin, who was already interested in the theater, a bit of swashbuckling for Michael, princesses for Jenny, and whatever else came to mind.

At the end I asked for their green cards. Then I did a stupid thing we all would later regret. I sent all four cards back to the U.S. Department of Justice, informing them that we no longer wished to reside in their country. How stupid a protest was that? I later asked myself. My two boys never really forgave me.

Steve McQueen's wife, Neile, and her two children joined up with Dixie and our three on the SS *France* for the voyage to Southampton, England. Steve was shooting in Europe and I was in preproduction at Pinewood Studios. Dixie and Neile arranged a magnificent going-away party on board, with all our trunks and cartons. Deecho arrived later and the poor animal was immediately thrown into quarantine.

Visiting Deecho became a regular feature of our first six months in England. For some insane reason, the British had a strict quarantine system for cats and dogs that kept the animals in captivity for months. Deecho was kept in Slough, a good forty-minute drive from Pinewood Studios where I worked. I would go there once a week, stopping in Twickenham to buy him a big beef rib bone at the butcher's so he'd remember who we were. I had promised the kids I'd make sure Deecho survived his imprisonment. Most days I had a chauffeur called Bert who knew all the back roads and short cuts and told tales about Noel Coward and his friends all the way to Slough and back. In happier times, Bert had been Noel Coward's dresser. When Deecho escaped from quarantine—he was one of the few dogs ever to succeed—Bert helped me explain to the police that the best way to bring him back was not to shoot him but to call "Deecho, come!" and he would come back. After our mad dash to Slough, he was captured and placed in solitary.

At first we lived in a furnished flat in Kensington, then bought Sean Connery's old house on Putney Heath and settled into London life. Jennifer enrolled at Miss Lambert's School for Young Ladies, began to speak English with a Mayfair accent for the neighbors and with a Cockney accent with Bert; the boys went to Herringswell Manor, a boarding school near Newmarket, and learned to live with shirts and ties. And, as I had predicted, they loved London but hated the weather.

I settled in at Pinewood Studios, about an hour's drive northwest of London. The studio restaurant, bar, and reception occupied the main floor of a lovely manor house. There were twenty acres of massive sound stages, studios, a gigantic pool, big enough to float a submarine that was used for some of the Bond pictures. My offices overlooked the formal gardens. There was a pair of French doors and a balcony. Whenever I drove to the lot I felt like I was going back into the forties. I somehow expected to run into Noel Coward, Leslie Howard, Charles Laughton. But it was busy with seventies movies.

There was Sean Connery doing Bond, the "Carry On" pictures, and now there was *Fiddler on the Roof*. I was going to put all the grief and disappointment of the sixties behind me—the assassinations of John F. Kennedy and Martin Luther King, the Vietnam demonstrations in Century City where Hal Ashby and I were beaten by mounted L.A. policemen, the assassination of Bobby Kennedy, all the causes and ideals I had believed in that now felt like defeat.

The first six months I studied the Jewish religion. I researched the photographs of Roman Vishniac and spent hours at the Jewish museum and research center. I read and listened. I immersed myself in Sholom Aleichem and Russian Jewish traditions because I felt it was important for audiences to feel what it was like to be living in those times. For me, with every movie there is a core, and it's the story I want to tell. And I ask myself, "Is the story worth telling? What is it about? Does it have some bearing on our lives? Is it important enough to spend a year and a half, two years of my life on?"

Fiddler on the Roof was a long, arduous undertaking. We spent almost two and a half years making that film.

Right from the start I knew it had to be shot in Eastern Europe. It was not only a question of the setting, it was the whole Sholom Aleichem world of old-fashioned shtetls, of people leading lives as they had lived them for generations, in an atmosphere where you can become used to the cruelties of your neighbors, the regular pogroms, and just carry on with raising your chickens and marrying off your children—those that survived.

I traveled to Hungary and Romania, Israel and Yugoslavia, searching for the perfect location. I decided to shoot the movie in a little town in Romania, near the Russian border, but we couldn't get insurance. We were too close to the Soviet border. Lloyd's of London agreed to Hungary, and for a while it looked like we were going to shoot somewhere on the Hungarian plains, near Budapest. I met with István

Dósai, the man who ran Hungarofilm. He and Endre Szilágyi were supportive. They laid on the hospitality, the limos to scout locations, the wine and the best food you could get in a communist country. Then they read the script and the deal was off.

"You have a pogrom in the movie," they said.

"Oh yes, and the Cossacks ride up and there is going to be a great scene with the feathers flying, and—" I was so enthusiastic, I hardly noticed they had gone glassy-eyed.

"Not in Hungary," they said. "The Russians would never allow it."

"But that was Czarist Russia in 1905, not the Soviet Union...not now!" I shouted.

They just shook their heads.

We ended up in Yugoslavia, near Zagreb. Tito, as I discovered, loved movies almost as much as he loved hard currency and he maintained one of the largest standing armies in Europe. Lloyd's of London were happy to provide the necessary insurance.

I wanted the film to deal not only with the breakdown of traditions, but with the pain and hardship of persecution. I wanted audiences to really feel the racial hatred. There is a moment at the end of the first part when the Russian bullies attack a wedding party. They rip open some pillows that were meant to be wedding gifts and goose feathers fly through the air like snow. This scene came from an old couple at a Russian kibbutz in Israel. They remembered this image from a pogrom they had witnessed as children in a Ukrainian village.

Certain images come into your mind when making a film, and that image for me was iconic. It somehow held all that hatred and sadness I wanted my film to impart, echoed in John Williams's fabulous rendition of the Jerry Bock and Sheldon Harnick score.

Tevye, the central figure in *Fiddler*, is a wonderful composite of several characters in the Aleichem short stories. Zero Mostel was perfect for the stage role in New York, as Joseph Stein created the character for the musical. He had the right sensibility, the moves, the ability to sing quietly or shout out the lyrics when he was in despair. But I wasn't sure. Zero seemed so American, so New York. He just wasn't Old World enough for the Tevye I thought Aleichem had written. We were approached by others—Danny Kaye, Danny Thomas, Alan King. Then Joe Stein suggested Topol.

Topol was a successful Israeli actor who had first played the role at the Habbema Theatre in Tel Aviv. When he was offered the chance to audition for the Hal Prince production in London, he had to learn English phonetically, word by word, inflection by inflection. In the beginning he couldn't understand the words. I was impressed with his voice and his stage presence when I went to see him on stage. He was big and powerful, strong; he didn't have the Mostel charm, he was tougher, more muscular and sexy.

When we met backstage I was surprised at how young he was. Tevye the character is somewhere in his mid-fifties, he has three grown daughters with marriage on their minds. This man, when he took off the makeup, was in his mid-thirties. The gray hair was a wig over his own long black hair, the girth had been added to his body in layers. But he had that don't-mess-with-me pride that the Tevye of my imagination had. He would be able to tell someone to "get off my land," and mean it. What's more, he was first-generation Israeli, his parents Russian Jews who had immigrated to Israel. He spoke with a heavy Israeli accent but sang clearly, with a clear voice. I was sure I had found the right man.

The Mirisches were harder to convince, but Joe Stein backed me, and I continued to assert that we would bring in the movie on budget—a rare feat in the business even now.

I don't think Zero Mostel ever forgave any of us.

Topol added dimensions to the character that were not part of the play. He made him more complex, so the tension between his old-world authoritarian role and his love of his daughter Chava seems to come naturally. Topol made us feel Tevye's heartbreaking struggle when he pronounces his daughter dead for marrying a Christian. Yet, unlike Zero Mostel, Topol didn't take over the movie, didn't dominate it as Zero had dominated the stage.

Topol suggested a couple of other Israelis from the Tel Aviv production for the parts of Golde and Perchik: Hanna Meron and Assaf Dayan, who was Moshe Dayan's son. Their agent announced they would come to London to audition. By now, both the Mirisches and Arthur Krim were willing to go with my instincts, and we paid their way. It was 1970. I was expecting them both to read and sing for us the next day at the studio. Topol called. "There has been an attack in Munich!" He was so agitated he could barely utter the words.

The El Al plane Hanna and Assaf were on had stopped to refuel in Munich. Passengers were bused to the terminal to wait till the Munich group joined them to board. It was on the bus back to the plane that an Arab terrorist pulled the pin from a grenade he had hidden in a briefcase. Though a young Israeli businessman threw himself onto the grenade, it exploded, killing one person and wounding twenty-three. Hanna Meron lost a leg. It was a tragic event on the world stage and for our production of *Fiddler*.

Norma Crane was cast as Golde and Paul Michael Glazer as Perchik. Sadly, Assaf Dayan couldn't handle the language. Paul Michael Glazer was young and inexperienced, but talented and enthusiastic and perfect for the part. The only problem was that his eyes were blue. So we had him wear brown contact lenses. Later he starred in the TV series *Starsky and Hutch* and is now directing and producing his own movies.

Norma Crane was diagnosed with breast cancer halfway through the studio musical recordings and had to travel to hospital most days for treatment. Watching the movie, you would never know she was in pain some days and how worried she was. She and I kept her illness a secret from everyone except Topol and Pat Palmer, the associate producer. What a courageous and talented performer she was.

I worked with Joe Stein on the screenplay. Having written the stage play, he knew all the characters inside out. It was not much of a stretch to enlarge the scene to include the whole village of Anatevka, not just Tevye's family. The film opens with village scenes that we staged and choreographed to "Tradition," the song that describes the Jewish family, its way of life, its customs and beliefs.

The Fiddler, another Aleichem character, was to start the movie, playing his fiddle on a rooftop in Anatevka at dawn, exactly as Chagall had painted him. Right away, I thought of Isaac Stern.

I had seen Isaac Stern play when I lived in New York. I realized he had to play the fiddler's opening music. He was a Russian Jew who was also an American citizen, and his music had the soul I was looking for. Sometimes when you make a movie, you get these crazy ideas that won't leave you alone, and sometimes they even turn out to be some of best ideas for the film. But getting Stern wasn't going to be easy.

Needless to say, his agent wasn't having any of it. Mr. Stern was booked from here to next year and couldn't consider anything new in his schedule for two years. At least. He could have added that flying to London to play on a soundtrack for a movie was beneath Mr. Stern's dignity, and did I know that Mr. Stern was the greatest fiddler in the world.

The Mirisches said no just as emphatically. Even if Stern were available, we couldn't afford him. But I believed I could talk him into it. I could sell him the idea. He was a Russian Jew. He knew how important the fiddler was to this production and exactly what he represented to his people.

I flew to Chicago and went to the apartment he was staying in at the time. Halfway along the hall I could already hear the music he was to play with the Chicago Symphony the next evening. I stood in the hallway, waiting for a pause in the music. Then I knocked timidly. He called out to me to come in, and suddenly, there he was, a small man in sweat pants playing Beethoven, accompanied by an older man on the piano. Neither of them stopped playing as Stern told me to go and pour two drinks in the kitchen. Kept playing when he asked me why I wanted him for this one song. And he seemed to listen while I went into my dance, telling him it's all about Sholom Aleichem and Chagall, and his family, how Aleichem's uncle used to get tipsy on the night before Shabbos and sit on the rooftop and play his violin.

Once he stopped and told the piano player to start a bit again. Later, he told me he had no time for movies. He was going to Brazil and Paris, then New York and London. Over the Scotch in the kitchen, I told him how the fiddler was the essence, the spirit of the whole story, and did he know that Tevye took the fiddler's spirit with him when he went to America.

"Isaac, you are a Russian Jew, and you should play the fiddler." I clinked his glass. Toasted Sholom Aleichem, and left. I'm not sure how I convinced him, but I know it wasn't the money. The $25,000 I offered, while much more than the Mirisches would have been willing to pay, was nowhere near what Stern would have been paid for a single recording even then.

The day he arrived in London I set the Chagall sketch on the glass wall of the studio where the London Symphony Orchestra was waiting, dressed as if for an evening performance. Stern wore his old sweat pants. He stopped and looked at the drawing, then the orchestra, then the drawing again. "Good morning, ladies and gentlemen," he said, at last. "The spirit of Chagall is with us. This will be a wonderful performance."

And it was.

I doubt if we would have been able to shoot the film in Yugoslavia without Branko Lustig. We found him through Yugofilm, Yugoslavia's own state filmmaking machine, mostly devoted to propaganda documentaries. Branko knew how to get things done, how to work with and around the system, knew his way through the bureaucratic jungle. What's more, he was Jewish and he knew Sholom Aleichem's stories. Only he and his mother survived Auschwitz, and he cursed the number tattooed on his arm. When he ate, one arm always encircled his plate—a sign of the struggle for food he'd experienced as a child in the camps. He definitely understood what the movie was about.

He and Robert Boyle, our production designer, found the locations we needed—Malagorica and Leckinek, both old Croatian villages about two hours' drive from Zagreb. He met with the commissars of each town, explained what we were going to be doing, rented barns, houses, had a town square created, a synagogue built. Robert Boyle did the drawings, Branko made sure the workers delivered. Already the first day, he had good news for me: Tito was giving us a cavalry regiment. Trained soldiers and trained horses, all we had to do was come up with the Cossack uniforms. He rented me a house in Zagreb, found a wonderful translator/secretary for me, an art history major, Lluba Gamulin, who spoke perfect English (she now runs an art gallery in Dubrovnik), and he hired all the extras, even the cows and the rooftops. All Branko's transactions were in cash. Pat Palmer gave him a wad of dinars every few days, and trusted him to use it as needed. He never betrayed that trust. And the movie, as I had promised the Mirisches, came in on budget.

Years later, Branko emigrated to the United States and produced *Schindler's List* for Spielberg. I was so proud of him when he received the Academy Award for best picture. Branko was a real survivor and we have remained friends. Topol and I have kept in touch, as he played his Tevye all over the world, and still does, but now he no longer has to wear gray wigs to cover his black hair, and his figure has become more like Tevye's. In the Australian theatrical production, two of his daughters played Tevye's daughters. He came to Toronto several years ago with a new production of *Fiddler*, which they rehearsed in Ontario before a new North American tour. We had a great reunion and I told him that I sang his song "Sunrise, Sunset" at my daughter Jenny's wedding in Caledon and everybody cried. (I didn't sing it nearly as well as he would have, but this was my privilege as father of the bride.)

Fiddler had eight nominations, including best picture, and won three Oscars: cinematography, sound, and John Williams for the score. As in 1967, in this 44th Academy Awards, I would again be denied the award for best director. That night it went to William Friedkin for *The French Connection* and to my great disappointment Topol lost to Gene Hackman for the same picture.

Lew Wasserman sent me a note of condolence implying that we were robbed. I was pleased for Ossie Morris and John Williams, who both thanked me from the podium, but it was a tough night for Dixie and me, and of course the Mirisch brothers and United Artists.

When a reporter shoved a mike in my face at the Governors Ball after the awards and asked how I felt about them, I could only smile and say, "An Academy Award is only important if you win it." I knew in my heart that *Fiddler* would become a classic and remain on the screens of the world and in people's minds long after *The French Connection* had faded away.

The night was not a total loss, because Charlie Chaplin was finally honored just a week away from his eighty-third birthday. Dixie commented, "You'll probably be that old when they honor you." We laughed, but our hearts still felt the rejection. In the coming year *Jesus Christ Superstar* would restore my faith in the movie industry.

I first heard of *Jesus Christ Superstar* when the BBC banned the British record album. They had found it offensive. Sacrilegious. I was intrigued and bought the two-record album. I think I saw it as an opera almost the first time I heard it. I loved the idea, the music and lyrics. The scenes began to form in my mind before the first record had finished playing. I was so excited, I invited David Picker of United Artists to our London house to hear it with me. He was in town to see a rough cut of *Fiddler*.

I played him "I Don't Know How to Love Him" and King Herod's song, and described how it would work visually, how each scene would develop, how the conflict between Jesus and Judas would drive the film. David looked at me like I was crazy. "But Norman, it's just two phonograph records."

He turned it down.

The musical score for the record was composed by the then very young Andrew Lloyd Webber, the lyrics were by his then partner, Tim Rice. I called their agent in London, David Land. He answered his phone with the broadest of Cockney accents, surprised anyone would want to know who owned "that stuff." "It's the boys, of course." He always referred to Tim Rice and now Lord Andrew Lloyd-Webber as "the boys."

"And who has the film and theatrical rights?"

"Decca, of course."

I knew that Decca Records was owned by Universal. I sent a cable to Lew Wasserman and told him if he ever contemplated making a motion picture of *Jesus Christ Superstar*, I was his man. I don't think he knew what I was talking about.

But this time I had made enough of an impression on the major studios that Wasserman was pleased to hear from me. And so it began. I met with "the boys." Rice was tall, burly, soft-spoken; Lloyd Webber was small, sharp-featured, angular, egotistic, so young he seemed still to be growing. They were both keen to work on the film version. They weren't worried about anyone accusing them of blasphemy; after all, they were using the New Testament for inspiration and this was just a rock opera based on the good, the bad, and the beautiful. In Tim Rice's defense, he was more interested in the character of Judas than that of Jesus. The whole betrayal theme excited me and I was filled with all kinds of strong visual images.

Robert Stigwood, a powerful and wealthy record impresario, was clever enough to buy out David Land's Agency and, of course, the contracts with the boys. He met with me and asked if I was interested in staging it for the theater. Apparently the record was now a big hit in America. I told "Stiggy" that I really didn't see it as a theater piece and I would keep working on the film concept.

When the Stigwood Broadway production opened in October 1971, the American Jewish Committee claimed the musical defamed Jews and incited hatred, that it showed Jewish clerics to be "satanically evil." The committee was particularly concerned with these lyrics sung by Judas: "My God, I saw him—he looked three-quarters dead!/And he was so bad I had to turn my head/You beat him so hard/That he was bent and lame..."

They said the "you" referred to the Jewish clerics, whereas it should have referred to the Roman soldiers, and so on, rather similar to the protest over Martin Scorsese's *The Last Temptation of Christ* and Mel Gibson's more recent *The Passion of the Christ*. But it was not until the film was ready for release, that I personally felt the full force of religious intolerance and fundamentalism. My biggest fear was what the Vatican or the powerful Southern Baptists might think about my interpretation. I never thought I was making an authentic religious dramatic story. This was a rock opera, highly stylized with modern elements. There were tanks, planes, and automatic weapons mixed with Roman helmets, swords, and spears.

The Broadway production closed after 3,242 performances. I had hired a talented young British writer, Melvyn Bragg, to help me with the screenplay. Melvyn later ended up as head of arts programming for London Weekend Television and author of a number of books. He was recently made a life peer by the Queen. But in 1972 he was in blue jeans and T-shirt as the two of us wandered all over Israel with tape recorders, listening to the music and lyrics and trying to figure out how the screenplay would work in a musical film with no text or book. Melvyn was cool. He was good-looking and something of an intellectual. He had very little experience in film, however, and was not nearly as enthusiastic about Andrew and Tim's work as I was. I think he felt Andrew's score was rather mediocre.

Since I had made *Fiddler* the year before, I was a big *macher* in Israel. Despite the sensitivity of the project, I had the full support of Golda Meir's government and could count on the minister of culture and of course Moshe Dayan, as well as Topol's friends in the Israeli cinema. The government was anxious to encourage filmmaking in Israel, and Pat Palmer promised our company could also try to bring a western film to shoot simultaneously in the country.

When Melvyn and I finally decided that the film should be shot as a play within a play, we sat down and wrote out the action sequences that would fit with certain musical passages and would interpret the story using Tim Rice's lyrics. We would open on an old Arab bus roaring across the Negev Desert, loaded down with props and costumes and, of course, our cast of young performers. They would come from America, England, Canada, and Israel.

Ted Neeley was a Southern rock and roller who was in a production at the Universal Theatre when I went to L.A. for casting and production meetings with Universal Studios. He missed the audition and later showed up at my hotel room. He tapped gently on the door and when I opened it, he was in full costume. His intensity, confidence, and wild falsetto wail convinced me, even though I would have a very slight and small man for the role of Jesus.

Judas was the toughest to cast. I loved Carl Anderson in the L.A. production, but he was black. I was deeply concerned that the racial overtones of a black Judas would affect the whole film. But this tall handsome kid, born in Lynchberg, Virginia, one of twelve children of steelworker James and seamstress Alberta, was destined to create this role on film. Both he and Ted would be forever the great team that continued in these roles for years after the film. It is estimated that Carl played the role more than twelve hundred times. Carl died of leukemia in 2004, on February 23. He and Ted were reuniting in a worldwide tour that was to open at the Vatican in the fall of that year. Before his death, Carl told an interviewer that he was glad he had persevered in his interpretation of Judas as more of a victim than a villain. He said, "I have lived to see the musical recognized as a masterpiece."

Of all my films, I consider *Superstar* to be the most inventive and visually interesting. Released in 1973, it was the first rock video before MTV. I used all my old live-TV musical shtick. Tremendous zoom shots, great swooping crane movements, and much of the camera work choreographed to the music.

Rob Iscove, our young Canadian choreographer, did a brilliant job with our dancers. Unfortunately he fell from the top of a Roman amphitheater in Bet Shean, smashing his jaw and breaking so many bones he had to be hospitalized in Tel Aviv for weeks before we could fly him home.

Richard MacDonald, our talented British production designer, also took a bad fall at the ruins in Avdat, but I suspect the reason was an overindulgence of arak, a strong Arab liquor. Regardless, he also was in the hospital for a long stay. It was a hard physical shoot. What with temperatures close to 120 degrees Fahrenheit at midday, we were forced to shoot only in the early hours of the morning and the few hours before sunset.

The year before, we had chosen the location for the last supper at Aqua Bella, so that green grass could be planted and watered in anticipation of our shoot. I wanted the scene shot outside surrounded by a green meadow. The crew was British and Israeli with three Italians, who handled the huge camera crane, which was shipped over from Rome. *Superstar* was the last film to be shot with Todd-AO lenses, which gave it the largest wide-screen image possible. With the London

Symphony, the St. Paul's Boys Choir, and the rock musicians from Deep Purple, under the baton of André Previn, the soundtrack was truly fantastic. Although there was no love lost between André and Lloyd Webber, the recording sessions were inspired. The filming was helped along by a healthy quantity of pot, which was relatively easy to obtain in the Middle East. With an excellent cast and crew, we enjoyed the country, especially on our weekends in Eilat.

This sun-drenched playground on the Gulf of Aqaba was our favorite spot for scuba diving, grilled fish, and beer. I had a young driver with a rented Jaguar sedan, and I luckily hooked up with a Haitian Jewish hotel manager and a tall blond French female architect who were both experienced divers. They took me under their wing and I experienced some fantastic dives among the deep coral reefs in the Red Sea. It all took place at a very hip spot called Raffy's, a bar on the beach with a grand piano and a few tables set in the water where you could eat and still stay cool. The heat was particularly tough for us Canadians. I had never experienced anything like it anywhere else. When we were shooting, young Arab kids would constantly come by with trays of water and no matter how many quarts you drank, you never had to urinate.

The dancers could work full out on some of the large production numbers for only about two or three minutes at a time. The only real problem we faced, though, was when there was an attack on the Golan Heights—then we would lose half our crew for a few days. Most of our grips and electricians were in the army. Everybody in Israel is in the army, both men and women over the age of eighteen. Midway through production, my agent Larry Auerbach and his wife, Carol, visited us in Beersheba for a few days.

"So this is 'the Desert Inn' in downtown Beersheba," Larry announced as he arrived at the hotel, which had no water, bad food, and a wheezing air conditioner. Larry had visited me on the set of *Fiddler* in Yugoslavia, where he had smuggled in fifteen pounds of kosher wieners from The Stage deli in New York for our July fourth barbecue in Zagreb.

While we were shooting *Superstar* in the desert, my partner, Patrick Palmer, was making another movie we had committed to deliver at more or less the same time as *Superstar*. We had maneuvered it to be also shot in Israel, in another part of the Negev, hoping we could share some costs and equipment. *Billy Two Hats* was certainly the first, and may have been the last, "kosher western" ever made. We had fellow Canadian Ted Kotcheff directing and Gregory Peck, Jack Warden, and Desi Arnaz Jr. starring, and a vast group of Jewish Indians and assorted Jewish cowboys and a western town that looked a bit like a kibbutz.

The idea of sharing equipment didn't work seamlessly. I remember the day I discovered that Ted Kotcheff had been promised our crane for a couple of days of filming an Indian attack. I needed the crane and the three Italian operators I had brought over from Rome with the crane at the same time for wide-angle shots of the crowds around Jesus. Greg Peck told me later how Ted had received the news: "Well, you kinda expect a bit of a temper in a guy from Bulgaria," he drawled, "but I've never seen anything like this." Apparently, Ted had gone into such a rage about the crane and my movie, he found a whole new series of swear words not even Greg had heard before, and when he ran out of those, he grabbed his Australian bush hat with both hands, threw it on the ground, and began to jump up and down on it like a character in a Chaplin film. When directors lose it, watch out!

Pat and Greg left for their trailers convulsed by laughter and left Ted with the mystified crew to reorganize the shoot.

I had worked with Ted many years before at CBC Television and knew he could make a tough low-budget picture on location. He did a great job and went on to establish himself as a top director and producer in film and network television. I think his film of Mordecai Richler's *The Apprenticeship of Duddy Kravitz* remains one of Canada's best films.

Dixie and the children joined me from London on school holidays. I rented an apartment in Tel Aviv, and Dixie brought our Japanese au pair to help out. To watch Dixie and Kiyoko do the shopping speaking no Hebrew or Yiddish was a real trip. We sent Kevin and Michael to a kibbutz to work for a couple of weeks just to toughen them up.

Pat Palmer produced *Billy*, while Larry De Waay and I handled *Superstar*. Universal Studios left me alone. Ned Tanen, one of Wasserman's top executives, made one visit, but unfortunately arrived at the High Holy days. "Why would you think I would be shooting during Yom Kippur?" I asked in astonishment as he stepped from his limo to be told we wouldn't be shooting for the next three days. "You're a Jew and so is half my cast and crew."

Ned looked awkward in his charcoal suit with shirt and tie. "I guess I wasn't thinking," he said. I knew that Wasserman had sent him over to report on the production.

"Why don't you come with some of the cast down to Eilat for the weekend? Relax, enjoy Israel. We're a long way from Hollywood. I'll have my editor, Tony Gibbs, show you some film on Tuesday."

Ned, not wanting to return to Tel Aviv, decided to join the *goyim* members of the cast at our hotel in Eilat. To see about twenty or thirty young attractive dancers and actors having a great time in the pool at the hotel was a little bizarre for the Jewish patrons. As evening came and Ned, Larry, and I returned from dinner, some Israeli cops were in the lobby looking for the person in charge. Since Ned Tanen was in a suit and represented Universal Studios, he took it upon himself to calm everybody down and promised the police that the unruly rock and rollers would behave and respect the other hotel guests on this High Holy day. I told my first assistant, Jack Reddish, who was a little drunk himself, to round everybody up. I explained, "They should put away the guitars and cool it until the sun comes up."

Later as we sat under a full moon on the fifth-floor terrace, Ned began to relax. Someone was passing around a joint and we gazed down at the softly lit pool and across the Bay of Aqaba toward the sparkling lights of Jordan. Things were decidedly mellow.

"Beautiful, isn't it?" I said. "Why can't people just live in peace with each other?"

Then Ned, his eyes wide, whispered, "She sure is beautiful."

That's when I saw what he was looking at. One of our young blond dancers was walking nude along the ledge of the terrace, apparently crossing from one room to another.

"Just close your eyes, Ned, and hope that no one calls the police again."

Ned laughed nervously, and soon we all murmured our good-nights. *Shalom, shalom.*

Ned Tanen left for the U.S. two days later. He apparently told everybody at Universal that we were right on schedule and the film looked terrific. That Jordanian weed must have been great.

Superstar was the first picture for which I had negotiated a gross participation. To keep the budget below $3.5 million, I had offered to work for no salary but just "a tiny tiny slice of the pie in case it makes its money back." Lew Wasserman gave me a cold stare. "You wouldn't be talkin' gross."

I explained that I was serious and felt that if I delivered them a finished film, I deserved a small part of the worldwide gross. I was producer and director and had co-written the screenplay. If Robert Stigwood had a piece, I wanted one, too. It was one of the best deals I ever made in my life.

The American release was marred by attacks from the Anti-Defamation League and almost every U.S. Jewish organization. I felt betrayed by many friends, especially after making *Fiddler on the Roof.* Golda Meir and the Israeli government were also criticized in the American press for cooperating and helping us make the film. Other countries, however, did not follow suit and the film had a tremendous reception in Canada, the U.K., in South America and even Japan. Dixie and I joined Ted Neeley on a promotion tour to Tokyo, Kyoto, and Osaka. It always amazed me that my two musicals, *Fiddler* and *Superstar*, were so popular with Japanese audiences. When I visited Tokyo in 2002 as head of the jury for the film festival, no one was interested in *A Soldier's Story, In the Heat of the Night,* or *The Hurricane.* But they loved *Rollerball*—my 1975 film—and Doris Day.

My only regret is that Carl Anderson did not live to perform at the Vatican. But I'm sure he's performing on a screen somewhere in the world at this very moment. Films are forever. The new DVD of *Superstar* will bring a whole new audience to this unique rock video. Like *Rollerball,* it was way ahead of its time.

12

Crowds Roar When
Lions Attack

In the not too distant future there will be
no wars, no poverty, but there will always
be Rollerball.

—Rollerball

When I was a kid, we listened to hockey on CBC Radio, Foster Hewitt
shouting, "He shoots, he scores!" We'd be dancing in the street if it was
the Maple Leafs and the winning goal was Syl Apps or Charlie
Conacher. My dad couldn't afford to take me to Maple Leaf Gardens,
but my gang played on an outdoor rink in Kew Beach Park with little
or no equipment—two *Saturday Evening Post* magazines tucked
inside big wool socks for shin pads, mittens for hockey gloves.

When the National Hockey League expanded into the United
States, hockey became a lot more violent than it had been in the days
of the Original Six. There were more players, higher stakes, and the
larger TV audiences loved the hits and fights, the crowds applauded,
the noise level grew, the players became bigger stars if they landed
more punches.

I remember one game in Chicago when one of the new breed of
"enforcers" threw a player against the boards and the whole place

erupted at the sight of blood on the white ice. The cops immediately moved down and into the aisles. They knew the mood of the fans, and they tensed.

Of course, there is nothing new about it, violence and entertainment have been linked since at least Roman times. In the vast arena of the Circus Maximus there was death every afternoon if the emperor chose. And the more difficult the times, the more people criticized him in the agora, the more he let the populace come and enjoy the gore, the violence, the deaths in the dust, where gladiators fought and lions devoured the enemies of the empire. Despite Hemingway's heroic portrayals, the bullfights were just another version of deaths in the afternoon, just another way to satisfy the blood lust of people who enjoy watching things die.

I've never really understood that common human urge. To this day, I don't understand why people love blood sport, what makes them run wild in the streets after soccer games and bash one another's heads in, what makes them howl for more when there is blood on the ice. But I have tried to grapple with it, tried to see it for what it is. That is one reason why I made *Rollerball*. It was my way of trying to understand violence and the high stakes involved in promoting violence—whether it's the emperor of ancient Rome, the owner of a sports franchise, the corporation that markets violent video games for kids, or films that glorify bloodshed, gore, and murder. The spurious pleasure they give the viewers is, for me, horrific, more disturbing even than gratuitous violence in the back streets and bars of most big cities.

The way we showed people's faces, their obvious delight in the blood, their almost sexual pleasure when they watch Rollerball—it was that transforming moment in the human psyche that makes crowds roar when lions attack. I wanted to make the audience think about that when they saw the movie.

Larry Auerbach had given me a copy of *Esquire* magazine with the short story, "Rollerball Murder," by a University of Arkansas professor called William Harrison. It had that sense of recognition I often feel when I come across a story that hooks into something I have been thinking about, something I have worried, like a kid worries a scab.

And this one had it all. It was about sponsored violence, and it was about a corporate society—the way the world would sacrifice the rights of individuals for corporate goals of profit. The multinational corporations, even then, before Enron and Worldcom, recognized no boundaries and no states. They operated above or beyond the law, much like they do today.

I was a passionate reader when I was growing up in the Beach, in the east end of Toronto. The area had always been working class, supporting the CCF, later the New Democrats (NDP), sometimes the Liberals, but never the Conservatives. I was a Kippendavie kid. Most of the families on Kippendavie Avenue were on relief, and everyone was deeply suspicious of the wealthy elite who lived in the large homes on Glen Manor Drive, or in Rosedale and Forest Hill. Later, like many of my street-smart friends, I was attracted to the ideas of George Bernard Shaw, Bertrand Russell, Norman Thomas, even Karl Marx. They were much more interesting and passionate than the stuffy Canadian establishment politics of Mackenzie King and R.B. Bennett. My boyhood friend Reid Scott, whom I knew from Cub Scouts right through high school at Malvern Collegiate, became the youngest provincial member of Parliament in history, representing the Beach area. He was a passionate member of the CCF and later became a provincial Superior Court judge.

One thing I've always been sure of is that I'm on the side of the working stiff and against the owners of the company store. I have always rebelled against authority—though the Navy knocked out some of my early rebelliousness. It did not, however, change my way of thinking. When I returned to university, I was tougher and even more determined to support every liberal cause that appeared, and I began to seriously study the history of the development of social justice in Western society. I was becoming a political animal.

I was devoted to my anthropology teacher, Professor Edmund Carpenter. He was a passionate and eloquent young American leftist who was later hounded off the University of Toronto campus by the RCMP. That was during the McCarthy era, and the long arm of the FBI and American paranoia reached up into Canada with little resistance from Ottawa, or from the president and chancellor of the university. It was the same outrage suffered by Reuben Shipp at the CBC.

Many years later Senator Keith Davey, who was at Victoria College (now Victoria University) with me, told somebody how he'd recruited me to work for the campus Liberal party. Little did he know that I was also attending rallies to support Joe Salsburg, our only Communist member of Parliament in 1948.

The whole idea of a class struggle, the excitement of worker solidarity against the oppression of capitalism, captured my imagination. No matter how naive or unsophisticated I was in 1948, these ideas influenced me in one way or another for the rest of my life.

Maybe this is why I have always felt that culture or the arts were pitted against commerce, that artists are often exploited and used by the networks and major studios. As I matured during my university days and became exposed to the teachings of different philosophers and historians, I began to question my simple ideas of right and wrong, and realized that life was a little more complex than I had first assumed. Politically I have always supported candidates and causes on the left of the political spectrum, both in the U.S. and Canada. From Robert Kennedy, Martin Luther King, and the American anti-gun movement, to Lester Pearson, Pierre Trudeau, and the Canadian coalition to ban land mines. So I guess when people accuse me of being a bleeding heart liberal and a propertied, leftish seeker of social justice, they are justified. It's true.

The summer of 1980 I met Pierre Elliott Trudeau for the first time. I was walking my dog along the beach close to our house in Malibu Colony when I saw a guy in a French bikini bathing suit with a woman wearing a wrap. I recognized her right away as Margot Kidder. It took a little longer to discover that the sporty-looking man with the full-body tan was Pierre Elliott Trudeau.

Margot told me she had brought him down to show him the beach, she had lost her car keys, couldn't get back and couldn't phone for help, everything was locked in the car.

"Can you help us out?" she asked in her warmly helpless way.

We walked back to our place, me wondering the whole time where in hell are the Mounties, the U.S. security detail, and why isn't some-one making sure our prime minister doesn't get stranded on a beach? Dixie was sitting outside on the deck, reading, when we arrived. She looked up casually when I explained about the keys and said I would drive them back. "Make sure you wash the sand off your feet," she advised the prime minister and went back to her reading as he hosed down his feet and Margot's. The following evening they invited us to an elegant dinner party in Malibu, hosted by the Canadian architect Arthur Erickson.

In 1981 when I was shooting *Best Friends,* I was invited by Allan Gotlieb, the Canadian ambassador to the United States, to attend a luncheon in the huge ballroom at the State Department during Prime Minister Trudeau's state visit to Washington. In his elegant Savile Row suit, with a red rose in the lapel, Trudeau stood before America's power elite and dazzled them all. His ease with languages amazed the diplomats, and his sharp and honest comments about our two coun-tries and their differences were eloquent and impressive. He was witty, erudite, and passionate.

At Sondra and Allan Gotlieb's official Washington residence that evening, in the company of Supreme Court judges, senators, con-gressmen, ambassadors, Pamela Harriman, Art Buchwald, and Ben Bradlee, editor of the *Washington Post,* Pierre danced the Charleston with Margot Kidder. No doubt about it, the Canadian embassy was one cool place that night.

Some years later, when Trudeau resigned as leader, I flew to Ottawa with Paul Anka and comedian Rich Little to appear at his farewell celebration at the Coliseum. I delivered the most heartfelt three-minute speech I have ever given. Though a great many people have tried to persuade me otherwise, I still think he was the best Canadian prime minister in the twentieth century.

I also had great respect and admiration for Mao Zedong, who united China into a world power during my lifetime. Despite human rights violations and heavy-handed politics, he did succeed in freeing one billion people from famine and serfdom.

I first visited China in 1976 before it was opened up to Western tourists. Ted Allan, a Canadian leftist who had served with the great Canadian humanitarian Dr. Norman Bethune and the republicans in the Spanish Civil War, asked me to help him make a film based on his book *The Scalpel and the Sword*, about the life of Dr. Bethune. The story moved from Montreal and Spain to China, where Bethune died while working as a medical doctor for the Chinese Communists.

We were invited to China by the Chinese government, which welcomed the making of a major motion picture on the life of someone they considered to be a national hero. It was, I thought, a real insight into a country at a time when all travel by Westerners was restricted and the United States did not even have an embassy. Because of Trudeau's close relationship with Zhou Enlai, Canada maintained an embassy in Beijing, as did the U.K. and Germany. Zhou Enlai and Mao Zedong had both died earlier that year—Zhou in January, and Mao in September. China had also experienced one of the worst earthquakes on record in late July, with more than 250,000 dead. So it would be a gross understatement to say that we were visiting China at a tumultuous time.

Accompanied by John Kemeny, Ted's producer, and Michael Spencer from the Canadian Film Development Corporation, we arrived in Beijing on a flight from Hong Kong in October 1976. The Gang of Four, including Mao's widow, Jiang Qing, had just been arrested and the situation was very tense. We were escorted everywhere by soldiers and accompanied by interpreters who spoke perfect English. They had all been trained by David Crook, who with his Canadian wife, Isabel, had been in China since the late 1930s. He had also served in the Spanish Civil War, fighting the fascists, and was now a professor at the Foreign Languages Institute at the University of Beijing. After Mao's death, he had been imprisoned by the revisionists but eventually released. He fascinated us with his firsthand account of the last thirty-five years in China's political history.

To the astonishment of the Canadian ambassador, we were invited to fly to Yunan to visit the caves where Mao had lived and written his famous articles during the Chinese civil war.

Crowds surrounded us at every turn. They were especially fascinated by Dixie, who had blondish hair in Little Orphan Annie
ringlets. I had brought a Polaroid camera. After taking a group photo,
I would wave the negative in the air and make strange incantations
and then watch everyone's amazement as the image slowly appeared.
I have never had a more captive and enthralled audience.

There were no hotels. No bathrooms. No toilets. No running water.
Few cars and no phones. Yet everyone seemed well fed and committed to helping one another. After my experience with Russian
communism in Moscow in 1966, this was refreshing, almost innocent
in its total dedication. To see hundreds of thousands of people all
dressed alike, all in the same color, all believing in the glory of their
promised destiny. At times one was just totally swept away by their
deep belief. This was brainwashing on a massive scale since no dissent
was tolerated. Tiny children in daycare centers would march in circles
chanting "Every grain of rice costs one drop of sweat."

When I returned to China twenty-five years after my first visit and
stayed on the twentieth floor of a modern hotel with full room service,
and saw firsthand the industrialization of China that has emerged so
quickly, I felt that I was witnessing a miracle. Only with a billion people
all pushing together could this be accomplished in such a short time.

Standing in Shanghai in 2000 counting twenty-six skyscrapers
being built simultaneously, I found it hard to remember how unde-
veloped it had been in 1976. Now people were rushing about in
Armani clothes and carrying cell phones. Traffic was clogging the
streets and the air was polluted. China was emerging as perhaps the
most powerful country in the twenty-first century. And Mao had
started it all.

I never ended up making *Bethune*. We couldn't get the financing.
The 1990 film was made by Canadian director Phillip Borsos, starring
Donald Sutherland, who was perfect casting for the charismatic
Canadian who had such a powerful influence on modern China.

When I returned to Malibu wearing my Mao hat, excited about
what I had seen, little did I know that the FBI would be staking out my
beach house some six months later.

During the last two years of his life, Jay Scott, the great film critic for the *Globe and Mail*, Canada's national newspaper, began to work on a book based on my films. He interviewed many of the people I had worked with over the years. And he urged me to request my FBI file under the Freedom of Information Act, which had been passed by Congress in 1966. My U.S. attorney, Roger Sherman, petitioned the Bureau twice. After months of stalling, we finally received a dozen pages from the FBI.

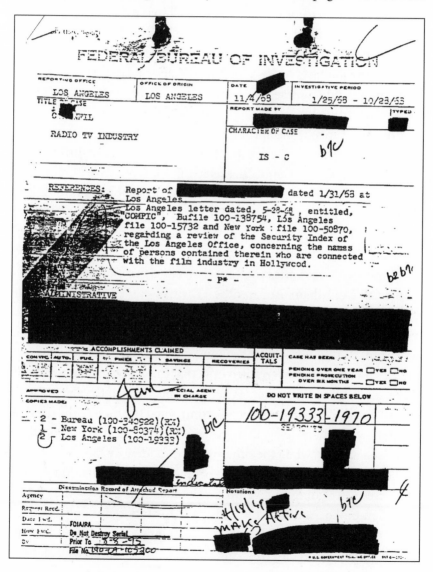

When I showed them to Jay, he laughed uproariously. "Man, they've blacked everything out! How the hell could you be any threat to the U.S.?"

It's always fascinated me that under Hoover the FBI could find the time to investigate people like me when there was such an abundance of crime, tax evasion, and real espionage taking place. It's common knowledge that there were thousands of files on individual citizens.

After I returned from my first trip to China in 1976, I had had my first encounter with the FBI. Paul Lin, a Chinese Studies professor at McGill University in Montreal, and his wife, Eileen, had been helpful in arranging contacts for us in China. Professor Lin was a supporter of the mainland Chinese government and was quite open about his views. He was invited to the University of California at Berkeley for a month of lectures in the spring of 1977. Since we had become close friends, I suggested they use our Malibu house as a base during their visit. Paul could travel up to Berkeley once a week to lecture. Eileen had a sister in Santa Monica and they had many friends in Los Angeles. Two, in particular, were also close friends of ours, Betty and Stanley Sheinbaum. Stanley was on the board of the American Civil Liberties Union and was politically active.

About two weeks after the Lins arrived at our home, I received a phone call from them. Apparently, a car was parked outside the gate night and day with two men inside. When they went out, the car followed them. They were upset and frightened. I called Stanley and asked him to find out what was going on. After a few calls to the Los Angeles police, it was ascertained only that the car was a rental and the lessee could not be identified. When the Lins went to the airport with some American friends, the friends confronted the men in the car that was following them. One man got out of the car and disappeared inside the airport, while the other refused to identify himself.

The Lins felt violated and left abruptly for Vancouver. I guess the FBI were never going to give up on the idea that I was some sort of Canadian pinko. And now I was also a Maoist in their books.

In April 1985 Farley Mowat, the distinguished Canadian author, was banned from entering the United States for "confidential reasons," according to the U.S. Immigration Service. This followed a speech in which President Reagan had praised artists in general and the freedom of expression that was so important to a free society like America. One moment praising the artist and the next, banning the artist. It's amazing how hypocritical governments can be.

All that latent socialism gave me the passion to make movies that extolled the virtues of the little guy, the guy who stands up to the powerful forces that deny his basic human rights. *Rollerball*, released in 1975, is one of those movies.

My L.A. agent, Larry Auerbach, once told a reporter, "I wish Norman would shut up about American politics—he is an outsider here." I think he was talking about my disillusionment with American politics in the 1960s, but he may as well have meant what I had wanted to convey with *Rollerball*. For me, the politics of corporations and the violence of the games the people watched were all part of the same pattern, the Circus Maximus of modern times. When Jimmy Caan and his team of players enter the rink and everyone stands for the corporate anthem before the games begin, I wanted to show the connection between violence and profit. And when Caan's character, Jonathan, faces off with the corporate leaders, I was showing the individual standing up against the pressure to be bought off by the comfort of not having to think for himself.

Jimmy Caan was the perfect choice for the great jock hero who tries to stand his ground, who misunderstands the larger focus of those who can buy and sell him. He had just finished filming *The Godfather, Part Two* and came out of the Mafia movie a hero. My main concern with Jimmy throughout the filming was that he wanted to do his own stunts. He was fearless. He had been a football player, a rodeo rider, and he was sure he could handle any physical challenge. We were shooting *Rollerball* in the days before computer animation, and I knew there would be difficult and dangerous action scenes.

But first, as I explained to Jimmy, we had to invent the game and the rules that the players had to follow.

William Harrison's short story had the barest of hints about what the game was—his interest was in the story, and the message. When we first met, he confessed he had always been fascinated by sports, by the audience they attracted, by their frequent brutality, but he had never given much thought to the rules they were played by. We sat on the terrace of my office at Pinewood Studios—an elegant eighteenth-century manor house—and we tried to make up the rules.

"Any game, Bill, no matter how mindless, has rules," I told him. "And most games have a ball, or something like a ball such as a puck, that everyone has to grab, throw, or snatch from another player, a ball that can land in a goal or hoop and give the fans a chance to roar their approval." By then, I had agreed to hire the soft-spoken Southerner to write the script with me. He was on sabbatical in England, enjoying the image of his small idea turning into mass entertainment.

I did my dance for United Artists, the men in their charcoal gray suits, watching and measuring how much the budget would be and would it sell. They were all there, Krim, Benjamin, Picker, and Bernstein, all dressed almost identically, silent, watching as I talked enthusiastically about "the game," the violence, the crowds, corporate society. In the end, one of them, I think Krim, asked if this was some sort of science fiction.

"Sure," I said, knowing they had been watching the grosses roll in from *A Clockwork Orange* and *2001: A Space Odyssey*. "It's my first film about a future society."

"The budget?"

"Five and a half million," Pat Palmer responded quickly. Pat had already prepared a detailed budget. He had been along for the ride on every picture since *Gaily, Gaily*, and stayed with *Rollerball* till the release of the film.

"Who's gonna star?"

"Jimmy Caan," I told them, having barely talked with Jimmy, but I knew him and knew he would like this role. He had done *Brian's Song*, a great jock film that everyone watched and cried through. *Rollerball* would be a good film for him. In addition, we had the same agent at William Morris—Stan Kamen.

As we were walking to the elevator, Krim said, "Okay, if you can do it for five and half, you've got a deal."

Bill Bernstein kept shaking his head. "Hell, Norman, if they wear those studs on their gloves, how the hell do they pick up the ball, never mind toss it? How do they hang on to the thing?" He rode down with Pat and me. All the way to Seventh Avenue, I began to frantically improvise the rules of the game, how the gloves worked, how the goal had a giant magnet, how the motorbikes and the players worked together. Only Palmer knew I was making it up as we went.

"Norman," he said when Bernstein had left, still shaking his head. "How in hell do we make this game work? How do we make this picture?" We began to laugh hysterically.

We worked out the whole game with tiny figures on a scale model of an arena, and ended up building the set on the site of the Munich Olympic Stadium. We found a German architect who had designed the bicycle track for the Olympics, and along with John Box, one of Britain's top productions designers, he constructed the perfect setting for the perfect blood sport played for high stakes for the entertainment of the masses.

Sir Ralph Richardson was a brilliant choice for the enigmatic keeper of the world's knowledge, which was stored in a giant computer in Geneva. Jimmy Caan turned out to be much more than a great athlete, he managed to convey the ultimate rebellion of the individual against all odds, however hopeless. The multi-talented John Houseman succeeded both as the evil corporate genius who understands the futility of individual action and envies the heroism of someone who tries anyway.

This was our vision of a future society in which political systems had failed and the multinational corporations now controlled all of society. Everyone was content, enslaved by the creature comforts provided by the multinationals.

Every day we shot on the track with some of the best stunt men and motorcycle riders in the world. Jimmy Caan and the other actors insisted on playing the game and doing their own stunts. I was filled with anxiety, fearing injuries to the cast. Today, of course, we have computer imaging, blue screen, and cable-assisted movement. There is little risk.

Sir Ralph Richardson was a true British eccentric. Already in his seventies, he insisted on riding a 350cc Harley Davidson to the studio every day, rain or shine. Wearing a huge canvas coat, goggles, and a helmet, he would roar onto the lot and skid right up to the stage door. Everyone would scatter when they heard him coming. He loved to go to lunch with me, where he would proceed to order a large steak and a bottle of the best claret, topped off by a pudding—and never picked up the check. He had a very talkative parrot, which often perched on his shoulder. Sir Ralph would forget the bird was there and take off on the motorbike, the bird screaming as he hung on for dear life.

When the movie was released in Europe, the reviews talked about the story, about the ideas Bill Harrison, Pat Palmer, and I were trying to convey about a future society. In the United States, moviegoers were excited about the violence in the game. How is it played? they asked. Can we open a franchise? Most American critics missed the point of the story.

In 2002 MGM/UA did a remake of *Rollerball* but left out the central political motivation of the story. It turned into a chaotic action picture. We pleaded with them not to proceed with the project but to no avail. It was an expensive failure.

F.I.S.T., released in 1978, also has that same sense of outrage I have carried with me since my childhood, together with the determination that the little guy could make a difference. *F.I.S.T.* is a story about the betrayal of the American labor movement. Sylvester Stallone starred as the Jimmy Hoffa figure, a guy who starts out with all the right ideals but is corrupted by power. It's the corruption, the betrayal of the ideals that really interested me about the story of the Teamsters Union.

I was fascinated by Joe Eszterhas's series in *Rolling Stone* about what had happened to Hoffa, about gangsters and high rollers, the violence that had become a hallmark of the labor movement in America. In hindsight, I can see why Arthur Krim said no. "Norman, no one is interested in the labor movement," he told me in his office after I described the movie. I stressed how important this movie would be. He just looked at me and kept saying, "It's expensive, it's period, and no one is gonna see it."

Later, we were sitting in one of those fine restaurants in New York where they give you linen napkins, and I asked the waiter for a paper one. I jotted down all the grosses from my movies, the money they would have seen roll in since they hired me, the grosses on *Fiddler*, *The Russians*, *Heat of the Night*, *Thomas Crown*. And I looked at him over the rim of my glasses. "Arthur, you owe me," I said.

He looked at the numbers. After a long pause, he sighed and agreed. "If you can get Stallone for the lead, we'll make it."

Sly Stallone had just finished making the first Rocky movie. He was a big star even by Hollywood standards. His film had won an Academy Award, he was macho America, he was a folk hero. At first he loved the story, he loved doing something totally different after Rocky, but he ended up wanting to change history. He kept going back to being Rocky, the hero, long after Jimmy Hoffa had stopped being heroic. He wanted Jimmy to survive.

I kept telling him that Jimmy Hoffa is somewhere under the New Jersey Turnpike, and that's how the film has to end. Sly had become so fixed in his hero role by then he simply couldn't face that his Hoffa character wouldn't be redeemed, wouldn't survive and somehow win.

Our relationship was never easy and became more difficult as we neared the end of the movie. Sly always considered himself a writer. He began to rewrite Joe Eszterhas's script. Joe went crazy and argued about every change. Sly pushed back. Joe, a burly Hungarian, challenged Stallone to a fist fight. I, of course, was in the middle. I couldn't lose Stallone—UA would cancel the picture. Yet my first obligation as a director was to the writer, to the story itself. I had worked with Joe on the script for more than a year. It had become a close relationship since Joe had never written a screenplay. I had become his mentor and tried to protect him.

Stallone had hit success early and unfortunately was not easy to deal with. He behaved like he believed his own publicity. Years later, I was told that Stallone considered me one of the best directors he had ever worked with, that he was proud of his performance in *F.I.S.T.* Strange.

I had a similar experience with Al Pacino in *And Justice for All*. I walked off the set once as we were about to shoot a scene for the third or fourth time, went outside and sat on the curb. Al looked around and noticed nothing was happening. "Why aren't we shooting?" he asked.

He was told it was because Norman had left.

"What's all that about?" he asked.

He was told I was going home. Pacino came out and sat down beside me on the curb.

"Look," I told him, "you see it one way and I see it another way. You might as well direct the picture, I'll go home."

He thought about it for a while, then he agreed to do the scene the way I had asked. He didn't want to be known as a difficult guy to work with.

Pacino is a brilliant performer, he can portray anger better than anyone I have ever worked with, better even than Steiger, who had been magnificent in *F.I.S.T.*, screaming at Stallone's Hoffa. Pacino, when he lets go his anger, explodes, it's like releasing a Doberman. But all the time he is in control. Pacino's last summation to the jury is a classic film moment. He received an Oscar nomination for it but didn't win.

In *And Justice for All*, I wanted to examine the American judicial system. I wanted to tell a story that made people think about whether the system still allowed for justice, as it had been designed to do, or was it now all about winning, plea bargains, and the legal maneuvering of counsel rather than a search for truth.

America is a litigious society. In twenty years, every tenth person in the U.S. will be a lawyer. There is one justice for the rich and another for the poor. I am convinced of it. The American Bar Association hated the film, but recently I was invited to a Harvard Law Society gathering to discuss the film, so maybe it did at least stir up some controversy.

Arthur Krim turned out to have been right about *F.I.S.T.* No one in America wanted to see a movie about the labor movement. For me, on a personal level, it was the least fun I had ever had directing.

The film I should have made, one of the ones that got away, was *The Dogs of War*, and for years after, I regretted my decision. I was immediately attracted to the book and to the author. Frederick Forsyth lived in an Irish country house with freshly painted shutters, a big garden, horses in the paddocks. He was a tall, good-looking man, at first about as welcoming as if we had drifted off the road by accident and were asking for alms. He had a natural suspicion of Hollywood. But he relaxed somewhat after a long walk in his garden, a couple of debilitatingly stiff drinks, and my telling him how I felt about his story.

We had already sold United Artists on making the film—this time it wasn't difficult since *The Dogs of War* was a bestseller. I worked on the screenplay with Abbie Mann, then later with Gary DeVore. We spent some time flying around war-torn Africa, meeting with mercenaries in Sierra Leone, Ghana, Gambia, Liberia. We would have included Uganda on our schedule, but the plane had barely landed when we were surrounded by gun-toting, uniformed thugs whose affiliation with Idi Amin's government was not much of a comfort. What we discovered was hardly surprising: most of the mercenaries were recruited by big corporations to protect commercial interests. The rest were bodyguards for corrupt leaders or were there to provide training for the palace guards. In the bush we also stumbled upon military units from Cuba and China. It's amazing what you can find when you travel light and move quickly down the back roads.

It would have been a good follow-up to *Rollerball* for me, but Pat Palmer and I had contracted to deliver *F.I.S.T.* at about the same time. So, while Pat and I were setting up *F.I.S.T.* in Illinois, we flew down twice to Belize, where *The Dogs of War* was being shot, to provide support and encouragement on a difficult location shoot. We were fortunate that a regiment of British soldiers had been stationed in the country to protect the Belize borders from Guatemala. They provided us with excellent extras and military advisers for the screenplay, which dealt with the forced takeover of an African country by a mercenary force.

Larry De Waay, my production manager on *Superstar*, and John Irvin, the British director, did a heroic job shooting *The Dogs of War* in the swamps of Belize. The film starred Christopher Walken, Tom Berenger, and Colin Blakely. Larry went on to have a brilliant career as a producer in the U.K. and Europe. He produced *Yentl* with Barbra Streisand in Prague and *Rob Roy* with Liam Neeson in Scotland. John Irvin went on to make *Hamburger Hill* and, most recently, *The Boys from County Clare*.

The Dogs of War is one film I would rather have directed than produced, but I was proud to be associated with it in any capacity. It had modest success in North America but was well received in Europe, where there is more interest in African politics and a better understanding of the underside of corporate power in poor countries.

Almost every film I have produced and not directed started out as a development that I personally wanted to direct for the screen. Producing alone has never had much interest for me. The excitement is always in the actual making of the film. However, starting with *The Landlord*, which served to establish Hal Ashby's career, I have produced six feature films, one cable movie, and two television series.

In the constant search for an indigenous Canadian story a friend, Joan Cohl, came across an unusual collection of short stories entitled *The Fencepost Chronicles* by W.P. Kinsella and passed it on to me. It dealt with life among the aboriginal Ermineskin band in Alberta. The stories were filled with strong, eccentric characters, like Mad Etta (the Medicine Woman), Silas Ermineskin, and his buddy Frank Fencepost. The book won the Stephen Leacock Award for Humour in 1987. The stories were filled with protest and past wrongs but captured the smart, ironic humor of modern native people. What a relief to meet such hip and enlightened characters.

I wrote to Kinsella and arranged to meet with him at my central Toronto offices, which are housed in a century-old building that was once a factory for building furniture. Occasionally, the sawdust still floats down from the wooden ceiling and lands on my desk. Kinsella, to my surprise, turned out to be a lanky ex-hippie who was teaching creative writing at the University of Calgary. He was pleased, I think, that I wanted to option one of his stories for a screenplay. It was called "Dance Me Outside." But he turned down my offer to write it. I had the feeling he rather dismissed filmwriting as something not requiring a lot of talent. An earlier book he had written called *Shoeless Joe* was adapted into a highly successful baseball film, *Field of Dreams*, starring Kevin Costner.

My son Michael suggested we try to involve a native writer. Tomson Highway, a native playwright from Manitoba, is a talented and sensitive writer who had recently authored a successful play, *The Rez Sisters*, and agreed to take on this task. After reading Tomson's first draft, I felt the screenplay needed more work and I brought in Howard Wiseman, a young writer, and finally, Don McKellar and John Frizzell, a more experienced team of film and television writers. By this time, I was deeply involved with *Only You* so I turned the project over to Bruce McDonald, the talented young filmmaker who had once been my driver on *Agnes of God.*

Bruce was as hip and out there as any of the native characters in the story. With Brian Dennis as producer, and Sarah Hayward from my company, we raised the budget from Telefilm, CBC, and Cineplex and made a deal with the chief of the Shawanaga Ojibway Reserve, just north of Parry Sound.

Dance Me Outside attracted and developed several talented aboriginal actors from various Indian nations across Canada, and Bruce gave it lots of energy, filled it with exciting visuals and a strong rock music score composed by Mychael Danna. It was well received at the Toronto International Film Festival in 1994 where it opened the *Canadian Perspective* series. It went on to win an award at the American Indian Film Festival in San Francisco and two Genies from the Academy of Canadian Cinema and Television.

In the spring of 1995, Michael and I met with Ivan Fecan, vice-president of CBC Television's English-language services, and sold him on the idea of a spin-off TV series called *The Rez*. Bruce directed the first three episodes and then we hired various young directors. The writing of over twenty-one half-hour episodes proved to be the most difficult part of that endeavor.

A year previously, in the spring of 1994, Ted Turner had announced he was going to finance six films dealing with Native American culture. I was anxious to continue working with stories about aboriginal people so I campaigned to produce a film for the Turner Network, based on Geronimo, the legendary native revolutionary.

The film was shot in desert locations near Tucson, Arizona, with Chris Cook of my L.A. office producing for our Yorktown Company. Ted Turner's then wife, Jane Fonda, was also producing a film in the series, and I was impressed that Turner Broadcasting was investing over $30 million in Native American stories.

Our film opened the series with the highest-rated television audience for a cable movie on the network, receiving so much attention it hurt the box office receipts of another feature film released by Columbia at the same time and with the same title. *Geronimo* cost a little over $6 million; their film was budgeted at five times that.

Two other feature films that I produced but did not direct were *Iceman* and *January Man*. *Iceman* was directed by Fred Schepisi, starring John Lone, Timothy Hutton, and Lindsay Crouse, and shot in various arctic locations. *January Man* was written by John Patrick Shanley and directed by Patrick O'Connor, starred my old friend Rod Steiger, with Kevin Kline, Susan Sarandon, and Harvey Keitel. Although I worked hard on all these projects, I have never considered them my films. Producing, no matter how much you are involved in the script, casting, locations, and budget considerations, is still not the same function as directing the film. Movies are, in the final analysis, a director's medium.

When shooting on *Iceman* began, I was still working on *A Soldier's Story* but I had to fly up to Churchill, Manitoba, and take over some of the rough location work for Fred Schepisi, who apparently broke his ankle during the first week of shooting. Pat Palmer, my co-producer, told me that Fred, in an attempt to prove that Australians were just as tough as Canadians, was injured in a hand-wrestling bout with a very large, strong Canuck. I have a suspicion that alcohol might have played a part in this event.

Having a director in a plaster cast on crutches at locations covered in ice and snow, accessible only by snowmobile and helicopter, was an enormous problem for everyone. In Churchill one weekend, I found myself on a Ski-Doo roaring down the railway line at temperatures close to minus 30. The camera assistants carried the unexposed film cans underneath their parkas, close to their bodies. At the last moment they'd load the camera while another assistant held a hair dryer full blast on their fingers so they wouldn't instantly freeze.

It was the first time I had seen a polar bear hunting on the pack ice of Hudson Bay. As a matter of fact, the bears were so plentiful that a siren would sound every so often, warning the local citizens of Churchill to grab their kids and sled dogs and bring them to shelter while the bear roamed through town.

One of my most hair-raising experiences happened on another *Iceman* location north of Stewart, British Columbia, which has the reputation of having the most snow in North America. The tiny mining town sits right on the Alaskan border—the local Mountie shares his jail cell with the Alaska state trooper.

The last scene in *Iceman* required a stuntman in bearskin costume to fall from the skids of a helicopter over vast arctic glaciers. Since Fred was still hobbling around in his cast, I volunteered to shoot the stunt. We would have to wait for the right weather conditions and the logistics would all have to be perfectly coordinated because lives would be at risk. Remember, this was 1985, before the era of computer imaging.

Dar Robinson was one of the best and most experienced movie stuntmen in the world. I had used him on *Rollerball* and his credits were exceptional.

On aerial stunts, weather is always the most important factor. The bitter cold was constant but what we needed was a clear day with little wind. Since the stunt would take place over glaciers with crevasses, it required park rangers on the ground with rescue equipment and small flags to mark the dangerous landing spots so that when the chutes opened they could help direct the stuntmen and pick them up immediately on their snowmobiles. My job would be to direct the sequence and make sure we did not have to do a retake. "This is an expensive shot," Pat Palmer, the line producer, kept growling, "let's not screw it up."

The four of us gathered every morning over coffee to examine weather reports with our helicopter pilot and the park rangers. After three days of waiting, we were given the green light. Dar got into makeup and costume. A single chute was strapped tightly to his chest under the bearskin. His long black wig was anchored to his head. The plan was he and the cameraman would free-fall from an altitude of 10,000 feet. When they reached the minimum height for a chute to open, Dar would tear off his costume, which was Velcroed carefully, and the shot would be finished. What if the Velcro froze? What if Dar's hands froze? What if they landed in a bottomless crevasse? What if the helmet camera jammed? These thoughts were whirling through my mind as we climbed into the Bell chopper.

The pilot had given us a distinct warning that when the two people jumped off, the helicopter would veer to one side and I must shift my weight immediately so we wouldn't flip over. A small helicopter is carefully balanced for weight and not generally used for parachute jumping. We climbed steadily in huge circles over the vast white glaciers, all of us listening to the steady beat of the blades. There was too much noise to talk.

Dar Robinson was chewing gum, trying to stay calm, going over in his mind every move he would have to make without a second of hesitation. I shifted two sandbags to my side of the helicopter and secured a thick rope around my waist, which was tied to the back of the pilot's seat. Dar smiled at my quaint safety rigging. I wondered what motivates someone to risk his life for a shot in a movie. Was it some sort of death wish? Was it the thrill of the ultimate gamble? Whatever fee Dar had negotiated with Pat Palmer, $10,000 or $20,000, at this moment I wouldn't jump for anything you could possibly give me.

The pilot turned and gave a thumbs-up. We had reached our altitude. I asked him through the intercom if the rangers on the glacier below were ready. "Everything affirmative." His voice was calm and thick with a Yorkshire accent. What was an English pilot doing up here, I wondered. "Are we ready?" I shouted at the two stuntmen, who smiled and nodded as if they were going to bail off a hay wagon. We slid open the door; a rush of arctic air filled the cabin. The noise was deafening. Dar very quickly turned to face me and stepped out onto the skids. He pressed himself against the window, hanging on to the tiny rain gutter with his fingers, which were poking out of cut-off woolen gloves. He clung there like a fly while the cameraman climbed out the door.

It was essential the two jump at almost the same instant. Dar, in his windblown wig and bearskin costume, looked unbelievably calm—like Sam McGee, sitting in the furnace. With a scream of "Geronimo!" he let go and the camera operator dived after him. The copter tilted immediately to a 45-degree angle as I slid toward the open door, frantically trying to claw at the floor. I could feel my feet hanging outside and suddenly, in a panic, I was filled with a strength I never knew I had as I yanked myself back inside with my rope and slammed the door. The pilot straightened the chopper immediately and we banked to watch the two bodies gracefully free-falling through the sky. It seemed they soared forever like two eagles in an updraft. "Open the chutes!" I pleaded to no one. "Please open the chutes!" Time seemed to stop. Then to our great relief, the camera operator's chute opened, and at the last minute, Dar's costume broke away and his chute blossomed in the cobalt-blue sky. I couldn't wait to get the camera back to base camp. In two days we could call the Technicolor Labs in Los Angeles and hopefully get a positive report on our exposed negative. We all had a great celebration that night and an even bigger one when L.A. called and said the shot was great and Dar could go home.

Stuntmen are a special breed, and movie-making has claimed too many of their lives.

13

The Truth Can Hurt You

Hatred got me into this place

Love's gonna bust me out

—*Rubin Carter, The Hurricane*

What makes a good picture? Ideas. It's the idea behind the screenplay that matters. It's the idea behind the work that makes a movie meaningful. A movie is like a painting, or a book: it can be entertaining, pretty, exhibit great technical skill, we can admire its brushstrokes, the attention to detail, the eloquence of its dialogue, the mastery of its composition. But if there is no essence, no meaning to the work itself, the audience, the viewer, forgets it. Every work of art that is important has a strong idea behind it. It's what grabs us immediately—at least that's how I see what good art is. It's what I try to reach for in most of my pictures: a thought-provoking idea, a strong theme. The films that remain with us are those that reveal some insight into human nature. These are the best kinds of films. They are about something, they communicate with their audience in an almost visceral way.

There are hundreds of films we have enjoyed or admired. There are a few we really love. That's what is so exciting about film: that it can speak intimately to each one of us, and some stay with us forever.

When I was thirteen years old I saw George Stevens's *Gunga Din*. Thanks to Aunt Bea, I already knew the Kipling poem by heart and loved every word of it. It is a poem about a dark-skinned, low caste water-boy in a British army unit fighting in Afghanistan's Khyber Pass, and it had everything going for it: it was about loyalty, sacrifice, honor, and it was, of course, also about racism. George Stevens had made a roaring red-blooded swashbuckler from the poem, and every kid at the Beach Theatre wanted to see it over and over. I could barely tear myself away from the screen. The movie had a stellar cast, though that would not have meant a lot to me, then. All I knew was that everything in that movie spoke to me. I didn't know that the trio of tough, rebellious British soldiers were Cary Grant, Victor McLaglen, and Douglas Fairbanks, nor that the movie was not shot in the Khyber Pass but in the California desert. I believed in the magic.

There are so many unforgettable great classic movies that still talk to audiences: *The Third Man*, an almost perfectly constructed film, Fellini's *8½*, John Huston's *The Treasure of the Sierra Madre*, Kurosawa's *Seven Samurai*, Bergman's *Fanny and Alexander*, and almost any movie directed by Billy Wilder. These are movies that continue to play in "the windmills of our minds" perhaps forever.

I have been thrilled this way in the theater, in the concert hall, art galleries, museums and, strangely enough, even in hockey arenas. The moment of truth, the sense that I am experiencing something of importance, always involves some insight into the human condition, some revelation about ourselves. That's what good movies are about. They involve us in the lives of others so that we see what they see, experience what they experience, and so provide a key to understanding or relating to our own experience.

For John Huston *The Dead* was such a movie. When the studios wouldn't support it, he made it independently, on a small budget, in a warehouse in Anaheim, in the stifling heat, struggling with his health. It was a tough shoot for a seventy-nine-year-old director with an oxygen tank on his back. But he finished it and was proud of his work. *The Dead* was his last film and, in my opinion, his most profound. It has been said that John Huston's last words, whispered into the ear of his nurse, were "Fix the bayonets...get ready for the charge." Perhaps he was preparing for a final battle.

I had met John Huston in the early 1960s. He was physically imposing, tall, with a shock of white hair, piercing eyes, his voice almost a whisper, his laughter infectious, his charm irrepressible. He smoked those thin cigarillos and loved to tell stories about his service in the Mexican cavalry, his attempts to find pre-Columbian art, his films and loves.

Of my own films, I think the most clear-eyed, those that go closest to the heart of the human condition, are *In the Heat of the Night, The Hurricane,* and *A Soldier's Story.* Some people tell me *Moonstruck* belongs to this group because it goes to the nature of love. The other three are all about being black in America. They deal with racial prejudice.

Americans love to talk about the Constitution and how it protects the rights of every citizen, but America is also a country based on racism, a country where prejudice has thrived. The South, so proud of its fine heritage, its passion for the land, its adherence to traditions, was built on the backs of African slaves. They don't talk about that too much in the drawing rooms of Georgia.

Every time a film deals with racism, many Americans feel uncomfortable. Yet it has to be confronted. We have to deal with prejudice and injustice or we will never understand what is good and evil, right and wrong; we need to feel how "the other" feels.

In an interview with Trevor Phillips of *The Guardian,* Denzel Washington said he understood that the racial prejudice that made it possible to own and treat slaves as chattel is something passed down from generation to generation; it's not easily obliterated, nor forgotten. Even now, despite his own celebrity, he feels it. Denzel is in both *The Hurricane* and *A Soldier's Story.*

When I signed Denzel to play the killer in *A Soldier's Story*, I knew he was destined to be an important movie actor. The camera loved

him. He was intelligent, rebellious, totally confident, and spectacularly talented. He was so confident he often thought he knew more
than the director, but he watched and learned. He never believed the
film was going to work until after he saw it finished. He didn't stop
being above it all until he saw the film with an audience and realized
how well it worked.

A few years later we took a long walk on the beach in Malibu
together. I told him he should play Malcolm X, that he should always
put the story and the director ahead of the deal. Money, I said and I
really believe this, is not the most important thing in an actor's career.
If you choose the right films, the money will follow.

His manager, Flo Allen, made the deal with Warner Brothers, and
Denzel did end up making the Malcolm X film. I had wanted to make
this movie. I didn't because Spike Lee also wanted to make it.

Marvin Worth, who did the documentary and had bought the
rights to the *Autobiography of Malcolm X*, signed me to direct. We had
a screenplay by Charles Fuller, who had written *A Soldier's Story*, and
an older script by James Baldwin and Arnold Perl. There were other
attempts at scripts, but none of them came close to working for me. I
wanted to know and understand the real Malcolm X, the person who
had made such an impact on America, both black and white, who was
the inspiration for generations of young, uncompromising black
men—men who would not be the Sergeant Vernon Waters of the
future, men who would not go to the back of the bus.

I had wanted to meet Betty Shabazz, Malcolm X's widow, and his
daughters. One of the daughters said they wanted me to make the
movie, but they could tell me little about their father other than what
I already knew. Betty Shabazz didn't come to the meeting in a New
York restaurant downtown. Marvin and I waited for an hour and a
half and then left.

The letter-writing campaign to get me off the movie had already
started. The media, ever hungry for a juicy tale, picked it up and
chewed it over. A white director making a film about a black hero?
And it was now all about me and Spike, and not about the story of
Malcolm X that we had both wanted to make. Lee went on talk shows

complaining that white directors should not make black movies, that he knew there were people who had been close to Malcolm X who'd talk to him and would never talk to me. As a white man, no matter how well intentioned, he maintained, I could never know Malcolm X. Prejudice was everywhere.

The letter-writing campaign escalated. Both Terry Semel of Warner Brothers, who had backed Marvin Worth, and Worth himself kept telling me they were still ready to have me direct, but the atmosphere had become too ugly.

In the end, the two of us met at Cibo's on Fifty-third near Fifth Avenue. It was at my invitation, through his agent. He wore his baseball cap and I wore mine. We talked about Malcolm. I wished him well with the movie. "One thing, Spike," I told him, "just don't screw it up."

That's how Denzel Washington ended up making the Malcolm X film with Spike Lee and not me.

It was the winter of 1983. I had just finished making *Best Friends*, a light romantic film written by Barry Levinson and his first wife, Valerie Curtin. It starred Goldie Hawn and Burt Reynolds and was a rather smart movie about marriage and friendship. Its title song, "Keep the Music Playing," written by my favorite composers, the Bergmans and Michel Legrand, became an enormous hit. Quincy Jones helped us to produce the soundtrack with Patti Austin and James Ingram.

My friend Charles Schulz—affectionately known as Chizz—called from New York and told me I had to drop everything and come see a play at the Negro Ensemble Company theater on Fifty-seventh Street. *A Soldier's Play* had opened in November to good reviews but not a lot of excitement. Still, Chizz insisted it would be perfect for me. Even before I left for New York, he sent me a copy of the script and admitted he was a friend of the playwright's, Charlie Fuller, and they had talked about my making a movie based on the play because they were both fans of *In the Heat of the Night*.

The play bowled me over. Adolph Caesar, Larry Riley, and Denzel Washington gave extraordinary performances—as they did, again, in the movie. The cast was mostly black. The story is set in 1944, in Fort

Neil, Louisiana, in the all-black 221st regiment of the U.S. Army. Sergeant Vernon Waters is shot and killed one night on a dusty road not far from the base. The white officers—only the officers were white in the all-black regiment—think it's a racial killing, one of several unsolved murders in the unit, but the camp commander is not too keen to find out who did it because it might anger the white towns-folk near the camp. This is, after all, Louisiana, in the Deep South, where hanging or shooting black men was not so unusual.

The Army, wanting to be seen as fair, sends a young, educated black officer to investigate: Captain Davenport, as polished as the white officers on the base, trained in law at Harvard, better able to understand the politics of the place. He sets out to discover as much as he can about the murdered Sergeant Waters. Davenport believes that in finding out about Waters, he will find out who killed him.

After the play, Charles introduced me to Fuller, a quiet, ruggedly handsome, very tall black man. He had been as anxious to hear my reaction as I was to tell him the play was brilliant and that I was deter-mined to make the movie, if he was willing. I discovered that the play had been somewhat inspired by the experiences of his father and his best friend, Larry Neale, a playwright himself, both of whom died while he was writing A Soldier's Play. The character of Davenport is loosely based on Neale and the play was dedicated to his memory.

We ate dinner at Tavern on the Green in Central Park. Long before it was over, we agreed I would go to a studio and ask them to put up the money, and that I would ask for over $100,000 for him to write the screenplay.

I didn't think it would be difficult to find the financing. I had made fifteen successful movies. But I was wrong. No one really wanted to put up the money. I discovered that Sidney Poitier had already tried to do what I was doing and been turned away.

I had been making a very commercial film for Warner at the time and, fortunately for me, they thought they could extend the contract if they bought the play as a gesture—"Let's keep Jewison happy." Barely a month after I first saw the play, and only a couple of months after it had opened, I had the rights. But I believe the studio had no intention of putting up the money to make the movie. I think they imagined I would get over it by the time the screenplay was finished. I wasn't. If anything, I was even more determined to make *A Soldier's Story*.

Both MGM and Universal turned me down. I tried to explain to Frank Price of Columbia that it would be successful commercially, that it was really a murder mystery with a new twist, that it would be a prestigious film for his studio to make. When he didn't react, I said I would make it for nothing. At this, he leaned forward and said, "You'll make the film for nothing?"

I said, "Yes, sir. But you wouldn't mind if I had just a tiny piece of the gross? Just in case I'm right and someone comes to see it, after all?"

He agreed to give me a budget of $5 million. Later, he told me he thought with that kind of commitment, there was a chance I might be right. In April, the play was awarded the Pulitzer Prize. Then it won the New York Drama Critics Award for best new play, the Theatre Club Award for best play, and went on to win an Obie.

Charlie Fuller and I spent many hours talking over how the script for the movie would work from the strengths of the play and adding parts the play couldn't accommodate. We talked about the nature of the army base, how the men were treated, how they responded to Davenport's arrival. We expanded Davenport's role for the film. More important, we talked about the whole pervasive culture of racism. The inverse racism of the kind Sergeant Waters is steeped in, the kind that denies any connection with the past, thrived in America while the movie was made. It was black against black racism, a reflection of the self-denial still apparent in America. When you have lived in a racist society for centuries, you can't help becoming part of the fabric of discrimination. It's like a disease, if you don't deal with it, you can't beat it.

The budget didn't allow me to sign established stars, but star talent we had anyway. Howard Rollins Jr., Adolph Caesar, Patti LaBelle, Larry Riley, Denzel Washington.

Production began on September 10, 1983, in Clarendon, Arkansas, a small community on the banks of the White River, then a few days in Little Rock, and nine weeks in Fort Chaffee, a big World War II vintage army base where German prisoners of war had been housed. Fort

Chaffee, now a National Guard base, is close to Fort Smith, a sprawl-ing town of some sixty thousand people, mostly white. We had a devil of a time engaging extras, mostly because the young black men of the town didn't want their hair cut off for the parts of army recruits. We hired as many black crew members as possible. We had black techni-cians, stunt coordinators, first assistant director, casting director, stylists, makeup.

Dixie came down to find a house for us. It had a little pond with koi carp. When you rang a bell they came to the surface to be fed. A couple of young Vietnamese kids who had recently arrived in America came every day after school to ring the bell and feed the koi their favorite foul-smelling crumbs. The kids watched us with as much curiosity as we watched them.

On Thanksgiving Day, Dixie cooked a huge turkey dinner for cast and crew. She was heroic, as were all the actors, going on day after day in the harrowing heat and dust of the base, up at six every morning to make the most of the day, and often carrying on late into the frigid nights. When Patti LaBelle sang her Big Mama number, you could see your breath it was so cold on the set of the bar.

Howard Rollins Jr. played Davenport with great panache and a constant sense that there is barely suppressed fury under the polish. He insisted on carrying an umbrella for the part, and wore dark glasses because General MacArthur wore shades. His father died of Lou Gehrig's disease while we were filming. Rollins insisted on finish-ing the scene he was shooting and gave an amazing performance. Later, I found out that he had dropped out of university against his father's wishes and had only recently succeeded in convincing Howard Sr. that he had the makings of a fine actor.

One day when we were filming, Bill Clinton, then only thirty-seven and already governor of Arkansas, stopped by to visit the set. Arkansas was a poor state and he was anxious to attract film production, much as Canada does its best to attract production now. He had instructed the people at the state film office to award a ten percent rebate for every dollar spent in the state. Since we would be working on such a tight budget, that had got our attention and we stopped looking elsewhere. I don't think the U.S. Army was wildly enthusiastic about a film dealing with a segregated regiment in World War II, but I was able to get permission through a friend in the State Department.

There was an important scene in the film where our black soldiers play a game of baseball against an all-white team. We found the perfect vintage stadium in Little Rock. With period costumes and a huge crowd of extras, it would add an exciting bit of visual drama to the movie. The day we shot this scene was the day Governor Clinton visited the set. He was tall, casually dressed in slacks and sports jacket, with a ready smile and an easy way with everybody. He seemed to be almost as excited about being on a movie set as our cast and crew were to meet him. He had read the play. He thought it had an important message. He was fascinated by the paraphernalia of movie-making. At one point I put him on a crane to show him how we could get a wide-angle shot of the whole stadium, and showed him how the zoom worked, and how we made our two hundred extras look like a huge crowd.

That first visit had made it easy for me to call on him later, when I needed some help with the last scene of the film, the one where over two hundred black soldiers march off to war. It would be a stirring, powerful shot panning along all those brave young faces, ready to fight for the honor of their country. My problem was we couldn't find enough trained extras with our meager budget. I explained the scene and fessed up to our problem. The governor said, "Hmm." Then he called in the general in charge of the National Guard.

On the second to last day of filming, all the black soldiers of the local contingent of the National Guard marched into Fort Chaffee, and we finished shooting *A Soldier's Story*.

Some ten years later, Dixie and I were invited to the inauguration of William Jefferson Clinton as President of the United States. Unfortunately, we were not able to attend, but in the fall of 1994 we were invited to stay at the White House. I was overwhelmed at the prospect, the monumental history of the place, but all Dixie could think about was how we would ever get home alive. "Everybody is a sitting duck in that place," she warned grimly. "Remember that incident with the small plane?" When Senator Barbara Boxer from California reassured her, she finally agreed to accept. She was somewhat comforted by the security clearance procedures and the armed marines, but kept looking over her shoulder as we were escorted into the White House and up the staircase to the Lincoln bedroom.

That evening we were premiering *Only You* with Marisa Tomei, Robert Downey Jr., and Bonnie Hunt for a celebrity Washington screening that would benefit AmeriCorps, the urban peace corps. First Lady Hillary Clinton was our guest of honor.

In the late afternoon, Dixie called me over to the window. President Clinton and Nelson Mandela had appeared on the lawn to give a press conference. I strained to hear but couldn't open the window. Dixie wandered off, looking for a spot where she could have a cigarette. She asked a maid, who showed her some stairs to the roof. Dixie climbed the stairs, put a brick in the door so she wouldn't be locked out, lit up, and strolled out onto the roof. Just at that moment, President Clinton was introducing President Nelson Mandela to the press on the South Lawn. Fascinated with his speech, Dixie leaned over the balustrade and had a front-row seat to a very historic occasion. Talk about security: I had to wonder whether the secret service even noticed her there.

That night I helped Dixie climb onto the high four-poster bed in the Lincoln bedroom. I've no idea when she finally drifted off, but I was far too excited to sleep. I sat at Lincoln's desk reading the handwritten Gettysburg Address and mused on the events of the Civil War that led to the Emancipation Proclamation in 1863, freeing four million slaves in these United States, signed in this very room. I wrote letters to my children on White House stationery, trying to capture the moment. I stared out the window at the marine guard, the lights spilling across the vast green lawn where the small platform stood, ready for the president to greet the next head of state.

At 7 a.m. a helicopter landed on the lawn. I shook Dixie awake and we both dressed and hurried downstairs to the sunny breakfast room on the second floor.

We had almost finished our coffee when the president arrived with a couple of his staff and a man he introduced as his brother-in-law. He was as relaxed now as he had been the first time we met: no fuss, no formality, and an interest in hearing our views. We talked about the problems of inner-city kids and our efforts to raise funds for young people who worked in the inner cities across America. We talked about gun control, and the president talked about *Soldier's Story* and why he thought it was an inspiring film that had stayed with him long after he had first seen it, and how important it was for young black Americans.

A Soldier's Story was rated R by the Classification and Ratings Board. I appealed and managed to have the rating reduced to PG-R, a classification attributed to movies with overly violent language and sexually explicit content that could be detrimental to young viewers. Jack Valenti, president of the Motion Picture Association of America, supported my appeal because there was little violence, no sex, and the language was suitable for the film.

Strange, looking back on it now, that anyone could find that film detrimental to young people. I made it for young people. I wanted them to know how heroic their forefathers were. How their fathers and grandfathers had fought for a country that wouldn't acknowledge them as equals with the white men who fought alongside them. How you could give your life in defense of your country but couldn't be led into battle by a black officer. Even in the eighties, it would have been hard to find a black face on the cover of *Time, Newsweek,* even *Sports Illustrated.* Just as Warner Brothers didn't believe *A Soldier's Story* would sell, the magazine publishers didn't believe a black face would sell.

I wanted my children and their white friends to see it and understand more about racism and its insidious spread over the centuries and into our lives. I wanted them to feel the outrage I had felt that day, years ago, when I was told I couldn't sit where I wanted on a bus in Tennessee, the uncomprehending anger I felt when I saw that black people could not use the same water fountains I used, that they couldn't use the same public toilets, yet I knew they were in the same war I had been signed up to fight.

Playing on the tracks outside Zagreb with Topol, *Fiddler on the Roof*, 1971.

With Carl Anderson as Judas, on location in Israel, 1972.

Floating in the Dead Sea with Jesus (Ted Neeley), *Jesus Christ Superstar*, 1973.

"You're changing, like a butterfly emerging from its cocoon … You're in love." Directing Cher in *Moonstruck*, 1987.

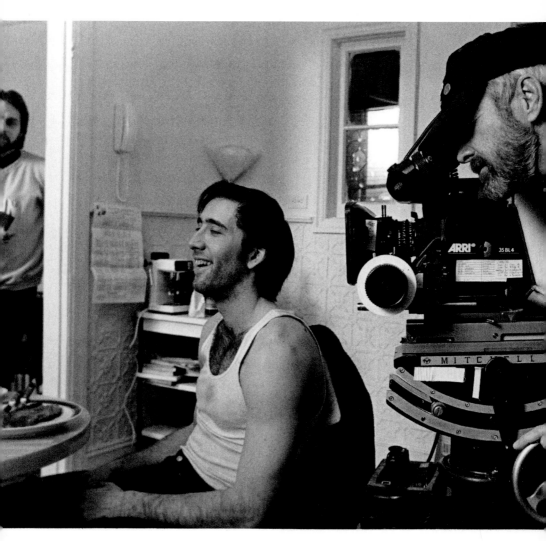

Setting up a shot with Nick Cage in *Moonstruck*.

With Vincent Gardenia (left) and Feodor Chaliapin Jr., who play father and son in *Moonstruck*.

Robert Weil (left) and John Mahoney enjoying Olympia Dukakis and her director on the set of *Moonstruck*.

On the set of *The Hurricane,* Denzel Washington and I react to the announcement of the Thalberg Award, 1998.

Doing my dance at the Oscars, March 21, 1999.

A Soldier's Story succeeded at the box office because people could sense the injustice, the unreasoning prejudice, the bred-in-the-bone, pervasive hatred that had only recently been part of America's everyday life. It's the same outrage I wanted the audience to feel when they saw the first part of *The Hurricane*. But there is something more important to take home from these films: the hope that there can be a better world.

I had been drawn to the story of Rubin Carter since the first time I heard Bob Dylan sing the story of The Hurricane:

> Now all the criminals in their coats and their ties
> Are free to drink martinis and watch the sun rise
> While Rubin sits like Buddha in a ten-foot cell
> An innocent man in a living hell

But it was David Picker, then an independent producer in New York, who first called me to say, "Norman, you've got to look at what happened here. It's got everything: a great story of injustice and reversal of fate, a moral hero, a happy ending...it's even got a bunch of wonderful Canadians. And you can shoot it in Canada." Even before he showed me the *Sports Illustrated* piece I was excited.

In 1985, Rubin's murder conviction had been thrown out by Judge Sorokin, and Rubin was now living in Toronto. But David couldn't raise the money to make the movie; the old markers he left behind when he was head of United Artists just wouldn't be played. I had all but given up on the idea when my agent called. Armyan Bernstein, another independent producer, had a script, the rights to the two books about Rubin Carter and, better still, he had Denzel Washington. I thought, I love Denzel, he is a wonderful actor, but how is he going to play a young boxer, the middleweight champion of the world?

That's what I said to him when we met in L.A. "Denzel, how old are you? Forty? Over forty? How the hell are you going to play this angry, powerful, little guy who was so fierce and strong he beat every opponent? He was a magnificent boxer, and he was in superb shape."

Denzel just looked at me. "I want to play the part more than any-thing else I've ever wanted," he said after a while.

"When you're out there alone in the ring, in that hot light, you're half-naked in a pair of shorts, there is nothing I can do for you. Can't protect you from the camera. Can't fake it."

"I know." Denzel smiled. Neither of us had mentioned that he was overweight and out of shape.

The press called the man The Hurricane because he erupted into the ring with such wild anger, such fury, his opponents backed off. "How the hell are you going to tap into that anger, Denzel?" He had become a star in a white man's world. How was he going to reach into that deep sense of outrage, the fury that was The Hurricane? "I need your anger, Denzel."

"I need to do this, Norman. I'll be ready."

I believed him.

Denzel trained every day for almost a year, dropped more than ten pounds, became a boxer; he was in such magnificent shape he could convince anyone he was fifteen years younger. And he did tap into a deep dark anger in his heart, and an even deeper feeling of peace, of hope, that gives the movie its light. Denzel gave the performance of his life.

On the surface, *The Hurricane* may seem to be a simple story of a man wrongly convicted of a double murder in 1966, who is finally vindicated and released from prison. For me, though, the soul of the film lay in the relationship between Lesra, a Brooklyn teenager who learns to read when he becomes interested in the first book he has ever picked up, *The Sixteenth Round*, and its author, the prisoner who has stopped communicating with the outside world. It's the story between Lesra and Rubin that's the emotional core of the film. Without Lesra picking up that book, nothing would have happened. That almost mystical moment is the magic that transforms the story into more than the sum of its many parts.

Think of this black kid in Brooklyn who couldn't read, yet he picked up the book and learned to read and to write so he could send Rubin Carter a letter. Then think of Carter, who had stopped opening letters, cutting himself off from his family, friends, certainly from the well-intentioned folk who had come to see him over his nineteen years in a cell, the lawyers who had appealed his case, the celebrities like Bob Dylan who had tried to help but failed. Yet he opened that one letter. Why?

To this day, Rubin is unsure. Perhaps it was the picture of the Queen on the Canadian stamp, simple curiosity, fate, perhaps, or something greater, though he would never say divine. But opening that letter led to his return to the world. He was touched. Maybe it was the first thing that touched him in thirty years. Maybe it was the first thing that ever touched him. That is the heart of the story I wanted to tell, that moment of simple human connection that changes two lives.

We talked about it when I first met Rubin. It was a sunny spring day. We went for a long walk around my farm in the Caledon Hills. He was a quiet, thoughtful man with a ready smile, who seemed at peace with the world, as if the violent past of his early youth had become only a story, as if the anger that had fueled him as a fighter, the anger that drove him nearly insane in his cell had been buried so long, it had disappeared. He talked about his growing up black in New Jersey, about the first time he crossed a white officer, about the first time he was in jail, and how he had been convicted and jailed for the double murder he did not commit. He talked about the sense of hopelessness in solitary, the certainty that he would never come out alive. And his reading, his determination that he would be able to see through the walls, to sense the sunlight that was denied him. He believed he had been able to do that once he dealt with his anger at the injustice, the hatred he returned to those who had hated him enough to put him behind the walls. That turning point became another key moment in the movie, another tour de force by Denzel.

One of my horses reared when Rubin and I came out of the woods and into the pasture near our house. I watched in surprise as this small, slight man walked right up to the horse as it reared again. Rubin placed his hand on its neck and stroked it, gently, until the animal quieted. The two of them seemed to breathe together and relax. Rubin talked softly, the horse responded. Then Rubin turned.

"How do you know so much about horses?" I asked him.

He had learned to ride after he came out of prison. "There is something magical about them," he said. "The joy of freedom when you're on a horse…"

Both Rubin Carter and Lesra Martin were in the audience when the unfinished film was screened at the Elgin Theatre in Toronto in September of 1999 as part of the Toronto International Film Festival. Also in the audience was the group of idealistic Canadians, the Association in Defence of the Wrongly Convicted, who had adopted Lesra into their unconventional "family" and powered the appeal that led to Judge Sorokin's reversal of Rubin's original conviction. There was an eight-minute standing ovation. The producers were so sure of its sweeping the Academy Awards that year, they didn't need to court the critics; *The Hurricane* would become the last film to open in the twentieth century.

The audience responded to the magic of the story. They were in the aisles at the Village Theatre in L.A. Judge Sorokin was there, the lawyers were all there, Denzel and the cast were all embraced. It opened to audiences across North America and they all responded the same way. Universal had never had a movie that drew ninety percent approval from audiences both black and white, both rural and urban. The head of Disney was quoted as saying, "It's the best film of the year." Denzel Washington won best actor in the Golden Globes, the first time an African-American had won the award since Sidney Poitier for *Lilies of the Field* in 1963. We were headed for the Oscars.

But right from the day the movie opened, I had a niggling sense of worry. It was something Bill Goldman had told me: "Never make a movie about people who are still alive." I guess every one of them has a stake in his own story, and they began to come out with their fists up as soon as they saw an opening.

In the *New York Times*, Selwyn Raab headlined "Separating Truth from Fiction in 'The Hurricane'" and ranted for two pages that ours was a Hollywood version of the story. He said that it was really he who had discovered the evidence that led to the overturning of Carter's conviction. Then Lewis M. Steel attacked in the *L.A. Times*: "History's on the Ropes in The Hurricane." Steel was part of the legal team representing Carter's co-defendant from 1975 to 1988. We had included Carter's attorneys, but Steel had been left out of the script. Armyan Bernstein said both of them were upset about being left out of the movie, adding that when something so successful happens everyone wants to be recognized for their contribution.

I think we didn't respond quickly enough. We trusted in the truths of the movie, in the audience's response, in the extraordinary performances. We had underestimated the power of the press, the *New York Times'* claim to unbiased reporting, the gullibility of our own Hollywood community. Were competing studios feeding the firestorm? We found ourselves on the defensive. How can you include everyone in one film? Why the need to present all three trials? Even the group of Canadians came under attack. Here was a bunch of people who had given up their own lives, committed a million dollars, moved down to New Jersey, all because they believed in Rubin's innocence, and they were pushed by a young boy's enthusiasm. Did I give them too much credit? What is too much for what they did?

In New Jersey, some bigoted radio talk shows chimed in, trying to throw doubt on Sorokin's judgment, detailing Rubin's early life as a young black troublemaker. Sure, the police chief in the film is a composite, we agreed, but there are people like that walking around New Jersey today, who have clung to their racist ideas, who would send Carter back to jail now, and some of those people are police officers. There had been a police chief, there were detectives, and there was a mayor—all with racially biased attitudes, willing to bend the law if necessary to gain a conviction. There was this man, a boxer, tough, belligerent, he had a criminal record, he talked about killing "nigger-hating" cops—given it's the sixties, it's a surprise he lived to be wrongfully convicted!

By the time Armyan and I wrote our response to Raab and Steel, too much mud had been thrown. The trouble with mud is it sticks. I believe if it hadn't been for the mud, Denzel would have taken home the Oscar for best actor in 2000. It broke my heart that he didn't. I know he deserved it and so did everyone else. I believe they all felt guilty.

The Academy voters had to give him best actor in 2001.

Armyan Bernstein was named ShoWest Producer of the Year in 2000.

Rubin now works with the Association in Defence of the Wrongly Convicted. He has attended a screening of our movie at the White House. He has addressed the United Nations. Though he separated from his Canadian champions a long time ago, he remains in Canada. Lesra Martin is a lawyer in British Columbia.

And I went on to make another movie.

14

The Oscars

Hooray for Hollywood

That shaky rather flaky Hollywood

—special lyrics by Alan and Marilyn Bergman

The call from Faye Kanin, the president of the Academy of Motion Picture Arts and Sciences, caught me totally by surprise. The Board of Governors was asking me to produce the fifty-third year of the Academy Awards for ABC in 1981.

I was in my office at Putney Heath Farm when I got the call. I told Faye I would get back to her by the end of the week. Putting the phone down, I gazed out at the tranquil autumn scenery. The trees had turned and the lawns were carpeted in shades of red and yellow with flashes of crimson. It was a long way from hot and sunny Los Angeles.

I hadn't produced live television since the first Judy Garland Special twenty years earlier. The Academy Awards is one of the biggest live television spectacles in the world. It's said the audience is well over one billion people. That's a big jump from the Canadian Broadcasting Corporation's "Big Revue" in 1952. These were some of the thoughts that raced through my mind.

I called Pat Palmer, my producing partner at our office in Culver City, to ask him if he thought we should get involved. Pat had never worked in television, but he was immediately taken with the idea. "How long would you be tied up?" he asked.

"The show is set for Monday, March 30. It will eat up at least four months." I was guessing.

Charlie Milhaupt, my associate, shouted from the background, "Do it, Norman! Bring some style and class to that show. It'll be a blast! I've always wanted to be backstage at the Oscars! You gotta do it once just to say you did."

Pat laughed. "It's the biggest show of the year. Think about it. You can count on us. We'll be there for you."

I hung up. Maybe they're right, I thought to myself. Maybe I should experience real terror once again before I die. After all, it's one of the last live shows left.

From the very beginning, working on the Oscars felt like trying to drag an elephant across the stage of the Dorothy Chandler Pavilion at the Music Center in downtown Los Angeles. Awards shows, by their very nature, are pretty boring affairs. How could I breathe more life into this one? How could I add some style and fresh ideas? The parade of stars on the red carpet with hundreds of cameras flashing and press from all over the world was always an exciting overture, but how could we jazz up the show itself?

The first thing I had to do was to get a commitment from Johnny Carson to be our master of ceremonies. He had done the last two shows and, in my opinion, was the best part of the program. He was faster and edgier than Bob Hope and had huge amounts of charm and, more important, the best writers in the business. I had booked Johnny on the *Andy Williams Show* over twenty years ago when he had his comedy act with a dummy called Deputy John. So we went way back.

Once Carson was set, I signed my pal Henry Mancini to conduct and arrange all the music. Marty Pasetta was the director and, as well as the Carson writers, I had three strong, experienced television writers: Buz Kohan, Rod Warren, and the legendary Hal Kanter. My associate producer, Michael Seligman, had done the last four shows and was a real team player. I asked for a lot of favors from old friends. Alan and Marilyn Bergman came on board to work on some special lyrics, and the talented Broadway and film costume designer, Theoni Aldredge, flew out from New York.

In early January, Charlie and I started calling every agent in town to negotiate for the lineup of presenters to appear on the show. The stars are what people want to see, but it's always difficult to lock in so many important people for a live performance that pays nothing. I soon found out it's the publicity people you really end up talking to, and they can be very protective of their clients. But they also are aware of the tremendous exposure offered by the Oscars, and that always works in the producer's favor.

As the weeks flew by, the tension and terror began to build. "Can we get Willie Nelson to fly in from Vegas or not?" I shouted at Charlie. "What about Dolly Parton, is she confirmed? Tell the choreographer Alan Johnson that I think we can get Lucie Arnaz to appear in the opening production number! Tell Pat Palmer to call the Bergmans and see if they can get to Dionne Warwick's manager!"

Charlie Milhaupt loved the action and he gave great phone. He was funny and very clever at juggling all those agents, managers, and PR people. He even managed to convince Luciano Pavarotti's manager that the Oscars would be the perfect platform for Pavarotti's first American television performance.

As the nomination ballots were sent out to all the Academy members, things began to fall into place. The five best picture nominations that year were *Coal Miner's Daughter*, *The Elephant Man*, *Ordinary People*, *Raging Bull*, and *Tess*. I thought Scorsese's *Raging Bull* was a lock.

As we began rehearsals on Monday, March 16, at ABC Rehearsal Hall 6 on Vine Street in North Hollywood, we had lined up an impressive roster of presenters. In alphabetical order, they were Alan Arkin, Dyan Cannon, Richard Chamberlain, George Cukor, Blythe Danner, Angie Dickinson, Lesley-Anne Down, Sally Field, Lillian Gish, Dustin Hoffman, Margot Kidder, Nastassja Kinski, Steve Martin, Mary Tyler

Moore, the Nicholas Brothers, Peter O'Toole, Luciano Pavarotti, Bernadette Peters, Richard Pryor, Robert Redford, Jane Seymour, Brooke Shields, Sissy Spacek, Lily Tomlin, Peter Ustinov, Jack Valenti, King Vidor, Sigourney Weaver, Billy Dee Williams, and Franco Zeffirelli.

I was especially excited to have arranged for two of the industry's oldest and most celebrated directors, George Cukor and King Vidor, to present the best director award. These two remarkable gents had careers that together totaled 118 years of movie-making. And they were still active. Two days before the show, I had to rush George Cukor to Carroll's men's shop in Beverly Hills to get him a decent tuxedo. His own pair of pants kept falling down. One of my biggest fears was that they would forget to bring out the envelope or be blinded by the lights. They were both over eighty.

About four weeks before the show I was called in for a meeting with the Academy Board. What would I think if President Reagan agreed to appear live on the show? I was stunned. I thought, how could anyone even suggest this? I looked at Faye Kanin and a group of board members. "I think the Academy would be compromised and ridiculed." I tried to control my anger. Someone pointed out that the president was an actor and a member of the Academy and it would make the evening a momentous occasion.

"This event is a celebration of excellence in film. It has nothing to do with politics. If you invite the president, you can have my resignation as producer right now." I was starting to tremble. A board member mentioned that Jack Kennedy had videotaped a few opening remarks when he was in office. And since Ronald Reagan was a former actor and so close to the film industry, it was only natural that he would want to offer his support. I realized a precedent had been set, so I suggested that if the president wanted to participate in a short video presentation I would have no objection as long as we could write the speech. So it was finally agreed that the White House would be informed of our decision. I left the meeting in a state of high anxiety.

Hal Kanter and I drafted a ninety-second opening speech for the president. I was asked if I wanted to go to Washington and personally direct the segment. I said it was only two weeks before the show and I couldn't leave rehearsals, but I did talk to the White House television director and sent him the script with certain requests for set-ups and locations. Ten days before the show, I received two videotapes. They had also sent the outtakes. I was fascinated: to watch President Reagan at work before the cameras was like watching a very smooth professional TV salesman at work.

On the day of the Academy Awards, President Reagan was shot by John Hinckley Jr. We were in the midst of dress rehearsal on stage at the Dorothy Chandler when the message came through from the ABC control room. Having experienced the assassination of JFK, Dr. King, and Bobby Kennedy, I immediately stopped what I was doing and asked the stage manager to get a network feed to the television monitor in my dressing room right away. "Everybody, just stay calm until we find out what's really happened." There it was on the television screen, endless repeats of Hinckley shooting the president and White House press secretary James Brady before being hauled down by a policeman and the Secret Service agents.

I could hear Henry Mancini and the orchestra rehearsing "Nine to Five" with Dolly Parton. I took a deep breath and turned off the sound on the set. "Get me Faye Kanin and then get me Johnny Carson—and then get me Lew Erlicht and Gary Pudney at ABC." I buried my head in my hands. "Shit! I knew it. Things were going too smoothly," I moaned.

Faye Kanin, the president of the Academy, was at her hairdresser in Beverly Hills. "We've got to postpone the show!" I shouted over the phone. "What if the president dies! We don't know at this moment how seriously he is wounded."

"But we have over two thousand for dinner at the Beverly Hilton! The flowers are on the tables! What are we going to do?"

"Well, I don't think it's the right moment to have a grand celebration of movies. I've got to talk to Johnny, he's on the other line."

"Johnny, it's Norman. Are you watching?"

"Of course I'm watching!" he answered.

"I don't think we can go on tonight," I said. "What do you think?"

"My first four minutes of the monologue are Reagan jokes," he muttered.

I said, "I'll call you back—let me talk to the network."

In the next hour we had assembled my staff and the top executives from the network. We were all crammed into my dressing room backstage. A network executive banged the phone down. "NBC's going ahead with the basketball playoffs," he snapped.

"Basketball?" I questioned. "Jesus, the president's just been shot and taken to Walter Reed Hospital and no information has been released about his condition. In most countries they would stop the commercial programming and wait to see what's happening!"

"We've booked the satellite time for a complete international broadcast. Do you know what that costs?"

Another network executive barked at me: "What the hell will happen to all the talent? How can we hold on to all these people? Willie Nelson is coming in from Vegas in three hours."

I turned to Charlie. "Ask Dolly if she will stop by—I think they've finished rehearsing her number."

A moment later Dolly Parton appeared at the open door. We all looked at her. "Dolly," I said gravely, "the president's just been shot."

Without hesitation she answered, "Well, don't look at me—I didn't do it!"

"But what if we have to postpone the show, will you be able to perform?" I asked.

"Honey, don't you worry—if we have to delay the performance, I'll be here for you. I'm not going anywhere."

I was relieved. "There is a precedent," I said quietly. "When Dr. King was assassinated, they postponed the Awards from April 4 to 10. In '68. I remember very clearly." Everybody nodded.

At 4 p.m. a press conference was called outside the theater. It was pretty frantic. Hundreds of print reporters, press photographers, and television cameras were there, representing most of the world's media.

I walked out, nervous and overwhelmed by the crush of journalists. Someone handed me a microphone and I began to speak: "Ladies and gentlemen, because of the grave situation regarding the president, it is the decision of the Academy to postpone the awards program for twenty-four hours. The old adage 'The show must go on' seems relatively unimportant at this time." Everyone began shouting questions. The next day it was announced that the president would survive.

We lost only one presenter, Kris Kristofferson, who had to film in New York. Everybody else hung in, and I managed to get Donald Sutherland to fly in to replace Kristofferson. Donald is a class act, and I was deeply grateful. Outside of paying off a symphony orchestra in Florida, which had been booked for a Pavarotti concert, we were charged only for the dining room staff's wages and the wasted food at the Hilton.

During rehearsals on Monday, March 30, I received a call from the White House. An official wondered if I would be interested in sending a network mobile camera to Walter Reed Hospital so the president could send live greetings to the Academy's international audience.

"Isn't the president hooked up to tubes and everything?" I asked, not quite believing what I was hearing.

"Yes, but we could remove everything for a few minutes for the camera." It was then I realized that when it comes to politics, true power is access to the media. I declined the offer but suggested we use the tape that President Reagan had done ten days before, with an opening from Mr. Carson. And so began my last experience in live television production.

The opening musical number, starring Lucie Arnaz, with special lyrics to "Hooray for Hollywood" by the Bergmans, was my homage to the town that had accepted and embraced me before I became a successful producer/director. The lyrics say it all:

Hooray for Hollywood
Once film has captured it
It's there for good
On celluloid it can survive forever

Alive forever
The one thing movies do best
Is arrange a meetin' with Buster Keaton
And fix it so you come up and see Mae West!

Hooray for Hollywood
That shaky rather flaky Hollywood
Exotic and neurotic Hollywood
High wire, dream supplier Hollywood

The number was staged in front of a cinema screen with rows of seats, and the dancers and singers burst out of the screen to fill the stage. The whole number built to a great tap sequence, which brought down the house.

There were two or three elements in the show that worked beautifully. The segment we put together of all the stars and famous personalities who had died during 1980 was extremely touching and has been continued in every Academy Awards show since.

The homage to Henry Fonda was my favorite. I had campaigned for him to receive an honorary Academy Award for his lifetime of work in the movies. He had starred in over eighty-six films and never won an Oscar. His performances in *The Grapes of Wrath*, *My Darling Clementine*, *Young Mr. Lincoln*, and *Mister Roberts* should have been recognized by the Academy. But then, he was in good company because the Academy had also ignored Charlie Chaplin, Orson Welles, Cary Grant, and Alfred Hitchcock, to name a few.

I had persuaded Robert Redford to introduce Henry. It was a bit of a coup because, apparently, Redford had never attended a show. But tonight he was nominated for *Ordinary People* as the director, so I knew he would be there.

And I had personally supervised the film clips that showcased many of Henry's great moments. We finished it with a clip from *On Golden Pond*, which he had just finished a few weeks before and which, of course, had not yet been released.

Henry was seventy-six and had to use a cane. When Redford

began his introduction, I was backstage and realized that Henry would need some extra time to get to his mark. So I ran to the green room and brought him down on the elevator and walked him out on to the darkened stage. He hung on to my arm as I searched for his mark. We were behind the giant screen and there were his films flashing by, reversed like a mirror. He squinted as he looked up at the screen. I shouted in his ear: "Look, Henry—you're Wyatt Earp. How old were you?"

"Forty. Look, there's Jimmy." He pointed with his cane at James Cagney in *Mister Roberts*. "This is my favorite speech—remember Tom Joad?"

We stood in the dark as we watched the clip from *The Grapes of Wrath*, the images towering above us. Then I noticed he was mouthing the words in perfect sync with the screen. My eyes filled with tears.

I squeezed his arm and whispered in his ear, "When the screen goes up and the spotlight hits you, Redford will be to your right. Just move to him; the microphone will be there." Henry nodded. He was shaking. I leaned in closer and shouted over the music and applause that was starting. "Stand still for a moment. Take your time. Make them stand up for you, Henry. You deserve it." I turned and ran for the wings as the screen began to rise. The audience was applauding. Henry straightened up, and suddenly he didn't need his cane. He stood tall and elegant. The audience began to stand and as he walked toward a smiling Robert Redford, the entire audience, all two thousand of them, rose in unison to their feet.

15

The Lamb of God

The reason why birds fly is simply that
they have perfect faith,

For to have faith is to have wings.

—*J.M. Barrie*

By the end of 1977 we had lived in over a dozen places. Some were exotic; some, like our Victorian mansion on the edge of Putney Heath that we had bought from Sean Connery and the rambling Alan Siple–designed house in Brentwood, were exceptional; some we even loved, but none of them felt permanent to me. Charlie Milhaupt had said it was some deep Canadian guilt that drew me back to the cold. But why I had to live on a farm, he never understood. What Charlie didn't know is that I come from a long line of farmers. My great-grandfather pioneered a farm on Rice Lake and all the Jewisons in Canada come from that area. Because I have always felt strange about the name, I searched for the family roots as far back as Yorkshire and, instead of Jews, I found Protestant farmers.

On one of the coldest days of the year, early January 1978, our recently hired real estate agent Myra Koster, Wally's widow, Dixie, and I were traveling up the Third Line of Albion Township, northwest of

Toronto, to look at another place Myra had found. It was a hundred acres or so that a man called John Ellis had farmed for decades. The roads were so icy we almost didn't make it. Dixie was suggesting we turn around and forget the whole adventure when our car slid into the frozen ditch on the side of the road. She relented when we caught sight of the farmhouse on top of a hill. And when we stood at its front window overlooking those glorious Caledon Hills, we both fell in love with the place.

Once again, we packed our bags, our furniture, and our beloved dog, Deecho. Like my friend the writer Mordecai Richler, I felt it was time to go home. I first met Mordecai in London. We both had young families and used to go to each other's places for backyard barbecues that lasted well into the night and early hours of the next day. He came from Montreal, and though he had been away for most of his life, Montreal never left his imagination. He had become an acclaimed novelist and I had made a number of movies.

We used to talk about films and books and the way Hollywood was in those days. I had tried to adapt one of his early books, *The Incomparable Atuk*. I'd worked with Don Harron and other writers but could never get the script to work. Mordecai was content to receive his option check every year, and would always send me a sarcastic note about how Atuk had become his annuity and he hoped I would never actually make the picture but would keep trying.

The day he told me he was heading home, I didn't realize I had been thinking about the same thing for a while.

"You've been living here for almost twenty years," I said.

"Maybe it's got something to do with my age," he said, "but I want to go back."

We had a big farewell party and he boarded a Polish ocean liner headed for Montreal. Only Mordecai would choose a Polish ship. I began to feel homesick after he left.

When we arrived at the airport in Toronto in late June of 1978, the immigration officer examined my bulging passport, full of residence visas and visitor's permits, stamps and certificates. He must have leafed through it three or four times before he asked me, "Mr. Jewison, where do you live?"

"I live here, now," I told him. "I'm coming home."

"From where?" he asked, suspiciously. "Where have you lived before?"

"Well, let me see. It was about three years in New York, nine in Los Angeles, eight years in London…" I was looking at Dixie for confirmation.

She had been giving the immigration officer one of her withering looks. There was a long pause. "Why the hell," he asked, incredulous, "are you coming back *here*?"

Welcome home, I thought. Only in Canada would an immigration officer think I was nuts for coming back. Deep down I was shaken. Had nothing changed? Was the old inferiority complex still around? Do we believe that we are still second rate? Did we still believe that our best and brightest had to leave to achieve?

The next time I crossed the border I tried a different tack. In response to the suspicious questions about what I was doing in Canada, I informed the officer I was a returning settler. In a way, that was true. I brought everything I owned back to Caledon, even the wine cellar and my proud Porsche from Stuttgart. I could bring in everything duty free as settler's effects. Since I didn't then, and don't now, have any desire to be a gentleman farmer, I wrote to my second cousin Barb Patterson and her husband, Jim Pipher. They had been farming in a remote area near North Bay and I had heard through the family grapevine that they had been looking to come south. "Why don't you come to Caledon," I asked, "and help me make something of this place?"

We fenced the property and bought six Polled Herefords. Little did we know that we would soon have a prize-winning herd. We leased additional land in the area and started a sideline tapping maple syrup from trees on the property. We now tap about a thousand trees in our own hardwood bush and have over a hundred head of cattle.

When I sit in my baggy jeans and work boots at a cattle auction or stand in the steaming sugar shack on a cold early spring night waiting for the next draw of golden syrup, I am as far from Hollywood as any northern farmer. I also feel strangely content. Like my granddad and his dad, and generations before them, I feel that I was born to be a farmer. I know I am happiest when I work the land. I often think it's a farm my great-grandfather Jewison, my grandfather, and my dad would have been proud to see.

The old intolerant Methodist, who never missed a Sunday service and didn't allow alcohol in his house, would have been less pleased with my relationship with God. Nor would my father, who made sure I went to church every Sunday, attended Sunday school, and never touched a drop of liquor in his life. (His sole self-indulgence was smoking cheap cigars on Saturday afternoons at the softball games in Kew Gardens.) I know my aunt Bea, who taught me the psalms when I was only five, wanted me to stay close to a Christian God even though I was convinced we were Jewish.

I have dovened at the Western Wall and left Him a message in the space between the stone blocks. But I have also prayed at a Sikh temple in New Delhi and knelt for morning prayers at a mosque in Hebron. The year we made *Agnes of God*, my two sons, Michael and Kevin, and my friend Tim Stewart went trekking in the Himalayas, Dixie thought in search of some mystical experience. I asked St. Peter for a small intervention while I was in St. Peter's in Rome, and I have lit candles for my friends in churches throughout Europe. Aunty Bea used to insist I go to Sunday school and I still remember her little mantra for days when things go badly: "The Lord is the strength of my life, of whom shall I be afraid."

I think most people, regardless of their religion, regardless of logic, want to believe in something outside of their everyday lives. Outside of themselves. *Agnes of God* gave me the opportunity to explore that timeless human conflict between believing what we can see and believing what we can't see or experience. It seemed to me then, as it does now, that the world is in dire need of angels.

In February of 1981 I was in Buffalo, directing *Best Friends* with Burt Reynolds and Goldie Hawn, when I had a call from a friend in New York, Jeannine Edmunds, who was also John Pielmeier's agent.

She wanted me to fly to Boston to see his new play, *Agnes of God*. It had just opened in New Haven. I had already read the play and thought it was brilliant, that her client was one of the really talented young playwrights in New York. Now, Jeannine and the producer thought there was something wrong with the play but couldn't quite put their finger on why it wasn't working on stage. Lee Remick, an experienced American actress and a friend of ours from London, was the psychiatrist, Geraldine Page was the mother superior of the convent. Amanda Plummer was Agnes. It was a stark stage with only three characters: everything depended on the ability of the two opponents—both intent on saving young Agnes—to represent their views passionately and convincingly. Both had to be strong.

I realized that Lee was too gentle, not tough enough for this role. Meeting with everyone backstage in Boston confirmed my suspicions. Lee didn't have a chance against Geraldine's impassioned mother superior.

The play opened on Broadway with Elizabeth Ashley playing the psychiatrist and it earned Geraldine Page a Tony nomination for best actress.

When I decided I wanted to make the film version of *Agnes of God*, Guy McElwaine, the president of Columbia Pictures, asked me what it was about. I said it was the struggle between Freudian logic and Catholic faith. Agnes was in the middle, pulled in both directions. She was an innocent no matter what had happened to her, and she stayed innocent. I said the film would test our ability to believe in miracles.

"You mean it's the one with the nun?" he asked.

"Yes."

"Oh," he said.

"A nun, a psychiatrist, and a mother superior."

"Who do you have?"

"Jane Fonda," I said, "would be fabulous. She is strong-willed, no-nonsense, a great star..."

"Will it be an expensive picture?"

"No," I said. "I'm changing the location to a convent in Quebec."

We went back and forth like this for a while, but in the end he gave me the money to purchase the film rights to Pielmeier's play.

I had barely started to worry about the casting when Anne Bancroft phoned. She said she wanted the part of the mother superior. When I said I'd get back to her, she persisted: "I'm married to a director, I know that none of you know how to make up your minds. I'm going to help you with the decision." Anne was then and still is married to Mel Brooks, one of the great comedic talents of my generation.

I told her she was too young and too beautiful for the part. "For me, you'll always be Mrs. Robinson," I said. She had starred with Dustin Hoffman in Mike Nichols's *The Graduate*—a clever movie and big box office hit. "You're sexy, sensual... I don't see you as a Mother Superior, Anne."

"Where are you?" she asked.

I said I was in my office down in Culver City on Washington Boulevard by MGM. The old Selznick Studios.

"I'll be right over," she said.

Twenty minutes later Anne Bancroft swept in, pulled up a chair, sat down, leaned across, looked me in the eye, and said, "So this is Mrs. Robinson? Look at these lines. Look at me." She wore no makeup, she was pale, there were dark half-moons under her eyes.

I said I just happened to have a nun's wimple and black veil and would she step into the bathroom and try them on. So there we were, five minutes later, Anne in the wimple and veil, both of us staring into the meanly lighted mirror, her hair and lovely hands covered by the nun's habit, and I realized she would be a superb Mother Miriam Ruth in *Agnes of God*.

The next week I had to tell a nonplussed Geraldine Page that she would not be carrying her Broadway role to the film. Both Geraldine and Anne were nominated for Academy Awards that year, and Geraldine, in an interesting piece of irony, won for Horton Foote's *The Trip to Bountiful*. Anne did not win for *Agnes of God*.

Anne, a Catholic, completely identified with the role she played. Later, she told Jay Scott in an interview that the title was particularly meaningful for her, as was the story. In the Catholic faith, there is the prayer: "Lamb of God who taketh away the sins of the world..." Agnes derives from the Latin word for lamb and that's what Agnes was: the Lamb of God who took away the sins; she brought the Jane Fonda character, the doctor, back to the Church. Anne said, "I mean that's what it's supposed to be. She is supposed to be sacrificed, and in the end, she is."

I chose Meg Tilly for Agnes. She had been cast in *Amadeus* that year but had broken her ankle and had to withdraw. She was a classic beauty and an accomplished actress. She also had the wide-eyed innocence of the young nun. I was sure she could convince an audience, albeit briefly, that she was the victim of immaculate conception, that the stigmata were real. In the courtroom there is a moment of complete pathos where she has lost—not her life—but her mind, and she carried it off more convincingly than anyone else could have done.

As I had told Frank Price, we'd shoot the whole film in Canada. Yes, it would be cheaper than a comparable production in the United States, but I now also had a chance to shoot my first movie in my home country, the first time I could use a Canadian crew and supporting cast, and the second time that all three of my children would work on one of my films. Of course, they had been hanging around the locations during their summer holidays almost from the time they could walk. They all knew to stand still when I said "Action!" including Deecho, one of the best dogs we ever had. He not only froze for "Action!" he ran as soon as he heard "Cut!"

The boys were with me in Fort Bragg, for *The Russians Are Coming*. They were in Yugoslavia when we shot *Fiddler*—you can just glimpse Kevin's face as one of the village children. Michael became an expert chicken wrangler: he was in charge of getting the chickens to cooperate. He had tied a bit of fishing line to one leg of each chicken and fed them plenty of seed to make sure they were happily pecking when we needed them for background. He was so good with chickens we put him in charge of the goats as well. All three of them were on hand for *Rollerball.* Jennifer worked in costumes, Michael in props, and Kevin, the eldest, had begun his apprenticeship with Dennis Fraser, the big

Cockney grip everyone acknowledged was the master of the craft. He continued to work with him on *Jesus Christ Superstar*. On *Agnes of God* Michael was location manager, Kevin focus puller, and Jennifer was Meg Tilly's stand-in.

I brought Sven Nykvist into the production because I knew he understood what the movie was about. He had been Ingmar Bergman's cinematographer for some of his greatest films. I had been entranced by *Cries and Whispers*. Kevin started to learn the craft from him while we were shooting in Canada. Later, he traveled with Sven all over the world under contract for other movies, became, himself, a camera operator, worked on a number of the Merchant-Ivory films, and on *Only You* in Italy in 1994. After leaving Sven, his mentor, he settled in Paris, fathered two beautiful daughters, Ella and Megan, and became a cinematographer. He was the cameraman on *La Mentale* in France in 2002 and, with me again, on *The Statement* in 2003.

I had the idea of setting most of the story for the film in an old convent in Quebec, wanting to create an environment at once unfamiliar and convincing. The atmosphere in Quebec was steeped in Catholic mysticism; it was a place where miracles were still expected to happen. Pat Palmer, my production partner, hired an all-Canadian crew. I was fortunate to get Academy Award–winning designer Ken Adam, who transformed the Rockwood Academy for Boys in Ontario into a convent in less than six weeks. Most of the scenes were filmed on this quickly assembled set in Ontario in the bleak Canadian winter.

As we neared the end of the movie, I began to fear that we wouldn't be able to end it right, that there wasn't going to be a point where I felt the film had done what we had set out for it to accomplish. The courtroom scene came closest, but lacked a moment that might linger in the mind. It was both too sad, and too predictable. We then shot a long walk of the nuns in the snow, with Jane Fonda arriving and a new scene with Anne Bancroft. None of it worked.

Then something magical happened. Meg Tilly—Agnes—was in the belfry of the convent church. It was about 18 below zero, the camera was too cold to touch, some of the crew had taken shelter. Sven, Kevin, and I were shivering in the bucket of the crane shooting a silent scene with Meg.

Suddenly, a dove landed on the bell near Meg. "Try to reach out and touch it," I told her. Slowly, she reached out her hand. When the dove didn't move, I said, "Can you try to hold it?"

She did. She held it softly in both her hands, kissed it, and then slowly let it go. It flew out over the snow-covered hills. The camera caught it all.

Sven and I looked at each other. "Cut," I said. Then, "Did you see that?"

They all nodded. Yeah.

And that was the end of our movie.

16

On Love and Other Human Follies

Loretta: You and I are going to take this to our graves.

Ronnie: I can't do that.

Loretta: Why not?

Ronnie: I'm in love with you.

Loretta (slaps him hard, pauses, slaps him again): Snap out of it!

—*Moonstruck*

My love stories have always been a bit zany and never entirely serious. It isn't that I don't think love can be serious, sometimes catastrophic, sometimes merely heartbreaking, usually intense and complicated, but I just see it as one of the ultimate human follies, less dangerous than rage, less harmful than hate, and a whole lot less likely to lead to general mayhem than envy. I have tended to show humanity as fallible, sensitive, befuddled, misled, but redeemable rather than mindlessly, relentlessly violent. I want people to recognize themselves in the movies I make. I don't enjoy no-brainer action movies. And I do not imagine those movies are for my audience. The audiences I have in mind when I make films are adults who know about love and sex. They have known betrayal and abandonment. They have been tempted and, sometimes, succumbed. They are neither perfect nor evil. They have jobs, families, mortgages, they do not dress in full leather and carry massive weapons on their hips, they are not action heroes. But when attacked, they defend themselves and will try to do the right thing. When they die, they usually stay dead.

The Thomas Crown Affair was a film about love as a game, style over content. *Only You* was about love as destiny, about a young woman's search for her perfect soul mate. *Dinner with Friends* was about marriage, divorce, and the fine lines in between. *In Country* is about family. *Moonstruck* was the ultimate romantic love story, irrational, compelling, physical, operatic. It's also about family.

It was originally called *The Bride and the Wolf*—hard to imagine a worse title for a romantic film. My friend the literary agent Jeannine Edmunds gave me the script, so I read it. Jeannine represented a number of young New York playwrights, including John Pielmeier and John Patrick Shanley. She had a great eye for wit, for credible dialogue, for talent. But *The Bride and the Wolf* was the kind of script that makes you suspect you haven't been offered a unique favor. In addition to having one of the worst titles I have ever seen on any cover, it was dog-eared, coffee-stained, well-thumbed. It was also excessively talky.

"Who's read this?" I asked Jeannine.

"Everybody," she said with characteristic frankness. "But that was before *Five Corners*. And he wrote this on spec, Norman. No one has actually made an offer." She told me the script had been written for Sally Field. She had seen the playwright's *Danny and the Deep Blue Sea* on stage and asked if he would write a film for her. He agreed to write it, but refused to accept payment until she read it and liked it. In the end, though she loved it, she couldn't get the financing.

I read it that night. There was something about the script that grabbed me and wouldn't let go. There was something grand, operatic, and terribly human about the story and the way the characters behaved. At that point, I had only a germ of an idea about how it might translate into a movie, but I did want to meet the author.

John Patrick Shanley arrived for our meeting very casually, a few minutes late, decked out like a student turning up for an afternoon tutorial. He was in his mid-thirties, tall, handsome, long-haired, shabby, wrinkled corduroy pants, trench coat, a look of casual disdain. A young New Yorker, not about to be impressed by a Hollywood director.

"So," he said in a broad Bronx accent, "what pictures have you done?" He sat on the arm of a chair, sipping his instant coffee with obvious distaste. He was tense, as if ready to leave at any moment.

"A few," I said. I knew I was being auditioned. "You?"

"One," he said. "You've seen it?"

I hadn't.

"How many have you made?"

"Twenty," I said, "give or take."

We talked about the premise of his story: of a woman who decides to marry a man she does not love because she no longer trusts herself to meet a man she could love. Then, once the marriage is all set, she does meet the right guy. The right guy, as luck would have it, turns out to have only one hand, a grief-stricken attitude to life, and is her fiancé's younger brother. What does she do? For me, the story had all the elements of love and betrayal that have haunted me for so long. And there is the whole large family with all their complex relationships, their loves and betrayals, Cosmo's lover and Rose's temptation, Cosmo's father and how he fits into the family.

Once he relaxed I told him I thought he had a lousy title, long soliloquies that lacked focus, but I thought we could make it into a wonderful movie without changing what he had set out to write in the first place. We talked about the moon, a central image in the play, and its effect on how people behave. Shakespeare, Aeschylus, Donne, and all the Romantics had written about the moon, just as his Cosmo keeps pointing at the moon, as if it could explain something about human behavior. One of the grabby lines in the script comes from Perry, the NYU film professor and would-be lover, speaking to Rose about one of his students: "She's as bright and fresh and full of promise as moonlight in a martini." I loved that line.

We played with titles, all with the word "moon," and a couple of days later settled on *Moonstruck*. By then, he had signed on to work with me on the rewrite. He was the fastest writer I have ever worked with, understood every suggestion, did the whole thing in about two weeks. He had an uncanny ear for dialogue, original, poetic, funny, real. I nicknamed him "The Bard of the Bronx."

I was thinking about how and where to pitch it when I discovered that both Alan Ladd Jr., president of MGM/UA, and his assistant, John Goldwyn, were in town for the 1986 Toronto film festival. I had first met Laddy when he was involved with *Star Wars* in London and once had dinner with Sam, John's grandfather, alone, in his private dining room after *The Russians Are Coming* was released. I invited them both to my office, only a five-minute drive from the Four Seasons Hotel, where they were both staying.

I did my dance around a highly original romantic love story, great music, low budget, classy, it's time to do something extraordinary like this, something that doesn't require a thousand extras and special effects...yadda, yadda.

John Goldwyn had seen Shanley's *Five Corners* and liked it, so he was already intrigued.

"Laddy," I pushed on, "I want you to read it on the flight home. You've got five hours. It's a short script and I need a quick answer. This is hot."

"That good, huh?" he laughed.

They finished their coffee and left with the script, now clean and freshly typed, in Ladd's briefcase.

John Goldwyn called at around four o'clock the same afternoon. He loved it. Didn't just like it a lot, he loved it. He thought it was wonderful.

"Tell Laddy," I said, hopefully.

"How much would it cost?" Alan asked the next morning, calling from the airport.

"Ten. Not more than twelve," I said.

"Who do you see in the lead?"

"Cher, I think..."

"Cher? Hmmm. We'll get back to you."

Two days later we had a deal.

I had first seen Cher in the *Sonny and Cher Show* back in the "I Got You, Babe" days. Even then, buried in all that schmaltz, she had a tremendous sense of humor and sharp comic timing. "Oh, Norman," she told me when we met in her home in West Los Angeles, "nobody took me seriously back then." No one did until they saw her in Bob Altman's production of *Come Back to the Five and Dime, Jimmy Dean*. Then there was *Silkwood*, a heavy role for a serious actress, and *Mask*, in which she played the drug-addicted mother of a disfigured teenager. Though I wasn't fond of the movie itself, she and that young boy gave riveting performances. I think everyone knew what a chance she had taken with those two films.

"Loretta Castorini is Italian, her hair black, done in a dated style, flecked with gray, she's dressed in sensible, unfashionable clothes of a dark color" according to the script. She had not a drop of Italian blood in her veins, Cher told me. Perhaps some Cherokee. Cherilyn Sarkisian Bono Allman was born into a messy family: her mother had been married eight times, three of those times to her father, an Armenian. She was worried about the Brooklyn Italian accent.

"No problem," I said, "we'll get a voice coach. The important thing is you can do the part from your heart." I think Cher is in touch with the reality of ordinary people. They identify with her because they see themselves. She has no pretense, doesn't play the star unless it's so outrageously played—the big wigs, the Bob Mackie gowns—that everyone is in on the joke. She was "streety," honest and pragmatic, the ideal Loretta.

She had already read the script. She had laughed at parts, but she was still shooting *Witches of Eastwick*, which was, apart from the humor, a very different part from Loretta.

"Cher," I told her, "you're my first choice of any actress in the world. If you don't do this, you're going to regret it for the rest of your life. Films like *Moonstruck* don't come along often. It's such an unusual part, romantic, playful, passionate..."

Later, she told me one of the reasons she agreed was that she thought she was taking a chance again. She liked the fact that Loretta got a second chance, and that she took it. What Loretta did was look in the mirror and say to herself "If you do this you're crazy," and she does it anyway. She falls in love with her fiancé's brother, who is neither safe nor reliably sane.

When I cast the movie, what I had in mind was an opera: Loretta is the soprano, Rose the alto, Johnny is the baritone, Ronnie the tenor, Cosmo the bass. Music was a very important part of the movie. Right from the beginning when Loretta strides through the streets of Little Italy, Dean Martin's "That's Amore" sets the tone for a film that is both unabashedly romantic and joyfully self-mocking. The audience is cued to expect love, passion, and fun. The first scenes with Loretta are intercut with Lincoln Center, where Puccini's *La Bohème* is preparing to open. I wanted Puccini's hauntingly romantic music to underscore our Brooklyn Italian opera with Dean Martin's "When the moon hits your eye like a big pizza pie, that's amore!" as an overture.

Olympia Dukakis as the unflappable Rose Castorini was easy— hell, I had wanted to work with her for years. I had seen Danny Aiello and John Mahoney in *House of Blue Leaves* on Broadway, Vinny Gardenia had been in several movies, some of them Italian. Julie Bovasso was not only a brilliant choice for Rita Cappomaggi, she was also a professional acting coach, one who knew exactly how to teach a Brooklyn Italian accent. Cher got it in under two weeks!

I had seen Feodor Chaliapin Jr. in *The Name of the Rose* and had a hunch he'd be terrific as the grandfather. I called Sean Connery and asked if Chaliapin spoke English. "Norman," Sean said, "he canna hear and he canna see but outside of that he is totally brilliant." Feodor was living in Italy at the time. He was the son of the great Russian opera singer Chaliapin and had actually met Puccini and Tchaikovsky. He told stories about having lunch with Stravinsky. He memorized the whole script so he wouldn't have to bother with trying to hear what was said. When he was in a scene, he watched for the other actor's lips to stop moving, then he gave his lines.

Ronnie was the hardest to cast. He was a tormented soul. Poetic. Dramatic. "Bring me the big knife. I'm gonna cut my throat!" "I lost my hand, I lost my bride. Johnny has his hand, Johnny has his bride!

You want me to take my heartbreak and put it away and forget it?..."
These are some of his lines and he has to be able to say them so as to
make the audience believe. Okay, so they can laugh a little, but they
have to like him at the same time and empathize with his torment.

The most tormented soul I knew who was right for the part was
Nicolas Cage. Nicolas, whose name had been Coppola, had decided
right at the start of his acting career to change it. He would not trade
on his uncle's famous name. He changed it to Cage after a comic-book
hero-for-hire who had been wrongly convicted, jailed, dunked in a
chemical bath that disfigured him, etc. Only a tormented soul would
pick a name in honor of a guy like that!

The trouble with Nicolas in 1986 was that he was death at the box
office. Most of his films had bombed. I had to ask him to test for the
part, though we both knew Nicolas didn't do tests. I told him the studio thought he was too young for the role. Cher was forty, Nicholas
twenty-three, and he had to be credible as her lover. She was playing a
thirty-seven-year old widow, but there was no indication of age for
Ronnie. I told him not to shave for a couple of days, wear a white shirt
and black tie but undo the black tie at the top. Formal but disheveled.
He came to New York and baked bread all night in one of those old
coal-fired ovens, and he worked on the accent with Danny Aiello so he
started to sound like him.

Cher supported the idea of Cage. She even agreed to do the screen
test with him: the one in the snow after the opera where Ronnie talks
about the pain of love. And he was wonderful.

We shot the exteriors in New York. The bakery is in Cobble Hill. It had
coal ovens, and an atmosphere we couldn't have duplicated anywhere
else. Loretta's grandfather (played by Feodor Chaliapin) lives in
Brooklyn and we shot all around a landmark house in Brooklyn, near
the promenade where the old man takes his dogs for their walks. It's
little Italy: family, working class, emotional. From there, there is a
grand view of Manhattan.

Because we couldn't count on Cosmo's moon appearing on cue,
David Watkin, our British director of photography and Academy

Award winner for *Out of Africa*, made us a portable moon of two hundred fay lights attached to a giant cherry picker. It could roll out over the Manhattan skyline when we needed it and cast its magical spell over the unlikely loves and betrayals of *Moonstruck*. It was so bright it lit up two city blocks and fooled the birds into singing their dawn songs.

Cher won the Academy Award for best actress in 1987, Olympia Dukakis won best supporting actress, and Shanley won the Oscar for best original screenplay. I was nominated for best director and as the producer for best picture but lost in both categories to Bernardo Bertolucci and his film *The Last Emperor*. You can't fight two hundred Buddhist monks and the Forbidden City.

When Cher stood in front of the microphone, she thanked only her hair stylist and makeup man. Three days later, she took a full page in *Variety* to thank the cast, the crew, even the director. Cher was also awarded the prestigious David di Donatello Award, the Italian equivalent of the Oscar. Olympia Dukakis, John Mahoney, and Danny Aiello all received a huge push in their careers from *Moonstruck*. Shanley went on to write and direct *Joe Versus the Volcano* for Spielberg.

For me, it was a moment of hope: that the pendulum was beginning at last to swing back from those endless, mindless action films, the obscene violence, the simplistic plots, to films where people actually talk to one another.

That was one of the things that had drawn me to *In Country*, the fact that people talk to one another, that they try so hard to piece together relationships, that the love of a young girl for her father can overcome the terrible self-hatred of a man who had sworn off human emotion so he could live with himself. *In Country* was also my tribute to the horrific trauma America had suffered—and is still suffering—as a result of the Vietnam war. The title of the film refers to time spent in Vietnam.

Eighty-two films about Vietnam had been made by the time I came to make mine in 1989. I think of it, even now, as a healing film, a film about love. And about real loss. It begins in Vietnam and ends with the Wall in Washington, and Bobbi Ann Mason's profoundly moving novel. It's about a rural Kentucky family—one I instinctively understood—grieving after the loss of a father, brother, son, and trying to come to terms with its reality. Frank Pierson wrote a sensitive and profound screenplay.

Bruce Willis did, I think, his finest bit of acting in that movie. He was already a big star then, but too often played the same character in different guises. The scene in *In Country* where he climbs a tree during a horrific thunderstorm and begs God to strike him dead is fully convincing, as is his stumbling relationship with the seventeen-year-old girl who is trying so desperately to understand something about her father, whom she had never known.

Terry Semel, then president of Warner Brothers, now the head of Yahoo, visited the set in Kentucky. Both he and Bob Daley felt that this was an emotionally charged movie. When the family drives to the Wall and Bruce Willis's character touches the name of his friend among the thousands of names, the film brings a kind of closure to the trauma of the war. It was not just the family on the screen, we were all weeping at the end of that movie. When we showed it to Warner Brothers' publicity and marketing bosses, they were all in tears.

When it was over, I walked off alone. It was a dark, gloomy afternoon. Raining.

In Country received a standing ovation at the Toronto Film Festival. In hindsight, though, I think the timing was perhaps too late. America had already done its crying.

It was the idea that attracted me to *Only You*: the conceit so many people have, that there is a perfect mate for each of us, that we are destined to be happy with one person and only one person, that the Prince will come and wake us from slumber, that the Princess will open her eyes only when we plant a kiss on her soft, lifeless lips. (I turned down the opportunity to direct *The Princess Bride* because I was convinced such a large conceit needed a much larger budget than the studio was willing to give me.)

Only You also gave me a chance to shoot in the best locations in the world with my two sons. As Dixie pointed out, we had graduated from Paducah, Kentucky, and Fort Smith, Arkansas, and finally got to go on locations that were truly beautiful, romantic, irresistible. Alitalia offered us free first-class flights. Our locations were Tuscany, Rome, Positano, Venice. In Rome we took a magnificent baronial apartment, in Venice we had a palazzo, in Positano we borrowed Franco Zeffirelli's villa where the best cook in Southern Italy presented his aromatic dishes on the terrazzo overlooking the turquoise sea. It was so exquisite Dixie ended up running a vast guest house for all our delighted friends from California, London, New York, and Caledon while we kept to our twelve-hour shooting schedule.

The story turns on a young woman's absolute, unshakable conviction that she is destined to find the right man, that everyone else is just a stand-in. Marisa Tomei, fresh from her Oscar for *My Cousin Vinny*, had the right mix of zaniness and charm; Bonnie Hunt, her sensibly married sister-in-law in the story, showed the right mix of good sense and hopeful romanticism; and Robert Downey Jr. was so convincing as the lover, I think the crew—most of them were Italian—had all fallen in love with him by the time the movie climaxed in Positano.

It was my sole movie with Robert Downey Jr. Everyone warned me about his drug problems, TriStar had trouble getting insurance for him on the movie without regular blood tests, but as far as *Only You* was concerned, he was attentive, professional, and the perfect romantic lead. Dixie and I took him to visit Gore Vidal and Howard Austen at their villa, high on the cliffs of Ravello on the Amalfi Coast. Robert was enchanted to be in the presence of one of America's most ascerbic and entertaining writers.

Only You provided me with the opportunity to work once again with Sven Nykvist. Ever since *Agnes of God*, my eldest son, Kevin, had been Sven's camera operator. Michael was associate producer and shot all the second-unit film. We loved working with the Italian crew. They were experienced, fast, and like all Italians, they were passionately opinionated about food, politics, and romance, in that order. We had heated arguments every day about where to go to lunch and what to order once there.

We were in the middle of shooting the day Federico Fellini died. We all stopped and stood with heads bowed, remembering him and all his brilliant films. He was one of the greatest filmmakers of our generation. *8½*, *La Strada*, even *Fred and Ginger* will remain with me forever. I once drove two hours from Rome to have lunch with Anita Ekberg, to listen to her stories from *La Dolce Vita*.

On that day in 1993, we toasted Fellini's memory with the best Italian champagne, shed a few tears, then went back to work, invigorated by the maestro's inspiration.

17

Other People's Money

I've always been fascinated by money and power. In 1997 when Peter Gzowski interviewed me for CBC Radio's *Morningside,* he wanted to talk about how we find money to make movies and why there are so few Canadian films. In the United States, the business of movies is big business, I told him. In Canada, it's an artistic sideline that no banks take seriously and few financial investors support. For the United States, the entertainment business is a major money-maker, it's big export dollars. It may be their biggest export now. Some years ago it passed aerospace as the largest export sector and even armaments have fallen behind entertainment. A big hit at the theaters can generate more money than an oil well.

Everybody asks me, Why don't we have more Canadian movies? Look at the British, the Australians, the Indians. The answer is we lose a lot of our talent to Hollywood, to New York, and to London. Our financial institutions don't have confidence in our talent. They will bankroll real estate and Cuban tomatoes, transit systems in Brazil and oil in Sudan, but go see a Canadian banker about a movie and he'll throw up his hands.

Ghostbusters is a Canadian film. It was written, produced, and directed by Canadians, and stars a Canadian. It was made in the United States because no one here will finance a blockbuster film like that. There isn't a whole lot I could do about that, but I decided to create a place where our talent pool could learn the art of filmmaking.

When I returned to live in Canada in 1978 there was no center for the advanced study of film. The United States has the American Film Institute, England has the British National Film and Television School, France has the Institut des Hautes Etudes Cinémato-graphiques, a distinguished film school. The Swedes, the Australians, even the Israelis have a national film center. Canada has the National Film Board, which makes wonderful documentaries but rarely ventures into feature filmmaking. Since film had become the literature for this generation, I was shocked at how far behind we were in the art of making motion pictures.

It certainly wasn't because of any lack of talent. The contribution of Canadians to Hollywood is staggering, from Mary Pickford, Marie Dressler, and Mack Sennett in the silent films, to Fifi D'Orsay, Walter Pidgeon, Fay Wray, Deanna Durbin, Ben Blue, Walter Huston, and Norma Shearer in the thirties and forties.

Just consider what we would have missed if it hadn't been for these Canadians: No "Injun Joe" without Victor Jory. No "Lincoln" without Raymond Massey. No *42nd Street* without Ruby Keeler. No "Tonto" without Jay Silverheels. No *Star Trek* without William Shatner. No *Airport* without Arthur Hailey. No *Godfather* without Al Ruddy. No *Ghostbusters* without Ivan Reitman. No *ABC News* without Peter Jennings. No *Saturday Night Live* without Lorne Michaels, and no *SCTV* without Canadian talent.

The skimming of the cream continued as Hollywood attracted Canadians Donald Sutherland, Christopher Plummer, John Candy,

Eugene Levy, Dan Aykroyd, Rick Moranis, Dave Thomas, Howie Mandel, Monty Hall, Leslie Nielsen, Martin Short, Geneviève Bujold, Margot Kidder, Arthur Hiller, Dan Petrie, Helen Shaver, Michael J. Fox, Mike Myers, Neve Campbell, and Jim Carrey.

What a roll-call of talent, and these are just a few of the high-profile stars; there are thousands of other Canadians employed in the film business. People in Los Angeles are always amazed when they discover how many of us are there.

In 1979 I sat on the board of the Toronto film festival, then known as the Festival of Festivals. Wayne Clarkson, chair of the board, was anxious to improve the Hollywood connection and compete head on with Venice and Montreal. Whether it's the Cannes Festival, Berlin, or Moscow, every festival wants the hot pictures, the biggest stars, the flavor-of-the-month directors.

I had just directed a new film, ... *And Justice for All*, starring Al Pacino, Christine Lahti, and Jack Warden. Naturally, there was a great deal of pressure for me to bring it to the festival before it was released. I contacted the marketing and publicity people at Columbia Pictures, the releasing studio, and explained how it was important that I support the Toronto festival since I was Canadian and also from Toronto.

The festival in 1979 was still growing and the major studios were still not that enthusiastic about bringing all the U.S. press to Canada for a press junket so far in advance of the film's commercial release. But since I was the producer and director, they agreed as long as the local Toronto critics would hold their reviews until the film opened commercially. "No problem," I was assured, "Toronto critics are professional; our papers have integrity." I knew all the international and domestic press would attend the world premiere but again I was assured that no one would review the film before it opened to the public; it wouldn't be right.

We convinced Al Pacino to come to the premiere, and it was an exciting night for me and for the festival when the film received a standing ovation. The next morning, we awakened to a trashy, negative review by Gina Mallet in *The Toronto Star*. "Why would the paper do that?" I yelled at everybody. "It's so perverse and mean-spirited! The film hasn't even been released," I wailed. Jay Scott, the critic for the *Globe and Mail*, just looked at me and shrugged. "It's a Canadian thing, Norman. You're just too successful."

I felt betrayed. The studio people were furious, and Al Pacino left the next day for New York. Our only consolation was that four or five weeks later the picture opened to good reviews across North America, and Al Pacino received an Academy nomination for best actor.

During the next twenty-five years, the Toronto International Film Festival has grown into one of the most important festivals in the world. I premiered *A Soldier's Story*, *In Country*, *Only You*, and a work-in-progress screening of *The Hurricane* here with great support from the Toronto audiences. The press here has always been tough on their own but I've become accustomed to it. I remembered what that immigration officer had said to me in 1978 when I moved back here to live.

In 1980 I met up with Dusty Cohl, an enthusiastic cinephile who was one of the founders of the Toronto International Film Festival. Dusty was a born promoter, a lawyer who always wore a cowboy hat and who seemed to know every deal-maker in town, a man with an astonishing range of political connections. He introduced me to all the film buffs and heavy hitters in Toronto.

Following the example of the American Film Institute, I began to search for an impressive venue for a production center and school. Dusty told me that the huge E.P. Taylor estate on Bayview Avenue, in the heart of an exclusive residential area in north Toronto, was going to be left to the city. Dusty set up a meeting with Mel Lastman, the mayor of the former City of North York, now part of the City of Toronto. Mel was a popular and powerful politician, a small man with a big voice, a tireless promoter who had helped make North York prosperous. As luck would have it, *Fiddler on the Roof* was one of the mayor's favorite movies.

I told Mel about the need for a film center and how Windfields, the Taylor estate, would be the perfect home for aspiring filmmakers who would enrich his city and our country in the years to come. I described how the American Film Institute began at Greystone, a large estate owned by the city of Beverly Hills. How Gregory Peck and George Stevens Jr. got the city to lease them the elegant vacant property for a dollar a year.

Mel smiled and winked at me. "That would be in American money."

I nodded and continued to plead my case.

Some weeks later I received a call from the mayor's office summoning me to a meeting at the Windfields estate with Charles Taylor, E.P.'s son. Charles was an interesting character. His passion was writing and therefore he understood the need to nurture creative talent. He was also one of the most successful horse breeders in North America, and his wife, Noreen, was a talented artist.

He explained that his father was seriously ill at his villa in the Bahamas and that the Windfields estate was definitely going to be left to the City of North York. The family, however, would have the right to approve future use of the house and all the outbuildings that covered the estate and parklands on Bayview Avenue. Since all this land was surrounded by million-dollar homes, you can imagine what the market value would be. There were stables, cottages, tennis courts, and paddocks on the property.

As Charles toured us through the mansion and grounds, he reminisced about his childhood growing up there. The Queen and the Queen Mother had both stayed at Windfields when they visited Canada. Charles said they loved horses, and his father would always make sure the famous Canadian-bred Northern Dancer, one of the greatest breeding stallions in thoroughbred racing, was on show in his stable when they were there.

Charles agreed to think about my proposal and discuss it with the rest of the family. Since the Taylor children had all grown up at Windfields, it was difficult for them to part with so many memories.

A few months later, I invited Charles and Noreen to visit the American Film Institute in Los Angeles. I'm not sure, but Dusty believes that was what finally convinced him to let us establish the first Canadian film center at his family's estate. Mel Lastman pushed it through city council, and we secured our lease for two dollars a year. Mel, ever the businessman, felt he had to double the City of Beverly Hills' charge.

There's an old saying "Never look a gift horse in the mouth." How was I to know there was no sewer hook-up to the estate? "You mean the place is on a septic tank?" I asked incredulously. "No wonder the apple orchard is so prolific; the Queen and everybody else has been providing fertilizer for all those years!" No sewers, not enough power, and the foundation was leaking. The roof needed to be renewed. My two-dollar lease had turned into a $2-million renovation

I assembled an impressive group to form our first board of directors. We wanted to keep the center independent from government control but I knew we needed one-third of our budget from the province of Ontario, another third from the federal government. We would attempt to raise the last third from the film industry and the private sector. To fill the role of administrator, I hired a smart, aggressive young woman, Mickie Currie Daniel, who worked for the Directors Guild of Canada.

To raise the first $2 million and open our new center by March 1988 required a powerful board of directors and enormous support from government officials and the public. I began meeting with everyone I knew, asking for help and advice. I started with our neighbors in Caledon. There was David Galloway, a brilliant young executive, and Tim and Nalini Stewart, who introduced Dixie and me to John and Isabel Bassett. Bassett was very un-Canadian in a way. He loved success. He loved Hollywood and Broadway. He was a great admirer of Bobby Kennedy, whom he had met and hosted in Toronto. He gave me a lot of solid advice even though we argued about everything political.

Garth Drabinsky, then CEO of Cineplex, came on board. It was his idea to establish a monthly fund-raising event called "The Reel Club." Always the salesman, he excitedly began to shout: "On the first Monday of every month I'll give you a theater. You will go to all the distributors and get the next hot picture a week or two before it opens, and we'll have a private preview for our select Reel Club Members. It will promote the films! The studios will support it!"

"That's a great idea," I shouted back. "Maybe we could also give them some free passes and a tax deduction."

He laughed and grabbed my arm tightly. "You get Famous Players to split it and you got a deal."

"Done!" I shouted. "It will be the sexiest, most fun, and the best bargain for a charitable donation in this town." And it was, and still is.

Eddie Cogan, a dapper Damon Runyonesque developer and promoter, got us some wealthy Italian contractors to dig the sewers for a song and a screening of *Moonstruck*. We made Eddie our first Foundation president. Marilyn Lastman, Mel's wife, who has the chutzpah and wit of a counterman at a deli, began arranging special events. I enlisted Brascan boss Trevor Eyton, Harold Greenberg, Rudy Bratty, George Cohon, and Murray Frum—all heavy hitters and influential board members. We hired Sam Kula, head of the film section of the National Archives in Ottawa, as our executive director and began recruiting our first twelve residents in the summer of 1987.

To give the place the necessary glamour, we enlisted Donald Sutherland as chairman and invited Christopher Plummer and Margot Kidder, Colleen Dewhurst, Dan Petrie, Kate Nelligan, Margaret Atwood, Ivan Reitman, and Lorne Michaels onto our board. Who wouldn't want to be involved with all these celebrities? Even Ontario premier David Peterson became a supporter and helped with the mandarins in Ottawa.

The first year of the Canadian Film Centre was pretty rocky. We enticed Peter O'Brian, a genial and enthusiastic feature producer, to take over the reins from Sam Kula. The center grew rapidly. Star directors like Clint Eastwood, Oliver Stone, David Cronenberg, Stephen Frears, Denys Arcand, Neil Jordan, and Michael Moore dropped by for seminars. Film stars like Kathy Bates gave workshops on acting, writers such as Hal Hartley, Frank Pierson, and Joan Tewkesbury discussed screenplays, and producers Saul Zaentz, David Puttnam, Lynda Obst screened their films for us. The place began to really cook. Under the expert guidance of Wayne Clarkson, who always reminds me he was appointed executive director on April Fool's Day 1991, and Deszo Magyar, Nancy Lockhart, Allen Karp, and dozens of talented and hardworking professionals, it has grown into Canada's leading national film center.

Wayne Clarkson, who once headed up the Ontario Film Development Corporation for the Peterson government, is in many ways our most talented film executive. He was responsible for encouraging feature filmmaking in Canada by both foreign and local filmmakers. During the last thirteen years under his direction, the CFC has graduated over seven hundred writers, directors, producers, and editors who, in turn, have injected energy and passion into Canadian film and television production. Wayne and his board of directors have pushed the film center to produce not only award-winning short films but also three or four feature films each year, and for the last four years, the center has sponsored one of the largest international short film festivals in the world.

During the early 1980s, Dixie and I held a barbecue at our farm in Caledon on the first Sunday after the Toronto Film Festival opened. It was an opportunity for us to bring together many of the visiting film artists and foreign press. The filmmakers loved it. It was a real outdoor Canadian-style barbecue held in a setting of acres of green fields, animals, and cool forests of giant sugar maples. In 1988 we moved our annual Toronto Film Festival barbecue to the twenty-two-acre Windfields site. In its first year at the center, we had 268 guests. By 2003 the crowd had swelled to over 3,000. The center barbecue had become the most celebrated schmooze-fest of the Toronto International Film Festival.

When Lyndon Johnson resigned the presidency, rumor has it he offered his silver-tongued Texan press secretary Jack Valenti his choice of various desirable appointments. One was the U.S. ambassador to Italy, but Jack had his eye on one of the top positions in Washington: president of the Motion Picture Association. As top lobbyist for the movie industry, he would inherit a handsome marble-lobbied building with a private theater, permanent offices with staff in Los Angeles,

New York, and Europe, and an unlimited expense account. He also would control the rating system on films, open up foreign markets, and appear every year at the Oscars as a celebrity presenter.

Jack is a smooth, dapper, experienced political insider. He has always carefully maintained his access to the Congress and the Senate just as he maintains his immaculately stylish appearance. His mentor in the film industry was Lew Wasserman, the legendary godfather of Universal Pictures, who taught him how to play hardball.

Valenti has ingratiated himself with the filmmakers and the stars and used that relationship brilliantly when dealing with foreign heads of state, ministers of culture, and foreign distributors. American films, television shows, and computer imaging dominate the screens of the entire globe. Much of it has to be due to the influence of America's Entertainment Czar who so eloquently has persuaded almost every country to drop quotas and protectionism and make a deal with the giant multinational American distributors.

Canadian filmmakers have always had a tough uphill battle. The cinemas across our country have traditionally been controlled by Americans. By far, the biggest distributors are the Hollywood studios. Alliance Atlantis, Odeon, and Lion's Gate are the major national Canadian distributors, but they are confined to foreign films and independents. Because of U.S. domination of the marketplace, Valenti has always been keen to keep it that way. We are the largest foreign audience for American films, but the U.S. has always considered Canada part of its domestic distribution. A series of Ottawa ministers responsible for culture have tried to loosen the stranglehold on our film and television distribution. They have battled Valenti and the studio system with little success. The same with the Europeans. When threatened with quotas or a tax at the box office, Valenti—with congressional support—threatens retaliation. Hardball is the American way. Cultural imperialism is denied by Jack. "Why don't you just make some wonderful films that everybody wants to see?" is his challenge. "If they are popular, we will distribute them," he promises. Valenti has always maintained that the marketplace should control what people see.

Despite resentment over these strong-arm tactics, I am grateful for Valenti's support for the Canadian Film Centre. He knew that the nourishment of young creative talent in filmmaking was important not only for the aspirations of the next generation but that it would continue to help feed the Hollywood dream machine. Or perhaps it was guilt or an attempt to placate Canadian anger and frustration. Whatever his motivation, he helped us pressure some of the most important American distributors to financially support Canadian talent.

Strange that I have only made two films about money: *Gaily, Gaily* and *Other People's Money. Gaily,* based on Ben Hecht's book, recorded his time with a cynical eye to the money-makers, the power brokers in Chicago, the financial heartland of America. It's where the railways met, where commodities were traded, the mercantile mart, where all the great architects came to display their prowess, where robber barons thrived, a city steeped in politics, scandal, power: the kind that money can buy. As Carl Sandburg wrote, "Hog butcher for the world...City of the big shoulders."

I had fallen in love with the book, with Ben Hecht's insight into the times it portrayed. I loved the fact that it was set in the Everly sisters' brothel, itself a symbol of everyone being on the take, and the irony that the most honest people were the prostitutes, the madam—wonderfully played by Melina Mercouri—and the virginal Margot Kidder, the girl who has not yet been bought by anyone.

The police are for sale, the politicians are for sale, the press has sold out. A kid so innocent he doesn't even notice his pocket is picked, or that he ends up living in a bordello, is the hero-anti-hero of the film. It was a young Beau Bridges' first starring role. George Kennedy played the wealthiest man in America, the Robber Baron. Hume Cronyn researched the period for days in the New York Public Library to make sure he was properly attired to play the politician Bathhouse Grogan, the guy who knows everyone's secrets. He spent twenty minutes with me on the phone one night discussing whether his hair should be parted on the side or the middle.

Henry Mancini composed the music for the first time in one of my movies. I had been trying to sign him to work with me since *Cincinnati Kid*, but he was always busy. In the process, we had become friends, skied together with his wife, Ginny, and family in Sun Valley and Klosters, Switzerland, where Dixie and I used to rent a farmhouse in December and spend Christmas skiing with the kids.

We shot the movie in dark grays and browns, beiges, ochers. Robert Boyle, the production designer, felt the film needed a diffused look. Most of the scenes were shot in Chicago until the cops became uncooperative. I thought one of them must have read Ben Hecht's memoirs.

It's a tremendous historical piece. It had wonderful reviews from Chicago writers, even the young Siskel and Ebert praised it as a satirical morality play, and Rex Reed wrote: "I can't think of anything in recent memory that has given me more pleasure." And the movie bombed.

Henry Mancini told me it was the title. It came from a Bliss Carman poem:

> Oh but life went gaily, gaily,
> In the house of Idiedaily,
> There were always throats to sing
> Down the riverbank with Spring…

He may have been right but I'll never know. In Europe it was called *Chicago, Chicago*. I don't think it made much difference.

My other film about money, *Other People's Money*, was based on a successful play and starred Danny DeVito and Gregory Peck. It was about the pig years of the eighties, but by the time it was released in 1991 the pig years were over, the lean years had begun and no one wanted to see it. The timing was wrong, but DeVito and Peck were powerful in their scenes of dramatic confrontation.

The cinematography by Haskell Wexler was brilliant and the idea behind the film, that the bottom line and profits are more important than jobs and employees, was as valid in corporate America in the 1990s as it is today. Like the film *Wall Street* that preceded it, *Other People's Money* was all about greed.

It was while I was shooting *Other People's Money* in a foundry town in Connecticut that I learned of John Huston's death. He had been one of my heroes. One of the best in this terrible business. A great storyteller. The last time I saw him had been at Burgess Meredith's house, just a few steps from my house in Malibu. It had been a beautiful day and the two old dudes were sitting on the deck soaking up the sun and sipping iced Dom Perignon. As I left, John said with a twinkle in his eye: "Norman, never mind the movies, just keep making that wonderful maple syrup."

In the fall of 2000, I made a documentary for the cable Disney Channel celebrating the millennium. A number of film directors were given a choice of subjects looking back at the last hundred years in American life. I guess because of *Moonstruck* and *In Country*, they wanted me to deal with family as a theme. I suggested comedy. In my opinion comedy in America is not only a constant essential but a need. Humor has always played an important part in the daily life of Americans. They love telling jokes. From the early days of theater and vaudeville right through the first silent films, then radio and television, humor has prevailed. From Mark Twain to Will Rogers, from Chaplin to Laurel and Hardy and Mack Sennett, Americans love to laugh. During the 1930s and 40s it was Jack Benny, Fred Allen, and Amos 'n' Andy who gathered America around the radio in every front parlor. It was Milton Berle, Bob Hope, Jackie Gleason, and Lucille Ball who had them glued to their TV sets in the 1950s and 60s.

Funny is money in America. Two of the highest-paid actors in recent times have been Jerry Seinfeld and Jim Carrey. Why? They can make us laugh. Comedy is big business and everyone involved in it is deadly serious.

Almost every week I used to get a call from Rod Steiger. When I answered it would always be: "An old guy goes to see his doctor—" or "A priest and a rabbi go into a bar—" always a good laugh that lifted my spirit. Rod died in 2002, and I miss him. I miss his jokes. I miss the laughs.

18

This Terrible Business
Has Been Good to Me

Never mind the gross, Top Ten or
Bottom Ten—just tell stories that move
us to laughter and tears...

—*Thalberg Award acceptance speech at the*
Academy Awards in 1999

It was Thursday, January 7, 1999, just as I was getting ready to shoot the first fight scene in *The Hurricane* with Denzel Washington and five hundred extras. We were filming in an unheated warehouse in the north industrial section of Toronto. The setting was a re-creation of the Pittsburgh Civic Arena and the fight between Hurricane Carter and Emile Griffith that had taken place in 1963—all shot in black and white. It was a very exciting and noisy scene: the period costumes, the arena filled with smoke, and the overhead lights filling the white canvas ring and spilling out into the press photographers and the excited faces of our screaming crowd.

It was at that moment that one of my assistant directors came over with a mobile phone and told me that the president of the Motion Picture Academy in L.A. wanted to speak to me immediately.

"Tell him I'm on the set in the middle of a camera set-up; I'll call him back later," I yelled above the noise.

He left, only to return a few minutes later. "He says it's really important that he speak to you now for two minutes. He's really insistent."

"Shit! I can't believe this!" I shouted and grabbed the phone.

"Norman, it's Bob Rehme, president of the Academy. Can you hear me?"

"Yeah, I can hear you. Bob, I'm in the middle of a shot here; can't this wait until..."

He was shouting, "Norman, the board of the Academy has just voted unanimously to give you the Thalberg Award at this year's Oscar ceremonies. I wanted you to hear it first before the press or anyone else. Congratulations, Norm, you truly deserve it. Now go back and finish your shot." He hung up.

Go back and finish my shot? I was totally speechless. Totally unprepared for this most prestigious award. I thought I deserved an Oscar for *In the Heat of the Night*. I had even prepared a speech for *Fiddler on the Roof* in '71. Everyone had told me I was going to get it for *Moonstruck* in 1987. By the time we were shooting *The Hurricane*, I knew I would never be recognized by the Academy. I thought too many considered me not only a runaway producer/director but a Canadian political dissident as well.

After I had recovered from the shock of the phone call, I was bursting to tell someone. I climbed into the fight ring and pulled aside Denzel, who was preparing for a shot and trying to keep warm in a huge terrycloth robe with a hood. "Denzel, you won't believe this but the Academy just called and they're giving me the Thalberg Award at this year's Oscars." Denzel whooped and shouted. He lifted me off my feet in a huge hug—then he grabbed the mike. "Ladies and gentlemen, I have some great news," his voice boomed. The cast and crew and hundreds of extras went silent. "Our director, Mr. J, has just received the film Academy's highest honor for consistent high-quality motion pictures."

The place broke into a cacophony of applause, whistles, and cheers. It was a truly exciting moment for me. Probably more meaningful than the real event at the Dorothy Chandler Pavilion in Los Angeles on Oscar night.

Having produced the Academy Awards show back in 1981, I felt that I was prepared for the event. On the Saturday before the show—it took place on a Sunday night in March—I arrived at the theater for the traditional dress rehearsal. Security was tight. All the stars who were serving as presenters were there, as well as Whoopi Goldberg and the cast.

Everyone appearing on the show received an enormous wicker basket filled with goodies. Everything from a Tag Heuer watch to perfume, free massages, portable CD players, miniature cameras, caviar, champagne, and special Academy sweatshirts. It was the biggest gift basket I had ever seen and was so heavy they had attendants carry it to my car.

After a short rehearsal where the producer Gil Cates reassured me that the three-and-a-half-minute montage from my films looked great and Nicolas Cage had rehearsed his introduction and I knew where to stand stage right and where I was to go, I was free to leave and tomorrow night someone would bring me backstage to the green room a good ten minutes before I went on. Three and a half minutes seemed rather short to sum up my life. "Keep your acceptance speech short, funny, and don't thank all your family and friends," barked Hal Kanter, one of the writers and an old friend. "Nobody gives a shit about your Aunt Ethel."

The next day was frantic around our Malibu home. Kevin, my eldest, had arrived from Paris. My daughter, Jenny, and her husband, David Snyder, had come from London, my younger son, Michael, from Toronto. We were all tearing around looking for cufflinks, irons, hair dryers. We had to be ready by three in the afternoon. The Oscars start at 5 p.m. live and you must be in your seat on time. The traffic was terrible. Every limo company from San Diego to Santa Barbara has its cars on the road Oscar night. The logistics and the security are a nightmare, with everyone's PR person trying to push them down the red carpet at the optimum time. The resulting crush of bosoms, perfume, Botox, and hair-spray all jammed together is enough to send you right back to the farm.

I was okay until I got taken backstage to the green room and saw Sophia Loren, who was nervously peering through her enormous glasses at her introductory speech. Nick Cage was pacing. Elia Kazan, who was about to receive an honorary award, looked totally out of it. Only Tom Hanks looked cool.

My heart started to pound as I looked at the screen and realized I was next. Ben Affleck and Robert De Niro were laughing at something, then Goldie Hawn grabbed me. "Congratulations, you sweet man! You deserve this! You look great!" She hugged me and left. I was frantic. I not only couldn't remember my first line, I couldn't remember my name. An assistant stage manager appeared and grabbed my arm. "Come on, Mr. Jewison, I'll escort you to your spot backstage."

"Yeah, okay," I mumbled. "There are only a little over a billion people watching…" I began to ramble in panic. Other people were passing me, Jack Nicholson, Uma Thurman, Jim Carrey. I was almost catatonic by the time we found my mark on stage right.

The stage manager pumped my hand vigorously and talked into the mike to the control booth. "I've got him on his mark. Okay. I'll tell him." He leaned closer and shouted into my ear over the sound of the speakers. "Naturally, we're running long, so keep it short and sweet. Congratulations, Norman. Remember, Nick is on your right and the award is very heavy. You really deserve this, man. I'll give you your cue…"

I was now completely rigid. I stared at the huge screen, watching the images, reversed, of course. My whole career, my life's work was laid out to the world in three and a half minutes. Flashes of *Fiddler*, *Superstar*, *In the Heat of the Night*, *Russians*, there's Steve McQueen and Faye Dunaway, there's Pacino, Cher slaps Nick once, then again, harder, "Snap out of it!" The audience roars, the screen starts to rise. I hear a voice boom: "Ladies and gentlemen—Norman Jewison!" The stage manager taps my shoulder.

I stepped out into the brightest spotlight I had ever seen, and I've seen a few spotlights over the years. For a moment I was totally blinded. Then, about twenty feet away, I saw the smiling face of Bill Conti, the conductor. I had worked with him on *F.I.S.T.* He was waving at me and mouthing the words "If I were a rich man" from *Fiddler*. "Sing it, Norman!" he was shouting.

was fascinated by the prospect of screening the film in front of a Bavarian audience. How will they react? Will they reject the premise of the film? Is guilt still a problem?

I recalled my first trip to Germany in 1963 and my visit to Dachau, the notorious concentration camp, close to Munich. I just had to see the site of what we had fought against in 1944. My limo driver kept saying, "*Dachau? Ich weiss nicht.*" He didn't know where Dachau was? Then I got it. He didn't want to take a guy with a name like mine—Jewison—to a place where Nazis murdered Jews. I insisted. I showed him the place on a map. In the end, he walked with me through the camp. I shed tears. So did the driver.

Surprisingly, the Munich audience seemed to embrace the film. Most of the film critics who interviewed me seemed supportive and praised the performances of Michael Caine, Tilda Swinton, and Jeremy Northam. They also seemed enthusiastic about the reception the film would receive when its German distributor released it. However, I have learned that you can never predict anything in the movie business and often people will praise your work in a personal interview and later print a negative review. Very few critics will be candid and tell you the truth face to face. Jay Scott, Brian Linehan, and Roger Ebert were always honest when discussing my work with me, but such critics are rare. At any rate, you can't make films to please the critics.

The Statement was not a commercial mainstream film. Its leading character played by Michael Caine is a despicable seventy-year-old, anti-Semitic French Nazi on the run for ordering the murder of seven Jewish civilians during World War II. Not exactly the kind of movie where you can root for the hero. It also dealt with the hypocrisy of the Vichy government and the support for fascism by right-wing elements in the Catholic Church. Clearly, they were two subjects in which an American audience had little interest.

Conclusion

In April of 2004, my dear friend Norman Campbell died. Norman was a prominent CBC television director and producer. We had started out together when CBC-TV went on the air in 1952. The news of his death hit the wire services.

That night, I was in our Malibu home with my son Kevin and my two French granddaughters, Ella and Megan. The phone rang. Kevin answered and it was a reporter from the *Los Angeles Times* inquiring if it was true that Norman Jewison, the TV and film director, had just passed away. Kevin listened, paused for a moment, then hollered loudly: "Dad, it's for you!"

Needless to say, the *Los Angeles Times* apologized. A few minutes later we received another call from a local TV station. I decided to use the quote from Mark Twain: "The reports of my death are greatly exaggerated."

The whole mistaken identity by the press was a little unnerving because it seemed my demise was something that everyone expected. The following morning at 7 a.m., the phone rang and it was my personal assistant, Liz Broden, calling from the Toronto office.

"Is everything okay?"

"Yeah," I answered grumpily.

It seems Piers Handling, head of the Toronto International Film Festival, had called Wayne Clarkson at 6 a.m. to find out if I had died. Wayne immediately called Liz. "Tell everybody I'm still alive!" I shouted and banged down the phone.

I looked in the mirror that night and understood why everybody had called. "It's true," I whispered. "You are one old dude." It's funny but I have never felt old. I don't even know how I got old. But looking in the mirror, I knew the truth that was reflected there. "Shit!" I said out loud to no one. "What the hell do I do now?"

Do I stop making movies? Do I stop farming? Stop skiing? Stop making maple syrup in the sugar shack next spring? Stop riding my horse Sullivan over the Caledon trails? How should you behave when you realize you're old? It had never really occurred to me until everyone was calling to see why I was gone. You mean it's time to go? I looked closely in the mirror. The baggy eyes, the thinning hair . . . it all seemed magnified.

I turned off the bathroom light and headed to bed. I noticed I was walking differently. My god, I'm shuffling along like an old *alte koker*. Maybe it's all in the mind—you're as old as you think you are. Bullshit! It took me a good hour to fall asleep, still wondering why everybody was so accepting of the news of my death.

Vladimir Nabokov said, "Other men die, but I am not other men, therefore, I'll not die." He died in 1977.

It's not that I'm afraid of death; as a matter of fact, it's a subject that has always held great fascination for me. It's just that I hate being old. So I decided I wouldn't buy into it. No shuffling, no complaining about aches and pains. No struggling to remember. No afternoon naps. Just keep working, laughing, drinking, and appreciating every smell, sound, taste, and touch that one can possibly experience.

We live in a world where fifty percent of the population of Africa does not have access to potable water and the infant mortality rate is a frightening ten percent in the first year of life. So I give thanks every day for the exceptional good fortune of my birthplace.

This summer I was at my farm in Caledon. I had been awakened at first light by my very neurotic, big-voiced Rhode Island Red rooster named Rubin, after my friend Rubin Carter.

I got out of bed, pulled on a pair of shorts and a T-shirt, poured myself a cup of tea, and walked outside in my bare feet. The sun was just beginning to rise and cast its yellow light through the huge maple trees that line our eastern rail fences.

Whether it was the wet dew on the thick grass that squeezed up through my toes or the early cries of crows, doves, and songbirds that began to fill the quietness, suddenly I was keenly aware of how magnificent it is to be alive. I wandered around the property for close to an hour, filled with a rush of exhilaration. The natural beauty filled me with love and hope.

I remember reading somewhere that after the premiere of *Waiting for Godot*, Samuel Beckett was asked why he had written such a depressing play. He replied, "Great art can never be an act of pessimism. Art comes from hope. The very act of writing something anticipating an audience is an act of hope."

I like that. Hope is what we have to hang on to. It's our anchor in a sea of despair. Hope, like faith, remains constant, independent of any evidence.

When we lose hope we lose everything. People who have no hope become desperate. But hope is a gift of the spirit. It is God's gift and is His wonder. Hope is eternal.

"A life which is unexamined is not worth living." My philosophy professor at Victoria College told me that fifty-six years ago. I think that's why I wrote this book.

My hope is that you liked it.

Norman Jewison Filmography

of Feature Films

---

40 POUNDS OF TROUBLE   1962
Universal (106 mins.)
director: Norman Jewison
screenplay: Marion Hargrove
cinematography: Joseph MacDonald
editing: Marjorie Fowler
art direction: Robert Clatworthy, Alexander Golitzen
music: Mort Lindsey
producer: Stan Margulies
main cast: Tony Curtis, Phil Silvers, Suzanne Pleshette

THE THRILL OF IT ALL   1963
Universal (108 mins.)
director: Norman Jewison
screenplay: Carl Reiner
cinematography: Russell Metty
editing: Milton Carruth
art direction: Robert Boyle, Alexander Golitzen
music: Frank De Vol
producers: Ross Hunter, Martin Melcher
main cast: Doris Day, James Garner, Arlene Francis,
                     Edward Andrews

SEND ME NO FLOWERS   1964
Universal (100 mins.)

director:	Norman Jewison
screenplay:	Julius Epstein
cinematography:	Daniel Fapp
editing:	J. Terry Williams
art direction:	Robert Clatworthy, Alexander Golitzen
music:	Frank De Vol
producers:	Harry Keller, Martin Melcher
main cast:	Rock Hudson, Doris Day, Tony Randall

THE ART OF LOVE   1965
Universal (99 mins.)

director:	Norman Jewison
screenplay:	Carl Reiner
cinematography:	Russell Metty
editing:	Milton Carruth
art direction:	Alexander Golitzen, George Webb
music:	Cy Coleman, Frank Skinner
producer:	Ross Hunter
cast:	James Garner, Dick Van Dyke, Elke Sommer, Angie Dickinson, Ethel Merman, Carl Reiner

THE CINCINNATI KID   1965
Metro-Goldwyn-Mayer (113 mins.)

director:	Norman Jewison
screenplay:	Ring Lardner Jr., Terry Southern
cinematography:	Philip H. Lathrop
editing:	Hal Ashby
art direction:	Edward Carfagno, George W. Davis
music:	Lalo Schifrin
producers:	Martin Ransohoff, John Calley
cast:	Steve McQueen, Edward G. Robinson, Ann-Margret, Karl Malden, Tuesday Weld, Joan Blondell, Rip Torn, Jack Weston, Cab Calloway

THE RUSSIANS ARE COMING!
THE RUSSIANS ARE COMING! 1966
United Artists (126 mins.)

director:	Norman Jewison
screenplay:	William Rose
cinematography:	Joseph F. Biroc
editing:	Hal Ashby, J. Terry Williams
art direction:	Robert Boyle
music:	Johnny Mandel
producers:	Norman Jewison, Walter Mirisch
main cast:	Carl Reiner, Eva Marie Saint, Alan Arkin, Jonathan Winters

Academy Award nominations: Best Actor—Alan Arkin, Best Picture, Film Editing, Writing

IN THE HEAT OF THE NIGHT 1967
United Artists (109 mins.)

director:	Norman Jewison
screenplay:	Stirling Silliphant
cinematography:	Haskell Wexler
editing:	Hal Ashby
art director:	Paul Groesse
music:	Quincy Jones
producer:	Walter Mirisch
main cast:	Sidney Poitier, Rod Steiger, Warren Oates, Lee Grant

Awards: Oscars for Best Picture, Actor—Rod Steiger, Screenplay—Stirling Siliphant, Editing, Sound
Academy Award nominations: Directing, Sound Effects

THE THOMAS CROWN AFFAIR 1968
United Artists (102 mins.)

director:	Norman Jewison
screenplay:	Alan Trustman
cinematography:	Haskell Wexler
editing:	Hal Ashby, Byron Brandt, Ralph E. Winters
art direction:	Robert Boyle
music:	Alan & Marilyn Bergman and Michel Legrand
visual effects:	Pablo Ferro
producer:	Norman Jewison
main cast:	Steve McQueen, Faye Dunaway

Awards: Oscar for Best Original Song
Academy Award nominations: Best Original Score

GAILY, GAILY   1969
United Artists (107 mins.)

director:	Norman Jewison
screenplay:	Abram S. Ginnes
cinematography:	Richard H. Kline
editing:	Byron Brandt, Ralph E. Winters
production design:	Robert Boyle
music:	Henry Mancini
producers:	Norman Jewison, Hal Ashby
main cast:	Beau Bridges, Melina Mercouri, Brian Keith, George Kennedy, Hume Cronyn, Margot Kidder

Academy Award nominations: Art Direction, Costume Design, Sound

FIDDLER ON THE ROOF   1971
United Artists (181 mins.)
director: Norman Jewison
screenplay: Joseph Stein
cinematography: Oswald Morris
editing: Antony Gibbs, Robert Lawrence
production design: Robert Boyle
music: Sheldon Harnick, Jerry Bock, and John Williams
producers: Norman Jewison, Patrick J. Palmer
main cast: Topol, Norma Crane, Leonard Frey, Molly Picon, Paul Mann,
                             Rosalind Harris
Awards: Oscars for Cinematography, Song Score—John Williams, Sound
Academy Award nominations: Best Picture, Directing, Best Actor—Topol, Art Direction,
Supporting Actor—Leonard Frey

JESUS CHRIST SUPERSTAR   1973
Universal (103 mins.)
director: Norman Jewison
screenplay: Melvyn Bragg, Norman Jewison
cinematography: Douglas Slocombe
editing: Antony Gibbs
production design: Richard MacDonald
music: Tim Rice and Andrew Lloyd Webber
producers: Norman Jewison, Robert Stigwood,
                             Patrick J. Palmer
main cast: Ted Neeley, Carl Anderson, Yvonne Elliman, Barry Dennen,
                             Joshua Mostel, Bob Bingham
Academy Award nominations: Music Scoring

ROLLERBALL   1975
United Artists (122 mins.)
director: Norman Jewison
screenplay: William Harrison
cinematography: Douglas Slocombe
editing: Antony Gibbs
production design: John Box
music: André Previn
producers: Norman Jewison, Patrick J. Palmer
main cast: James Caan, John Houseman, Maud Adams, John Beck,
                             Moses Gunn, Ralph Richardson

F.I.S.T.   1978
United Artists (145 mins.)
director: Norman Jewison
screenplay: Joe Eszterhas, Sylvester Stallone
cinematography: László Kovács
editing: Graeme Clifford
production design: Richard MacDonald
music: Bill Conti
producers: Norman Jewison, Patrick J. Palmer
main cast: Sylvester Stallone, Rod Steiger, Peter Boyle, Melinda Dillon

. . . AND JUSTICE FOR ALL   1979
Columbia Pictures (117 mins.)
director: Norman Jewison
screenplay: Valerie Curtin, Barry Levinson
cinematography: Victor J. Kemper
editing: John F. Burnett
production design: Richard MacDonald
music: David Grusin and Alan & Marilyn Bergman
producers: Norman Jewison, Patrick J. Palmer
main cast: Al Pacino, Jack Warden, John Forsythe, Lee Strasberg,
                       Christine Lahti, Sam Levene
Academy Award nominations: Best Actor—Al Pacino

BEST FRIENDS   1982
Warner Brothers (116 mins.)
director: Norman Jewison
screenplay: Valerie Curtin, Barry Levinson
cinematography: Jordan Cronenweth
editing: Don Zimmerman
art direction: Josan F. Russo
music: Michel Legrand and Alan & Marilyn Bergman
producers   Norman Jewison, Patrick J. Palmer
main cast: Burt Reynolds, Goldie Hawn, Jessica Tandy
Academy Award nominations: Original Song

A SOLDIER'S STORY   1984
Columbia (101 mins.)
director: Norman Jewison
screenplay: Charles Fuller
cinematographer: Russell Boyd
editing: Caroline Biggerstaff, Mark Warner
production design: Walter Scott Herndon
music: Herbie Hancock
producers: Norman Jewison, Patrick J. Palmer,
                          Ronald L. Schwary, Charlie Milhaupt
cast: Howard E. Rollins Jr., Adolph Caesar,
                          Denzel Washington, Art Evans, David Alan Grier,
                          David Harris, Wings Hauser, Larry Riley, Dennis Lipscomb,
                          Robert Townsend, Trey Wilson, Patti LaBelle
Academy Award nominations: Best Picture, Supporting Actor—Adolph Caesar, Writing

AGNES OF GOD   1985
Columbia (98 mins.)
director: Norman Jewison
screenplay: John Pielmeier
cinematography: Sven Nykvist
editing: Antony Gibbs
production design: Ken Adam
music: Georges Delerue
producers: Norman Jewison, Patrick J. Palmer, Charlie Milhaupt,
                          Bonnie Palef
main cast: Jane Fonda, Anne Bancroft, Meg Tilly
Academy Award nominations: Best Actress—Anne Bancroft, Supporting Actress—Meg Tilly, Scoring

MOONSTRUCK   1987
Metro-Goldwyn-Mayer (102 mins.)
director: Norman Jewison
screenplay: John Patrick Shanley
cinematography: David Watkin
editing: Lou Lombardo
production design: Philip Rosenberg
music: Dick Hyman
producers: Norman Jewison, Patrick J. Palmer
cast: Cher, Nicolas Cage, Vincent Gardenia, Olympia Dukakis,
                          Danny Aiello, Julie Bovasso, John Mahoney, Louis Guss,
                          Feodor Chaliapin Jr., Anita Gillette
Awards: Oscars for Best Actress—Cher, Supporting Actress—Olympia Dukakis, Writing
Academy Award nominations: Best Picture, Directing, Supporting Actor—Vincent Gardenia

IN COUNTRY   1989
Warner Bros. (120 mins.)
director: Norman Jewison
screenplay: Frank Pierson, Cynthia Cidre
cinematography: Russell Boyd
editing: Antony Gibbs, Lou Lombardo
production design: Jackson DeGovia
music: James Horner
producers: Norman Jewison, Richard Roth
main cast: Bruce Willis, Emily Lloyd, Joan Allen, Kevin Anderson

OTHER PEOPLE'S MONEY   1991
Warner Bros. (101 mins.)
director: Norman Jewison
screenplay: Alvin Sargent
cinematography: Haskell Wexler
editing: Lou Lombardo, Michael Pacek,
                         Hubert C. de Bouillerie
production design: Philip Rosenberg
music: David Newman
producers: Norman Jewison, Ric Kidney
main cast: Danny DeVito, Gregory Peck, Penelope Ann Miller,
                         Piper Laurie

ONLY YOU   1994
TriStar (108 mins.)
director: Norman Jewison
screenplay: Diane Drake
cinematography: Sven Nykvist
editing: Stephen E. Rivkin
production design: Luciana Arrighi
music: Rachel Portman
producers: Norman Jewison, Robert N. Fried, Charles Mulvehill,
                         Cary Woods
main cast: Marisa Tomei, Robert Downey Jr., Bonnie Hunt

BOGUS   1996
Warner Bros. (111 mins.)
director: Norman Jewison
screenplay: Alvin Sargent
cinematography: David Watkin
editing: Stephen E. Rivkin
production design: Ken Adam
music: Marc Shaiman
producers: Norman Jewison, Arnon Milchan, Jeff Rothberg
cast: Whoopi Goldberg, Gérard Depardieu, Haley Joel Osment,
                         Andrea Martin, Al Waxman, Ute Lemper, Nancy Travis,
                         Denis Mercier, Sheryl Lee Ralph, Don Francks, Mo Gaffney

THE HURRICANE   1999

THE HURRICANE   1999
Universal (145 mins.)
director: Norman Jewison
screenplay: Armyan Bernstein, Dan Gordon
cinematography: Roger Deakins
editing: Stephen E. Rivkin
production design: Philip Rosenberg
music: Christopher Young
producers: Norman Jewison, Armyan Bernstein, John Ketcham
main cast: Denzel Washington, John Hannah, Deborah Kara Unger,
                         Vicellous Reon Shannon
Academy Award nomination: Best Actor—Denzel Washington

DINNER WITH FRIENDS   2001
HBO (94 mins.)
director: Norman Jewison
screenplay: Donald Margulies
cinematography: Roger Deakins
editing: Ronald Sanders
production design: Peter S. Larkin
music: Dave Grusin
producer: Patrick Markey
main cast: Dennis Quaid, Andie MacDowell, Greg Kinnear, Toni Collette

THE STATEMENT   2003
Sony Picture Classics (120 mins.) USA/France/Canada
director: Norman Jewison
screenplay: Ronald Harwood
cinematography: Kevin Jewison
editing: Andrew S. Eisen, Stephen E. Rivkin
production design: Jean Rabasse
music: Normand Corbeil, Paul Intson
producers: Norman Jewison, Robert Lantos
main cast: Michael Caine, Tilda Swinton, Jeremy Northam, Alan Bates,
                         Charlotte Rampling, John Neville

Note: This is an annotated filmography. Only the Academy Awards are listed.

Index

as editor, 104, 107, 109–12, 152
and *In the Heat of the Night*, 148, 150–51
Ashley, Elizabeth, 244
Asner, Ed, 139
Association in Defence of the Wrongly Convicted, 228, 229, 230
Atwood, Margaret, 266
Auerbach, Carol, 188
Auerbach, Larry, 17, 93, 188, 193, 201
and NJ's television career, 45–46, 47, 58, 61
Austin, Howard, 258
Austin, Patti, 218
Axelrod, George, 87
Aykroyd, Dan, 261–62
Aylesworth, John, 43, 52

Badham, Mary, 67
Bahm, Marty, 135
Baker, Charlie, 61, 117, 118
Baldwin, James, 154–55, 217
Ball, John, 134
Ball, Lucille, 271
Balmy Beach Canoe Club, 15
Bancroft, Anne, 135, 161, 245–46, 247
Banff (AB), 33
Barbarella (dir. Vadim), 97
Bardot, Brigitte, 163
Barker, Michael, 276–77
Barrett, Sweet Emma, 101–2
Barris, Alex, 43
The Barris Beat (CBC), 43, 45
Bassett, John and Isabel, 265
Bates, Alan, 276
Bates, Kathy, 266
BBC (British Broadcasting Corporation), 37–39, 184
The Beach (Toronto), 11–12, 15–16, 22, 160, 192
left-wing politics in, 194–95
movie theater in, 16, 215
Beckett, Samuel, 281
Begelman, David, 49–51, 54–55, 57
Being There (dir. Ashby), 98
Belafonte, Harry, 49, 134, 140, 152
Belafonte N.Y. (CBS), 49
Belize, 207–8
Belmondo, Jean-Paul, 160

Benchley, Nathaniel, 116–17
Benchley, Robert, 117
Bendix, William, 43
Benigni, Roberto, 276
Benjamin, Bob, 12, 13, 202
Bennett, R.B., 194
Benny, Jack, 24, 271
Bentine, Michael, 38
Berenger, Tom, 208
Bergen, Candice, 163
Bergman, Alan and Marilyn, 170–71, 218
and Academy Awards show, 233, 237–38
and *In the Heat of the Night*, 148–49, 150, 156
Bergman, Ingmar, 215, 247
Bergman, Ingrid, 115–16
Berle, Milton, 271
Berlin Film Festival, 127, 129
Berman, Shelley, 44
Bernard, Tom, 276–77
Bernstein, Armyam, 225, 229, 230
Bernstein, Bill, 12, 13, 202–3
Bertolucci, Bernardo, 256
Best Friends (dir. Jewison), 196, 218, 243, 287
Bethune, Norman, 197
Bethune (dir. Borsos), 198
The Biggest Thief in Town, 40
The Big Revue (CBC), 41–42
Bikel, Theodore, 129
Billy Two Hats (dir. Kotcheff), 189, 190
Billy Wilder Award, 24, 277
blacklist. *See also* Cold War; McCarthyism
CBC and, 43–44, 195
in Hollywood, 140, 173
Black Panthers, 155
Black Power movement, 153
Blair, Bobby, 21–22
Blake, Robert, 139
Blakely, Colin, 208
Blanchett, Cate, 276
Blondell, Joan, 106
Blue, Ben, 261
Boatwright, Boaty, 67, 68, 133
Bock, Jerry, 178
Bogart, Humphrey, 103
Bogus (dir. Jewison), 18–19, 289
La Bohème (Puccini), 254
Bonanza, 57

Bondarchuk, Sergei, 129, 138
Bonnie and Clyde (dir. Penn), 152, 163–64, 171
Boone, Pat, 62
Borsos, Phillip, 198
Bound for Glory (dir. Ashby), 98
Bovasso, Julie, 80, 254
Box, John, 203
Boxer, Barbara, 223
Boyle, Robert, 123, 182, 270
The Boys from County Clare (dir. Irvin), 208
Braden, Bernie, 38
Bradlee, Ben, 196
Brady, James, 235
Bragg, Melvyn, 186
Brando, Marlon, 152
Brandt, Willy, 129
Bratty, Rudy, 266
Brian's Song (dir. Kulik), 202
Bridges, Beau, 172, 269
British National Film and Television School, 261
The Broadway of Lerner and Loewe (CBS), 49
Broden, Liz, 280
Brokaw, Tom, 277
Brooks, Mel, 245
Brooks, Richard, 152
Brown, Helen Gurley, 87
Brown, Les, 77, 79
Brown, Ray, 148
Buchwald, Art, 196
Bujold, Genevieve, 261–62
Bullitt (dir. Yates), 158, 161
Burton, Richard, 49, 160

Caan, James, 201, 202, 203
Cable, Howard, 41
Caesar, Adolph, 218, 220
Cage, Nicolas, 255, 274, 275
Cagney, James, 239
Caine, Michael, 276, 277, 278
Caledon Hills (ON), 227, 241, 242–43, 267, 281
Calley, John, 102, 109
Calloway, Cab, 106, 110
Campbell, Glen, 149
Campbell, Neve, 261–62
Campbell, Norman, 279
Canada. *See also specific cities*; Canadians
and China, 197

Photo Credits and Permissions

Photos that follow p. 64

1. At the Ed Sullivan Theater, New York, 1958. (CBS)
2. My mother outside Jewison's Dry Goods, Toronto, late 1930's. (Family photo)
3. Camping with the Cub Scouts at Highland Creek, 1934. (Family photo)
4. Gracie Fields introduces me to live TV at the CBC, Toronto, 1957. (Robert Ragsdale)
5. With Julie Andrews, *The Broadway of Lerner and Loewe*, New York, 1959. (CBS)
6. Working with the brilliant Luther Henderson. (Friedman Abeles)
7. Trying to direct Frank Sinatra, *The Judy Garland Show,* Los Angeles, 1961. (CBS)
8. Setting up a shot, *The Judy Garland Show*, Los Angeles, 1961. (CBS)
9. Taking a break on the set of *The Thrill of It All,* 1963. (Universal)
10. Dick Van Dyke and Elke Sommer in *The Art of Love*, 1965. (Universal)
11. Directing Claire Wilcox in *40 Pounds of Trouble,* 1962. (Universal)
12. On the set of *Gaily, Gaily,* 1969. (United Artists)

Photos that follow p. 128

1. On the set of *The Russians Are Coming,* 1966. (United Artists)
2. A family outing on location, 1966. (Beverly Rockett)
3. With Alan Arkin, in *The Russians Are Coming.* (United Artists)
4. Creating drama in a game of stud poker, *The Cincinnati Kid,* 1965. (Metro-Goldwyn-Mayer)
5. In my naval uniform, I hitchhiked through the American South in 1946. (Family photo)
6. A moment with Sidney Poitier, *In the Heat of the Night,* 1967. (United Artists)
7. Rehearsing with Rod Steiger—I'm playing Sidney. (United Artists)
8. Dixie joins me on location, 1967. (United Artists)
9. With Governor Bill Clinton on the set of *A Soldier's Story,* 1984. (Ron Phillips/Columbia)
10. Denzel Washington entertains the crew at my expense, *A Soldier's Story*, 1984. (Columbia)
11. Directing the "Chess with Sex" scene in *The Thomas Crown Affair,* 1968. (United Artists)

Photos that follow p. 224

1. On the tracks outside Zagreb with Topol, *Fiddler on the Roof,* 1971. (United Artists)
2. With Carl Anderson as Judas, on location in Israel, 1972. (Universal)
3. Floating in the Dead Sea with Jesus (Ted Neeley), *Jesus Christ Superstar,* 1973. (Universal)
4. Directing Cher in *Moonstruck,* 1987. (Metro-Goldwyn-Mayer)
5. Setting up a shot with Nick Cage, *Moonstruck,* 1987. (Metro-Goldwyn-Mayer)
6. With Vincent Gardenia and Feodor Chaliapin Jr. in *Moonstruck.* (Metro-Goldwyn-Mayer)
7. Olympia Dukakis and her director on the set of *Moonstruck.* (Metro-Goldwyn-Mayer)
8. On the set of *The Hurricane,* 1998. (Ken Regan/Universal)
9. Doing my dance at the Oscars, March 21, 1999. (Kodak Entertainment Imaging)